# Symbol and Privilege

# THE ANTHROPOLOGY OF FORM AND MEANING

# SYMBOL AND PRIVILEGE

⟨∿⟩

*The Ritual Context of British Royalty*

ILSE HAYDEN

The University of Arizona Press
*Tucson*

THE UNIVERSITY OF ARIZONA PRESS

Copyright © 1987
The Arizona Board of Regents
All Rights Reserved

This book was set in 10/12 Linotron 202 Bembo.
Manufactured in the U.S.A.

Library of Congress Cataloging in Publication Data

Hayden, Ilse.
Symbol and privilege.

Bibliography: p.
Includes index.
1. Monarchy—Great Britain.    2. Rites and ceremonies—
Great Britain.    3.Great Britain—Kings and rulers.
4. Symbolism in politics—Great Britain.    I. Title.
DA112.H38   1987        941          87-10934
ISBN 0-8165-0906-9 (alk. paper)
ISBN 0-8165-0906-9

British Library Cataloguing in Publication data are available.


Credit Line: Photographs on pages 22 68 70 75 89 138 and 156
are used by kind permission of The Photo Source, London, England.

*To T. O. Beidelman,*
*friend and mentor*

# Contents

## Reference Material

# Illustrations

# Acknowledgments

This book is a revised version of a thesis submitted in partial fulfillment of the requirements for the degree of Doctor of Philosophy at New York University. My special thanks go to Tom Beidelman, my thesis adviser, for steering me toward this topic of royal rituals, which was, when all was said and done, great fun; and to John Buettner-Janusch who, as chairman of the Department of Anthropology, saw to it that University funds were made available for my field research. I am also indebted to William Nathaniel Harben, whose letters of introduction were the thin edge of the wedge into royal circles once I got to England.

I benefitted greatly from the cogent and insightful comments made by Michael Marcus, Arnold Pickman, and Dean Gilliland, who read the manuscript at various stages of preparation. Similarly, I appreciate the efforts of the anonymous reviewers whose suggestions were most helpful in shaping this book. Regarding the transformation of a thesis into a book, I am most grateful for the unfailing support and patience of J. David Sapir.

Writing a dissertation or a book is an overwhelming proposition, or at least I found it so. During the course of this ordeal I was dependent upon the many kindnesses of my stalwart friends. My debt to Caroline Katz is enormous. More than anyone else she comforted, coaxed, and teased me out of the black moods that afflict those confronted with the empty page. I also owe much, but can only give short shrift, to Andrew Slivka, Anne Bard, W. L. Schonfeld, Priscilla Scherer, John Caronna, the Meinels, Rob Schwarzenbach, Diana Wall, Rob Beecher, Marshall Mount, Kathleen Andrews, Joe Kohlfuss, Deon Bezasuet, Mindy Eschen, Rachel Kaplan, Barbara Clayton, my dogs Beau, Chuck, and Oliver, and to the Porytkos, my landlords, for not evicting me during the writing of this book.

# I

⸙

# Royal Symbolism:
# An Introduction

Royal public events and occasions generate and sustain an immense royal iconography. By iconography I mean the images and symbols associated with the modern British monarchy of which the dominant one is Queen Elizabeth II. Although photography is now the major medium through which these images are projected, it is not the only one. Some media are traditional, like the coins and stamps of the realm, or even the royal coat of arms displayed by merchants who have served one or another of the royal households. Other media are of more recent vintage, such as the televised extravaganza, or royal souvenirs, those everyday items embossed with a royal likeness.

These various and disparate devices may be responsible for intruding royal symbolism into daily life, but they are not the source of its significance. Like all symbols, royal ones depend upon the contexts in which they are displayed and cannot be understood apart from them. The roster of royal occasions—coronations, royal weddings, palace garden parties—is the elaborate ritual backdrop against which royal persons are displayed and from which their meaning as symbols derives.

To state that the Queen is a symbol is also to ask what she symbolizes. She, of course, symbolizes Great Britain. Indeed, the Queen's profile is the only logo appearing on British stamps. To assert the Queen's identity with the nation is to say everything, and to say nothing at all. The Queen is also a symbol of cosmological order. In her are embedded notions of history, of tradition, of civility, and what it means to be a person. These notions and sentiments are the warp and woof of the fabric of a society. They are held in common by members of a society, and can, if we switch metaphors, be seen as a kind of social glue.

Such cosmological notions direct the interactions of those who share them. One kind of interaction that this book is particularly interested in is that of domination. Domination is made manifest in hierarchy, which is premised upon the belief that some categories of persons are better than others. This sentiment is one that is also implicit in the Queen.

Thus, the meanings inherent in the Queen can be contradictory. On the one hand, she unifies all her people, while, on the other, she is a means of categorization, sorting her subjects into the socially superior and inferior. In this, the Queen resembles other symbols. It is not unusual to find that symbols not only have many referents but that these referents can also be contradictory. This is part of their allure, especially so since the essence of social life is that of paradox.

Related to the tendency of symbols to make contradictory statements is the ability of symbols simultaneously to reveal and conceal. Symbols reveal aspects of the social reality that are difficult to articulate even as they conceal others.

When we look at the Queen, we find her in the company of certain exalted persons. In these configurations we glimpse a secret enclave of privilege whose domain is the apex of the social hierarchy and whose inhabitants are exemplars of cultural ideals. But we are allowed only a glimpse, for the conventions of the public presentation of the Queen obscure that world.

Most anthropologists accept the fact that symbols make statements. But no one has ever said that symbols always make true statements. A less cynical way of addressing the chimerical nature of symbols is to say that they seem to be making one kind of statement when in reality they are making an entirely different one.

This book, then, is an examination of royal symbols and the ritual contexts in which they are displayed. The research is based primarily on published texts and periodicals that reflect the immense interest and curiosity that people have in the British Royal Family. Although I spoke with individuals connected with the Palace, I was not made privy to any information that was not already in the public domain. Obviously, much goes on behind the scenes that would be fascinating. But that privileged world is not easily entered. There may, indeed, be a lack of fit between what royals actually do and what they seem to do. This, however, makes no less intriguing the neat picture that is publicly presented.

My argument, in brief, is that the Queen has more power than is generally realized and that the highly romantic images of the monarchy mask and legitimize a whole system of social and political privilege that participates in the Queen's unacknowledged authority.

Considerable pains are taken to present the Queen as a "mere figure-head," with no actual power. For example, a British Information Service pamphlet states that "with the establishment of responsible government and of the modern party system, the withdrawal of the monarch from active participation in politics had become complete" (1975a:1). Now, no one would argue that the Queen personally and solely exercises supreme executive, legislative, and judicial power; however, it remains arguable whether the withdrawal of the monarch from politics has been complete. The Queen is still privy to all the doings of her government; access to information has always been a prime source of power.

Harold Laski wrote in 1932 of the Queen's grandfather, George V:

> The influence of the Monarch is wide and pervasive, and it is felt in a score of different ways. He has the right, at the earliest possible stage, to see all the papers; he must be consulted, and he can express his views. It is clear enough that a monarch who takes his duties seriously is a force to be reckoned with in our system. It is not merely that his place at the very centre of affairs gives him an opportunity of continuous scrutiny and knowledge. It is not only, also, that what comment he may choose to make must be treated with a respect not normally accorded to the opinions of other men. We are still a highly deferential people; and the immense social prestige of the Monarchy gives to the King's views a weight and authority it is impossible to ignore. (Laski 1932:34).

Additionally, one has only to read the memoirs of Richard Crossman (1975), a Labour Cabinet member, to see that the British are still a highly deferential people, especially to the Queen.

On an average the Queen meets once a week with the Prime Minister when she is in London. It is on the occasion of these meetings that the Sovereign exercises her three constitutional rights: to be consulted, to warn, and to encourage. Although these may appear to be negligible rights, they can become a formidable means of participation when exercised by a well-informed individual. And the Queen, from all accounts, is a highly informed person.

To prepare for the weekly consultations with her Prime Minister, the Queen diligently works at her "Boxes." Every day the dispatch cases, or "Boxes," are delivered to the Queen wherever she may be. The cases contain, along with the minutes and agenda of Cabinet meetings, documents and telegrams from the Home and Foreign Offices, which she must read and sign. "Doing the Boxes" is a tedious and time-consuming chore, and one for which Edward VIII, the Queen's uncle, for example, had no patience. "Alarm began to be felt in the Cabinet Office when highly confidential documents began to return obviously unread, occasionally marked with slopped cocktails and the rings of wet glass bottoms, and, worst of all, after extraordinarily long delays" (Lacey 1977:58).

The Prime Minister is not the only government official with whom the Queen may meet. She may also confer with the Cabinet, the advisory body formed by the Prime Minister and composed of sixteen to twenty-three prominent members of his or her party. The Queen is also instrumental in the formation of this group; members need the Queen's approval for their appointment. If the Queen vetoes a particular individual, the Prime Minister can either resign or give way (Stewart 1967:39). Since meetings with the Queen are secret, it is impossible to tell how extensive the Queen's influence is in the creation of a Cabinet.

Once chosen, the Cabinet meets frequently. These meetings are not open to public scrutiny. Minutes are kept but not published. "It would be a breach of the Official Secrets Act for a Minister to divulge what was said at a meeting" (Stewart 1967:54). The only individual outside the Cabinet who is privy to these minutes is the Queen. Not only does the Queen regularly read them but she can, if she wants, discuss any matter contained therein with any one of the Cabinet Ministers. "In these discussions on policy the Queen may express her own opinion freely, on two conditions. The first is that it must not be made public. . . . The second condition is that, in the last resort, the Minister's wishes would prevail" (Stewart 1967:39).

Like the Queen's opinion of potential cabinet ministers, discussions with Her Majesty are strictly private, that is, "privileged." This makes it difficult to assess the degree of her participation in the affairs of state.

> There is never enough information [about the Sovereign's role] to enable a contemporary (unless in a special coign of vantage, such as, most obviously, the Prime Minister) to make a reasoned assessment of the position. The political role of the reigning sovereign is, of all the processes of the British Constitution, that least known to five preceding reigns. . . . The darkness in which the subject is enveloped is generally lightened only by death—by the posthumous publication, that is to say, of the biographies or memoirs of those concerned or of the rawer material of their papers. (Hardie 1970:1)

Thus, "the dividing line between Constitutional and personal monarchy is more shadowy than is sometimes thought" (Lee 1927:35). Regardless of where that line falls, it is fair to say that the Queen's formal jural power may be limited but that her informal influence is enormous. Ironically, the mistaken belief that the Queen is merely a figurehead has enabled the Queen to build up, over the course of her reign, a tremendous moral power—one that has increased because she has been so chary of using it. The Queen's power is a point, though, that can only be suggested here. Its proof is beyond the scope of symbolic anthropology.

## The Ceremonial Monarchy

If the Queen's participation in government is obscured by the British attitude that government is best shrouded in secrecy and kept from the public eye (Shils 1956:51), then the Queen's ceremonial role is one that brings her out into a full glare of publicity, making her most familiar to her subjects. Royal events are the ritual contexts in which the Queen is displayed to her people. These occasions can be roughly divided into two classes, which I have called the grand and the minor.

The grand occasions are those affairs from which are derived the most majestic images of the Queen—the Coronation, the Opening of Parliament, and the Service of the Order of the Garter (to name a few). These grand events have "mythohistorical" themes. They distort time and thereby accentuate awareness of it. They proclaim the continuity of past and present.

The past "seems to come alive," as media commentators effuse on these occasions. It "comes alive" in the presence of medieval, Tudor, and Jacobean costumes, anachronistically jumbled together with those of later eras. On these occasions history and myth merge as the senses are assaulted and overwhelmed. The brilliant red and gold tabards of the Heralds; the gleaming cuirasses of the Household Cavalry; the clip of hooves; the cacophonous music of the massed bands; the skirl of pipes; even the pungent smell of the horses and their inevitable droppings all contribute to the theatrics of the moment. A grand event, as the saying goes, is something to write home about. Who cares if the devices used are not exactly historical? The fiction of these occasions is that they are relics out of time immemorial. They were, however, made up in the late nineteenth and early twentieth centuries. Nevertheless, archaic modes of transportation (carriages, horsebacks, and sidesaddles), as well as fancy dress (capes, plumes, and ribbons), give the impression of venerable age.

This distortion identifies the Queen and her family with the traditions of the realm, that is, the timeless moral order. One does not see just the Sovereign ride by on these occasions but rather all the Sovereigns from the Conqueror on down. Thus, grand events are the contexts that imbue this flesh-and-blood symbol, the Queen, with much of her meaning. The passions stirred by these spectacles spill over from the Queen to her family who escort her, support her, and assist her.

The grand occasions seem to arouse in those assembled, whether along the procession route or in front of television screens, beliefs and sentiments held in common. These events represent the effervescence of the collective consciousness. As Durkheim put it:

> We have here a whole group of ceremonies whose sole purpose is to awaken certain ideas and sentiments, to attach the past to the present or individual to the group. (1967:423)

Although they awaken sentiments of national identity, they also intrude notions of class privilege into the consciousness of those who witness them. Participants are cleaved into those who stand and watch and those who serve. The Queen is always attended most closely by the Royal Family and her Household. The Household, who are often titled individuals, are also her personal friends and so share the private life of the Queen.

It would be naive to assume that the class affiliations of those in attendance upon the Queen are lost upon the spectators. The grandness of, say, a Coronation, may obscure such notions of class but does not obliterate them.

The social order of Great Britain—"the rich man in his castle, the poor man at his gate"—is glossed by an appeal to a romanticized national history.

The minor event contrasts with the grand both in scale and content. The grand occasions celebrate continuity with the heroic past. The minor ones extol continence: the theme of class privilege predominates.

The minor events slip by relatively unnoticed. Yet they consume more of the Queen's time than do the grand ones. "The most regular employment of the Queen and her family is to make visits all over the United Kingdom to open factories, schools, and other enterprises: to inaugurate, to commemorate, to congratulate, to approve, to meet the people" (Howard 1977a:29). They slip by unnoticed because, unlike the grand events, which are associated with national shrines, they are staged in places that are remarkable only for their ordinariness. Moreover, they are not good theatre; they lack red carpets, lavish costumes, and trumpet fanfares.

Although the lesser events pale in comparison with the grander ones, much of their appeal derives from the aura with which the royal person is infused on those other, more magnificent occasions. The Queen may inspect an iron-works in an unremarkable afternoon outfit, looking like many other upper-class matrons. But the image of the glorious Queen, riding up the Mall at the head of her troops, or progressing with her Knights Companion of the Garter, hovers about her, informing the perceptions of those who see her in what can only be described as an incongruous setting for the Queen of England.

The emphasis is always on civility and etiquette. These too underscore the legitimacy of the realm. When the Queen drops by, everybody is on his best behavior, and, being most mindful of his manners, is eager to put the best foot forward. But the manners of upper-class people are "better" than those of the middle and lower classes. Upper-class people can be trusted to know how to act in the presence of the Queen. Accordingly, they have far greater access to the Queen on these occasions. Thus etiquette, which makes obvious social hierarchy, is a dimension of world view. Courtesy, or civility, is a manifestation of the collective conscience. "The common sentiment thus animating all the members is outwardly expressed by certain gestures" (Durkheim 1965:410). These gestures are those of manners, which make royal occasions "unqualified exhibitions of niceness," to use Noel Coward's phrase.

The minor events dramatize class differences and accentuate the awareness of social distance. The grand occasions obscure those internal divisions by dramatizing heroic traditions and national identity.

The Queen, in addition to her public duties at home, averages two major foreign visits a year. These travels can be either Commonwealth tours or state visits to countries outside the Commonwealth. They fall midway between the lesser and the grand occasions. In terms of media coverage and the prodigious planning necessary for these journeys, they are very grand. But in terms of what the Queen does when she is abroad—inaugurate, congratulate, and commemorate—they resemble the lesser events.

At home, the Queen reciprocates the hospitality that she received abroad by entertaining heads of state. She becomes the hostess of the United Kingdom. Dignitaries often stay at one of the royal residences—Buckingham Palace, Windsor Castle, or Holyrood House. "The heads of state [are] paraded in a state coach beside the Queen through the streets decorated with their national flags. [They are] wined, dined, and danced at Covent Gardens, escorted around steelworks and schools and made speeches by the Queen" (Howard 1977a:29). Ronald Reagan went riding with the Queen in the grounds of Windsor Castle.

## The Aristocracy

This book is also about class, namely, the aristocracy. The monarchy makes very little sense without it. Yet this symbiosis is glossed over in popular books on royalty in which the monarchy is described as if it were somehow tacked onto an essentially egalitarian, modern democracy. This approach is also evident in the posing of such questions as: what if the monarchy were abolished. Answers are usually couched in parliamentary terms: the government would proceed very well without the Queen, and so forth. Despite the Queen's covert participation in government, the significance of the monarchy does not lie primarily in the administration of the state. Rather, much of the meaning of the monarchy derives from its position in British society. Specifically, the lives of royalty are closely interwoven with an amorphous group variously called the hereditary aristocracy, the upper class, the ruling class, or the elite. Social class, any class, is a difficult concept to define to everyone's satisfaction. For example, one individual may appear to one group as absolutely top drawer, while to another, quite middle class.

Despite such difficulties, it behooves me to try to define what I mean by the "aristocracy." The aristocracy is the top pinnacle of a hierarchical society. Simmel wrote that such a group "must be 'surveyable' by every single member of it. . . . Relations of blood and marriage must be ramified and traceable throughout the whole group" (1950:90). To say that such relations must be "traceable throughout the *whole* group" is clearly an ideal. Nevertheless, in Britain the highest echelons of the aristocracy, that is, the nobility, do seem to be able to do that. The Spencers, for one, can trace their relations to the Dukes of Marlborough, Abercorn, Bedford, and Devonshire *inter alia*. Whether the whole nobility is able to survey all such ramifications at any particular moment is, of course, debatable. There are limits to how many relatives a human being can keep track of.

No one would argue that the nobility, that is the titled, are not aristocrats. Currently, there are some one thousand of these hereditary peers. But they are not the only ones who are permitted the luxury of a title. The wives, sons, daughters, and occasionally grandchildren of peers are allowed the use of what are called courtesy titles. For example, the "commoner," Diana Spencer, was able to use the title Lady, as a courtesy to her father, the peer, Lord Spencer. Winchester estimates that there are approximately 7,000 such individuals (1982:17).

But the limits of the aristocracy are not defined solely by titles. For one thing, English primogeniture forces younger sons out beyond the pale of the titled, and thus easily recognized, nobility. Yet these younger sons and their children, as do their titled brothers and cousins, possess the same attitudes, values, and intangibles that constitute class affiliation.

Another difficulty in differentiating British social classes is the English "cult of gentility." Many try to appear better than they are. This is not a new phenomenon. As Stone wrote of the eighteenth century, "the middling sort" did not resent their social superiors. Instead, they imitated them, "aspiring to gentility by copying the education, manners, and behavior of the gentry" (1984:409). He adds that the great strength of the elite "was its success in psychologically co-opting those below them into the status hierarchy of gentility." This is a situation that still exists in Britain today. The minor royal event, as we shall see, makes manifest the aspirations toward gentility on the part of the middling sort. The emphasis upon etiquette on these occasions confirms the success of the elite in co-opting those below into the hierarchy of gentility.

The aristocracy, then, comprises all the Dukes, Marquesses, Earls, Barons, and Baronets, as well as their immediate families who are often courtesy-titled. Beyond these 7,000 or so individuals are their ramifying webs of kinship, which ultimately merge with an equally amorphous group called the upper middle class. But the nobility and those with noble connections do not exhaust the aristocracy. The "aristocracy" also includes a great number of devotees of the cult of gentility who have great wealth and/or hold high office and who imitate the nobility.

I think Nancy Mitford, in writing about upper-class (U) vs. non-upper-class (Non-U) linguistic usages, summed up the British class system most effectively:

> Most of the [1000] peers share the education, usage, and point of view of a vast upper middle class, but the upper middle class does not, in its turn, merge imperceptively into the middle class. There is a very definite borderline, easily recognized by hundreds of small but significant landmarks. (1956:6)

This upper middle class is in effect the "aristocracy." They are one percent of the population, that is, about 500,000, and control a disproportionate amount of wealth and political power, despite the fact that Britain is a parliamentary democracy with a nonpartisan civil service recruited from the universities by competitive examination. These individuals also have a disproportionate access to royalty.

Yet, the aristocracy remain sociologically invisible. Not only do they have the means to protect their own privacy, they also cultivate the habit of silence. In short, the aristocracy keep themselves separate so that others can feel their superiority (Simmel 1950:364). The aristocracy is, in effect, a secret society that others "through their hostility and envy, involuntarily acknowledge [their] higher value. . . . Secrecy and mystification amount to heightening the wall toward the outside, and hence to strengthening the aristocratic character of the group" (Simmel 1950:365). Secrecy, then, serves two purposes. It is an instrument of rule and a means of symbolic mystification. Both dovetail around the Queen.

## The Queen's Two Bodies

The Queen, as we have seen, is a symbol. But she is also a person, an individual. This twoness of the Queen enables her to rouse much stronger sentiments than could an inanimate emblem like a flag.

The seductiveness of the royal person as a symbol is apparent at royal public events. These events capitalize on the Queen's physical presence even while many aspects of her physical body are scrupulously denied. Much of the appeal of the Queen as symbol derives from her personhood, but the messiness of being a person must not be allowed to intrude upon the dignity of the institution of Queenship. The Queen cannot be shown sitting on the edge of her bed clipping her toenails. The messiness of the person is, of course, traceable to the possession of a body. Bodies are subject to their own ineluctable rhythms. Yet the Queen's physical and potentially embarrassing body does not detract from her appeal. Rather, it enhances it. She is human but does not "screw up." Her dignity, deriving in part from the almost suprahuman control of that body, is more impressive than if she were made of cast iron (Beidelman: personal communication).

This royal control of the treacherous body is not exclusively the Queen's. As Cecil Beaton writes:

> . . . The Royal Family seem to have acquired a communal manner of behavior. They have developed an instinctive self-protection so that they should not bump into each other or stumble down a step. They move in slow motion with care and fluid grace: their technique is so perfected that it appears entirely natural. (1973:113)

This problem of the relationship of the natural body to the royal dignity is hardly a modern one. Indeed, it had troubled Tudor Crown Jurists who had had to grapple with the problem of the sale of some lands from the Duchy of Lancaster. They concluded that Edward VI had made the unprecedented sale in the capacity of his natural body, which could make mistakes, and not in that of his Body Politic, which could not (Kantorowicz 1957:1). This fiction that the King had two bodies—a body natural and a body politic—was a convenient heuristic device for dealing with many sticky problems of kingship. Although this notion may no longer have the legal importance today that it had in the sixteenth century, it remains a useful way of looking at the public presentation of Elizabeth II. She clearly has two bodies. On one hand, she is an ordinary human being with her individual likes, dislikes, and idiosyncrasies. On the other hand, she is an immortal institution upon which her own individual personhood must not encroach.

There is a rough correlation between the Queen's two bodies and the two classes of royal public events. The grand occasions often present the Queen in the guise of her body politic. The "fancy dress" of these occasions transforms her into an *effigy* of kingship. But when the Queen visits a factory, she does so as an "ordinary" person. She comes dressed in everyday clothes, talks to ordinary people, and concludes her visit by attending to at least one function of her natural body: she takes refreshment, usually tea, with her hosts.

More important, however, than the correlation of the two bodies and two classes of events is the correlation between the two bodies and the dramatic oscillations of publicity and privacy that characterizes royal life. Prince Charles once said that to be royal is to lead a "fish-bowl" existence. At the same time, Starkey can write of "the veil of silence which blankets the everyday life of royalty; the impenetrable secrecy of royal palaces . . . the extraordinary anonymity of the servants of the royal household" (Starkey 1977:220–21).

These seem to be mutually exclusive observations, but each is true because it refers to one of the Queen's two bodies. The Queen's body politic is relentlessly on display. Her body natural is assiduously hidden by "the impenetrable secrecy" of the Palace. But the Palace is not just a famous building surrounded by high walls. It is an institution with its own personnel, divided into Staff and Household. Among the latter are the Queen's courtiers, drawn from the hereditary aristocracy. Courtiers have always been privy to the bodily secrets of royals.

In the sixteenth and seventeenth centuries, kings and queens got up and went to bed surrounded by their courts. This is not to say that they lacked any sense of what we could call delicacy about the body natural. A sense of this can be gleaned from the autopsy reports of Queen Anne (1714) and her son, Henry, Duke of Gloucester (1700). The body of Prince Henry was given a thorough autopsy, while only the most cursory look was permitted into the body of his mother, the Queen (see Appendix A). Queen Victoria also shared this sentiment that the handling of the dead royal body natural by commoners would constitute *lèse majesté*. Accordingly, her grandson, Kaiser Wilhelm, measured her for her coffin since "the Queen in her will [had] forbidden undertakers" (Talbot 1980:42).

Although modern courtiers do not cluster round the Queen's bed as she rises, they guard her personal privacy which, in turn, enhances her symbolic power. This private service is a mark of aristocratic privilege and a source of their immense social power. But it is a privilege that is hidden in the shadows cast by the Palace walls. Paradoxically, the aristocracy become visible in the refracted light of the royal publicity, yet remain anonymous. This is a major theme of this book.

One final word. The Queen of England strikes many as a most peculiar topic for social anthropology. Yet, interest in divine kingship—and all sovereigns are divine—is almost as old as anthropology. A bibliography of the anthropological literature on African kingship reads like a who's who of British social anthropologists. Most of the guiding lights of the discipline tried their hand at this topic despite one considerable obstacle: fieldworkers were hampered by a dearth of extant societies with actual kings. Thus, most accounts of divine kingship in African societies were "based on informants' stylized accounts" (Richards 1968:24). Oral traditions were the primary sources of data. But an oral tradition

> gives too static an impression. It does not reflect the ebb and flow of beliefs which, to my mind, are characteristic of such systems. All rulers without standing armies or other institutional means of control have to balance on the knife edge of their people's belief, but in cases of divine kingship the pose is surely a particularly precarious one, between god and man, between the *rex* and the *dux* for instance. (1968:24)

In the 1920s and 30s, the British monarchy was experiencing just such an ebb and flow of sentiment. The collapse of the other European monarchies—especially the Hapsburgs, the Hohenzollerns, and the Romanoffs, and somewhat later the Abdication crisis—made the Windsors' position quite precarious indeed.

One wonders why these earlier anthropologists, given their interest in divine kingship, did not examine British kingship. The only anthropologist who seems to have taken notice was A. M. Hocart, whose essay, "In the Grip of Tradition" (1970a), addressed the unfitness of Wallis Simpson as the King's consort.

Even today the British monarchy is virtually ignored by social scientists. Perhaps this neglect is due to a pervasive academic prejudice that the "royal show" is a modern form of bread and circuses, that is, harmless enough but not to be taken too seriously. Perhaps this neglect is not so cynical as all this. Anthropologists have always studied others so that we may learn more about ourselves. Distance has been an essential aspect of sociological investigation. It is necessary for observation. It is no accident that the first science was astronomy, that is, the study of that which is farthest away, and the most recent ones—anthropology, psychology, and so forth—are those which examine ourselves. It is hard to see what we ourselves are doing. Early Africanists searched often in vain for actual kingdoms ignoring the perfectly viable one of their own homeland as their intellectual descendants continue to do today. But anthropologists, having honed their skills amongst simpler peoples during most of this century, are now turning to the study of their own cultures.

Despite this interest in our own ways, the British monarchy remains out of bounds, more so than other social institutions. Indeed, one could say that a conspiracy of silence surrounds the extraordinary and probably unique hierarchical system of privilege that emanates from the monarch. Why? Because those who are close enough to see what goes on behind the Palace walls keep their lips buttoned in the hope that they too might be co-opted into that system via highly coveted awards. Blabbermouths are not knighted. Nor are they retained as friends or servants. Neither do they keep the affection of princes.

Nevertheless, the British monarchy remains a source of highly visible symbols in whose presentation can be discerned a certain world view, or cosmology. Moreover, these symbols, intertwined with the distribution of social honor, are like cosmetics which when applied make that world more attractive and desirable.

# II

⟨ᴠᴠᴠᴠ⟩

# The Queen Is
# What the Queen Does

## The Ceremonial Monarchy

Fergus Miller, in *The Emperor in the Roman World,* seeking to map "certain essential elements in the structure and functioning of the Roman Empire," wrote that "the Emperor was what the Emperor did" (1977:6). This can also be said of Elizabeth II: the Queen is what the Queen does. And what the Queen does reveals some interesting, though contradictory, aspects of British society. Some of her activities are highly publicized. Others are concealed. For some reason, pictures of the Queen in her primary residence, Buckingham Palace, are unusual. Most "at home" photographs seem to be taken at Balmoral. Some of her activities are not exactly concealed, but neither are they publicized, for example, her constitutional obligation of conferring with the Prime Minister; of reading and signing state papers; or presiding at Privy Council meetings. Few photographs of these events exist.

This chapter, however, is concerned with those very visible activities that constitute the ceremonial monarchy. The mystique of the Queen is enhanced on these occasions, which display her in spectacular setting. They also present "a relatively condensed and therefore highly general definition" of the society and its environment (Bellah 1968:13:408). In this condensed vision of British society made apparent on the occasion of a royal event we confront a basic truth about human social organization: no society has "a totally consistent system of ideas and values" (Beidelman 1970:2). Royal public occasions dramatize certain thematic elements important to a modern nation state. One prevalent theme of royal ceremony is the distinction between the Sovereign and the sovereignty she embodies, that is, between the Queen's body natural and her body politic. This distinction proclaims the contractual nature of a society composed of legal equals. But as George Orwell observed, some are more equal than others. This, too, is a theme that imbues royal ceremonial.

Let us turn our attention now to the ceremonial activities of the Queen. So important is such ceremony to the monarchy that each reign is bracketed by a ritual dyad: the Sovereign's Funeral and the successor's Coronation. These are clearly the very grandest of all royal events. They set each reign apart from that which came before.

The new reign begins—symbolically, if not legally—at the conclusion of the predecessor's funeral. Despite the legal maxim that the new reign commences the instant that the old sovereign expires, the death of a British monarch is still followed by an interregnum—even if it is merely a ceremonial one. The king's successor remains socially invisible (and thus, in a sense, nonexistent) throughout the funeral period while the dead monarch is accorded sovereign honors. It is only at the end of the Royal Funeral that any ambiguity about who is the undoubted incumbent of the kingly office ceases. The Coronation, which may follow the funeral by as much as eighteen months, merely confirms—sanctifies—the transference of sovereignty which occurred when earth was sprinkled on the dead king's coffin, consigning him to the grave (cf. Hayden 1975).

The impression given by all royal ceremony is that it has been faithfully and exactly reenacted since time immemorial. Nowhere is this more evident, or more important, than in the Coronation, which proclaims the legitimacy of the succession by stressing the continuity of the realm. The Coronation is indeed an ancient rite, but it is also one which has evolved, undergoing many changes over the years. A great number of those changes occurred at the Coronation of William IV, who became king in 1830. His "Penny Coronation" mercilessly cut many of the more picturesque figures who had previously taken part. The Royal Herbswoman no longer scatters flower petals and scented herbs in the path of the procession into the Abbey. Similarly, the "Chief Cupbearer, the Sergeant of the Silver Scullery, the Dapifer, the Grand Carver and the Chief Larderer passed from sight . . .[and] the holder of the Manor of Addington in Surrey could no longer come forward to present the King with a mysterious mess of dilligrout" (Baker 1977:64).

Although we *know* that the coronations of the twentieth century were very different from those of, say, the thirteenth and sixteenth centuries, they are still *thought* to be replicas of the earlier ones. The Coronation is a form of eternal return, which converts the flow of unilineal time into an endless and reassuring cycle. Side by side with this notion of cyclical time is the realization that time flows inexorably. "European time is a continuum. Whatever point we start at, each succeeding generation increases the distance from that point. Our grandfathers were nearer to 1066 than we are" (Evans-Pritchard 1939:214). These two kinds of time are reconciled in the Coronation.

Each coronation, of course, increases the distance from 1066; yet the ceremony's emphasis upon tradition *seems* to decrease the distance from that date which lies "beyond the limits of historical time" and is a point where history "merges into myth" (Evans-Pritchard 1939:215). Individual kings come and go. But the King is forever; he is beyond time (Kantorowicz 1957:171–72).

The Royal Funeral would also seem to have survived for centuries. This illusion is all the more remarkable since the modern Royal Funeral is clearly a twentieth-century invention, beginning fittingly enough with the funeral of Edward VII. This particular royal occasion came into its own with the funerals of the fifth and sixth Georges, almost exact replicas of each other and separated by a mere seventeen years.

The modern Royal Funeral is as impressive as the Coronation, although the exigencies of death and decomposition do not permit the luxury of the extensive planning that is devoted to a Coronation. Nevertheless, the Funeral is the only royal occasion that extends for several days. The Funeral of George VI, for example, took nine days. The King died on the 6th of February 1952, and was finally buried on the 15th.

> Only the Sovereign is entitled to a Royal Funeral by right. The honors and dignity of a State Funeral may however be accorded to members of the Royal Family and also to outstanding national figures as approved by the Sovereign. In the last two centuries only three people have been granted State Funerals; the first was Lord Nelson in 1806, followed by the Duke of Wellington in 1852, and within living memory, Sir Winston Churchill in 1965. (Paget 1979:148)

The Funeral of Lord Mountbatten in 1979 makes four. Royal Funerals are organized by the Earl Marshal and the College of Arms; State Funerals are the responsibility of the Lord Chamberlain's office. It is interesting to note that three of the recipients of State Funerals were peers. The fourth, Sir Winston Churchill, was the grandson of the Duke of Marlborough and would have inherited the title had his uncle died without male heirs.

The Royal Funeral and Coronation are "rites of passage." There are, of course, other royal passages that are opportunities for public celebration. A rather memorable one was the wedding of the Prince and Princess of Wales, followed five years later by that of the Duke and Duchess of York. The appeal of these occasions is that they are, as Bagehot wrote, brilliant editions of universal facts. People mourn when sovereigns die and rejoice at the marriage of princes. This outpouring of sentiment contributes to the fiction that the populace somehow participates in the monarchy and is on a par with royalty.

The essential form of royal occasions furthers the illusion of public participation. Most events are essentially elaborate processions that allow maximum, though fleeting, exposure of royal persons to the greatest number of people. These parades often start from Buckingham Palace and progress by a roundabout route to one ritual center or another where the actual ceremony, attended by a far more select group, takes place. The occasion concludes with an equally meandering return process. All public royal rites of passage (except funerals) end with the balcony appearance of the Royal Family. Charles and Andrew rode in open carriages to be married and on their return kissed their new brides on the balcony.

## The Annual Events

In addition to the celebration of the marriages, deaths, and coronations of royal persons, there are a number of annually occurring events that are ceremonial highpoints of the year. Unlike the rites of passage, these recur every year. They are the Christmas Broadcast, Royal Maundy, the Birthday Parade/Trooping the Colour, the Garter Service (though not as inevitably annual event as in 1984, when by the Queen's decision it did not take place), Royal Ascot, the Opening of Parliament, and Remembrance Sunday. Most incorporate decidedly odd elements whose explanation is that they are "traditional." These are not the only annual royal activities but seem to be the most important ones, especially in terms of media coverage.

The Christmas Broadcast is the stiff and oft spoofed speech the Queen makes on Christmas Day: "I am speaking to you today from my home. . . ." Although it may not strike many as being especially grand, it is the most regularly occurring of the annual events. Moreover, it is particularly tantalizing in its peek into the secret world of the Queen's private life. In recent years, it has been televised and shows the Queen with her family (e.g., in 1984 the occasion also included footage of

Prince Henry's christening). The Broadcast is the only fixed royal occasion. The others are moveable feasts, so to speak.

Two of the most intriguing events are Royal Maundy and Remembrance Sunday. Although they are separated from one another by some six or seven months, they are oddly related in that these occasions bring the Queen into contact with elements from which she is normally shielded: death and money. Similarly, these occasions are easily identified by the flowers with which they are associated: red poppies (Remembrance Day) and spring bouquets (Royal Maundy). They are also those rare times when the Queen appears to give something away. At the Maundy Distribution, the Queen gives little leather purses to specially selected paupers. On the Sunday nearest Armistice Day, the Queen leads the nation in mourning, placing the first wreath at the Cenotaph. I say "appears to give something away" because the Queen does not actually supply the wreath and purses.

## Royal Maundy

The Maundy Distribution is made on Maundy Thursday, the day before Good Friday. Its site alternates between Westminster Abbey and a provincial cathedral. In 1955 it was held at Southwark Cathedral, which was then celebrating the Golden Jubilee of its diocese. In 1979 the Maundy Distribution helped celebrate the 900th anniversary of the Consecration of Winchester Cathedral by William the Conqueror.

The event is easily recognized by the distinctive bouquets that the Queen, clergy, and other participants carry. "The traditional nosegays carried by the principal people taking part in the service were originally a precaution against infection" (Wright 1973:20). Let us not forget that nosegays were carried by people of quality as safeguards against the bad smells of poor, unwashed people. Thus, the distribution of the Maundy Money is not so much an act of humility as it is an expression of *noblesse oblige*. The Maundy bouquets insinuate that there is something rather distasteful about the Queen's mixing with poor people.

Be that as it may, the Maundy Service recalls the Last Supper when Christ washed the feet of his disciples, over the objections of Peter.

> When it was Simon Peter's turn, Peter said to Him, "You, Lord, washing my feet? . . . I will never let you wash my feet." "If I do not wash you," Jesus replied, "you are not in fellowship with me." (John 13:6–8, *The New English Bible*)

The distribution of Maundy Money brings the Queen into close contact with paupers. The distinctive bouquet that she carries protects her from the odor of the unwashed, reaffirming that some people are better than others. *Photograph by Tim Graham by permission of Sygma.*

The Queen, of course, washes no one's feet, even though medieval kings did so as an expression of their common humanity. Instead she distributes money. Like the Royal Funeral, this particular ritual has been grafted onto a preexisting religious service found in *The Book of Common Prayer.* The choir sings and the lesson is read. The Queen is escorted down the aisle by bishops, clergy, Prince Philip, Yeomen of the Guard, and a number of orphans and fatherless children. The recipients themselves average eighty years of age, are poor, and have been chosen because of their lives of Christian service and their longevity. Their number increases as the Queen ages. In 1985 the Queen was fifty-nine years old; thus fifty-nine women and fifty-nine men received the royal largesse. In 1987 there were sixty-one men and sixty-one women.

The Queen moves twice among their ranks. A Yeoman of the Guard holds the silver tray with the purses. The first distribution of white and green purses (white for men, green for women) is in lieu of clothing. At the second distribution, two purses tied together are given to each recipient.

The red purse contains 3 pounds in place of clothing which was given in earlier times, 1½ pounds for provisions, and 1 pound for the redemption of the royal gown (which Queen Mary Tudor gave to the most destitute woman present at the 1556 Maundy service), making a total of 5½ pounds. The white purse with the long red strings contains the silver Maundy coins, in sets, and consisting of the same number of pence as the Sovereign has years. Because of the historical associations the amounts distributed have varied little from earlier centuries, but the gifts are highly prized by the recipients for to be included in the list is considered very much an honour. (Wright 1973:24)

Honor aside, the gifts are also highly prized because they can be sold for much more than their intrinsic value to the collectors who gather outside the cathedral awaiting the service's end. Recipients probably do feel honored to be asked to participate in the Maundy Service, and to be so close to the Queen. But it is certainly a dubious distinction to be selected solely because one conforms to the definition of "poor beggar." Elizabeth II is not the only monarch to make distribution to the poor in modern times. Haile Selassie did also, although the Ethiopian distribution had a somewhat different tone than Royal Maundy.

I also took care of another bag, a large one that was filled with small coins on the even of national holidays. On such occasions our august ruler went to the most crowded and lively quarter of Addis Ababa, Mercato, where on a specially constructed platform I would place the heavy, jingling bag from which His Benevolent Majesty would scoop the handfuls of coppers that he threw into the crowd of beggars and other such greedy riffraff. The rapacious mob would create such a hubbub, however, that this charitable action always had to end in a shower of police batons against the heads of the frenzied, pushy rabble. Saddened, His Highness would have to walk away from the platform. Often he was unable to empty even half the bag. (Kapuscinski 1983:38)

The Maundy Service is remarkable for another reason: it is one of the few occasions on which the Queen appears when she is not associated predominantly with aristocrats. True, she is escorted by the clergy, the Lords Spiritual of the realm, but she is also escorted by orphans and fatherless children. Perhaps this is significant, since "patricians" (i.e., aristocrats) were defined as those who knew their fathers. Patricians, like royalty, can trace their illustrious heritage for generations. Furthermore, the whole ceremony focuses upon senescent paupers. The Queen is clearly out of her element on this occasion, a fact that cannot be hidden for all its medieval allusion and embroideries. Social distance is maintained by the Queen's failure to wash the feet of the participants and thus to enter into fellowship with them.

## Remembrance Sunday

Remembrance Sunday is as unusual as Royal Maundy. The ceremony is essentially one of mourning, and mourning does not become the Queen. This is an ancient proscription. A sixteenth-century writer observed of kings that "it is not fitting to their sacred persons to associate themselves with things funereal" (in Giesey 1960:7). Similar notions prevented Queen Victoria from attending one of the grandest public occasions of the nineteenth century, the funeral of the Duke of Wellington in 1852.

> All the great of the land were there, save only the Queen, who could not attend the funeral of a subject, however eminent; she watched from Buckingham Palace and Saint James's Palace; the [funeral] car halted before her so she could take in the scene. (Morley 1971:86)

So important is this stricture that even Elizabeth II attended the funeral of her own father as the daughter of George VI rather than as "Queen of England." Her presence at a subject's funeral, that of Churchill, on the other hand, was a remarkable exception. Churchill, in death, had achieved a quasi-royal status; his state funeral had been organized by the Earl Marshal, the impresario of Royal Funerals, and not by the Lord Chamberlain's office, which is normally responsible for such occasions.

This prohibition against the public association with mourning extends to other members of the Royal Family as well. Like the Queen, they do not normally attend funerals. In their stead, a proxy (e.g., Lady-in-Waiting or Equerry) is sent to the funerals of nonroyal acquaintances and people of prominence. When a head of state or foreign royal dies, however, the Queen is represented at the funeral, usually by one of her male relatives. The attendance of the Princess of Wales at the funeral of Princess Grace of Monaco was most unusual. I can recall no other instance of the Queen's being represented by a female relative. In this case, it was also a mark of Monaco's ascendance in royal circles. When Grace Kelly married Prince Rainier II, the only royal who condescended to attend the wedding was the deposed King Farouk. The Principality of Monaco in 1956 was regarded by other European royalty as something out of a comic opera.

That the Queen, then, who is normally shielded from death, should lead the nation in mourning its war dead makes the occasion remarkable. The ceremony at the Cenotaph, Sir Edward Luyten's monument to the war dead, is a most moving one. The brief religious ceremony is conducted by the Bishop of London. The Last Post is sounded. Two minutes of silence are observed. Then the Queen steps forward from the ranks of the assembled armed services, the British Legion, and the various war-

The Queen places the wreath on the Cenotaph on Remembrance Sunday. Dressed in black, she expresses the gratitude of the nation to the war dead. It is one of the few times that the Queen gives anything away. *Keystone Press Agency Ltd.*

time organizations. She is dressed in black, another departure for the Queen, red poppies pinned to her coat. The other royal ladies, watching the ceremony from the purple-draped balconies of Whitehall, are also in black. The Queen places the first wreath, often of poppies, at the base of the monument. Prince Philip places the second one to the right of the Queen's. Prince Charles places the third to the left. The Queen Mother sends a wreath, though she does not place it there herself.

After those of the Royal Family come the wreaths of politicians, Commonwealth High Commissioners, and the chiefs of the armed and civilian services, "until the base of the Cenotaph [is] hidden by poppies, laurel and yellow chrysanthemums" (Howard 1970:2). The bishop leads those assembled in prayer. The hymn, "O God, Our Help in Ages Past," is sung, and the crowds disperse.

The ceremony at the Cenotaph is actually the second part of what is called the Festival of Remembrance. On the preceding Saturday, called Poppy Day for the artificial poppies and wreaths made by disabled servicemen that are sold throughout the Commonwealth, an evening service is held in the Albert Hall. This program consists of performances by military bands and choirs, displays of gymnastics and military drills, and a muster of past and present servicemen. It is attended by the Queen and Royal Family. The service concludes: "When more than a million poppy petals, one for every man killed in the armed services since the beginning of the First World War, float down from the ceiling" (Trent 1966:31).

Remembrance Sunday is also unusual in that the Queen expresses gratitude, acknowledging her indebtedness to those who died in Britain's wars. To be indebted is, of course, a morally inferior position, and the Queen cannot be inferior to anyone. There is, however, more to this than meets the eye. Dying for one's country is heroic; an act which, *ipso facto*, transforms the essence of even the most socially inferior. The war dead are the nation's heroes who by virtue of their ultimate sacrifice have been elevated to the same exalted plane that the Queen inhabits. Embodied in the Queen are the heroic traditions of the realm. The traditional Oath of Fealty, sworn to sovereigns by their vassals, concludes with "to live and die against all manner of folk." The war dead did just that and in the process became the Queen's Chevaliers. Thus, the Queen's indebtedness is attenuated.

Another aspect of the ceremony indicates that the Queen is not as indebted as might first appear. The dead are anonymous by their very number—their quintessence embodied in a nameless warrior, the Unknown Soldier. The Queen, in contrast, is anything but anonymous, and so inhabits an elevated plane of existence.

## The Trooping, the Garter, and Ascot

June is the climax of the royal ceremonial year. Three of the most colorful events of the calendar fall in this month: the Birthday Parade, the Service of the Order of the Garter, and Royal Ascot. These events fall within two weeks of one another. They share a common thematic element—the horse. For example, to Troop the Colour, the Queen rides sidesaddle to Horse Guards in the company of mounted members of the Royal Family and the Officers of the Household Brigade. The Service of the Order of the Garter has the Queen progressing from Windsor Castle to St. George's Chapel in procession with her Knights Companion. Although horses do not actually appear on this occasion, knights, by definition, are horsemen. Royal Ascot is, of course, nothing more than a horse race. Its most indelible image is that of the Queen and royal party arriving in horse-drawn carriages.

Trooping the Colour marks the Queen's official birthday, usually celebrated on the second Saturday in June. Whereas a number of the grand occasions are religious in part (e.g., the Coronation, a royal wedding, a thanksgiving service, Royal Maundy), the core of the Birthday Parade is an arcane and elaborate piece of military choreography. I have yet to find an explanation of why these maneuvers should have become associated with the Sovereign's birthday.

Colours were originally displayed daily so that troops would be able to recognize them in battle. The Colours were not only displayed, they were also "trooped," that is, "saluted by beat of drum" (Paget 1979:29). The Colours trooped at the Sovereign's Birthday Parade are not from any regiment; rather, they are those of the Sovereign's personal troops, the Household Brigade, who guard Buckingham Palace, among their other duties. Incidentally, the regiments of the Household Brigade are socially the smartest regiments.

> The [Household] Brigade is made up of five regiments—the Grena-diers, Coldstream, Scots, Irish, and Welsh Guards—with the first two carrying the most *cachet*. There are two cavalry regiments, the Lifeguards and the Royal Horse Guards (the "blues"). [Since Perrott wrote in 1968, the Blues have been amalgamated with the 1st Royal Dragoons—the "Royals"—and are now the "Blues and Royals."] In the latter, which are regarded as top of the league for smartness, between five and ten per cent of the officers are titled or heirs to titles, and there are close connections with the landed gentry. In school background they show a much higher proportion of recruits from Eton than from other public schools. (Perrott 1968:142–43)

The Queen is Colonel-in-Chief of these regiments. She wears the uniform of the regiment whose colors are to be trooped.

The maneuvers are complicated. Thus, I shall quote at length Sir Julian Paget, an officer in the Coldstream Guards, who commanded the ceremony in 1962.

> The parade is complex and the standard is high. Over 1400 officers and men, and some 200 hundred horses take part, and they come from six to eight different units stationed in different barracks around London. There are over 400 musicians from ten different bands and corps of drums who march and play as one. Some 113 words of command are given by the officer in command of the pa-rade. (1979:30)

Precisely at 11:00 A.M. the Queen enters the parade grounds as the Na-tional Anthem is played.

> The parade begins with an inspection, the Queen riding slowly down the ranks of all eight guards, and then past the Household Cavalry. As she resumes her position, the Officer Commanding

gives the one single dramatic word of command, "Troop." A brief pause, and the massed bands strike up the traditional air, "Les Huguenots," to which they slow march across the parade ground and then back in quick time. (1979:31)

The most solemn moment occurs when the Colour is brought forth by the Escort Party and saluted. The Escort and whole parade present arms while six bars of the National Anthem are played, and the Colour is trooped down the ranks. At this point the actual Trooping is over, but not the parade. First the Foot Guards, and then the Household Cavalry march past the Queen. (Until 1939 the Household Cavalry preceded the Foot Guards "but, it is alleged, the Foot Guards objected to marching through the droppings inevitably left by the horses, and successfully argued that those on foot should march first" [Paget 1979:33]).

The precision of the movements of horses and men makes this a very impressive ceremony. (During every Trooping a number of foot soldiers faint, probably because of the heat generated by their bearskin hats. But this does not compromise the impression of precision since they manage to faint at attention.) Clearly, the message is one of the orderliness of society, an orderliness that radiates from the Sovereign.

When the parade is over, the Queen leads her personal troops back down the Mall to Buckingham Palace where they all march past her again.

> The last Guard marches past, and onto Chelsea Barracks to dismiss. The Queen turns, and rides between the . . . Guards into the Quadrangle of Buckingham Palace, where footmen appear with carrots on silver trays for the horses.
>
> The Officer in Command of the Parade follows the Queen into the Quadrangle, dismounts, usually with some relief, and accepts a welcomed Royal invitation to some refreshment. (1979:33)

The whole Royal Family then appears on the balcony of Buckingham Palace.

The Order of the Garter is the premier and most exclusive order of knighthood in the world. One could, of course, argue that the Order of the Thistle, which has fewer knights (sixteen knights of Scottish descent to the Garter's twenty-five), is more exclusive. The Garter, however, is generally considered to be the top of the pile. In a way, it is difficult to reconcile the immense prestige of this order with its insignia—a piece of underwear. Although the emblem is worn by knights in full view just below the knee, it is nevertheless a piece of underwear. Legend has it that a lady—variously identified as the Countess of Salisbury, Queen Philippa, or Joan, the Fair Maid of Kent—dropped her garter at a ball. Edward III, the founder of the order, seeing her consternation, picked it up and buckling it around his own knee, uttered what became the order's motto: *Honi soit qui mal y pense* (dishonored be he who thinks evil of it) (De la Bere 1964:59–60). The Queen wears the emblem on the left arm just above the elbow for formal occasions, such as an audience with the Pope.

Almost every year, the Order convenes at Windsor Castle for a luncheon given by the Queen in the magnificent Waterloo Chamber. This communal meal signals that the Queen does not disdain fellowship with her Garter Knights. A religious service follows in St. George's Chapel. St. George's Chapel, "home of The Order of the Garter and necropolis of modern royalty," and Westminster Abbey are "Royal Peculiars." "A Royal Peculiar is the peculiar name for a Church directly linked to the Sovereign and independent of all provinces of archbishops and dioceses of bishops. The Archbishop comes to a Royal Peculiar by invitation only, whereas he comes to any other church in his province by right" (Howard 1977a:90).

When new knights are inducted into the Order of the Garter (announced on St. George's Day, April 23rd), there is an investiture in the Castle before they are installed in the Chapel at the start of the annual service (see Appendix A for the Order of Service).

Although the Order is over six hundred years old, it was only four decades ago that it was added to the list of annual royal public occasions.

> It was in 1948 that King George VI gave orders that thenceforth that year was to be accepted as the sexcentenary of its foundation. It was on St. George's Day of that year that, accompanied by his queen, his mother [Queen Mary], his daughter [Princess Elizabeth] and his son-in-law [Prince Philip, Duke of Edinburgh], he went in a procession of Knights to the chapel of the order [Saint George's Windsor] to give thanks on this six hundredth anniversary. (De la Bere 1964: 58–59)

The Garter service is the most private of the public royal occasions. Neither the Service, the Investiture, the Installation, nor the luncheon are made public. The procession, however, of the Queen and the Knights of the Garter from the Castle to St. George's Chapel is comparatively public, but is watched only by individuals who have obtained tickets allowing them into the Castle compound for the occasion. One source of such tickets in gift is the Dean and Canons of Windsor.

The procession, incidentally, is very amply photographed. Indeed, one might even say that this event is overrepresented in royal iconography. Photographs of the Queen, accompanied by her Knights of the Garter, or massed on the steps of St. George's with the Royal Family, are a favorite theme of souvenir postcards and posters.

Ascot is royal on two accounts. The track itself is on Crown land, and the races themselves have enjoyed royal patronage since the days of Queen Anne, who decided that Ascot heath should be turned into a race course (Laird 1976:8). In the twentieth century the association of royalty with the races has become particularly strong. Edward VII, while still Prince of Wales, conferred the immense social cachet upon the races that Ascot still enjoys today. So dearly did he love it that, when he died, Queen Alexandra requested the races be held despite the observance of mourning—thus the famous Black Ascot of 1910; none of the Royal Family attended, however.

Nonetheless, it seems a peculiar addition to the roster of royal public events. After all, it is nothing more than a week of horse racing, that is, sporting events that the Queen would seem to attend primarily as a private person as she does the other big races like the Derby or Goodwood. Paget includes Ascot in his book of British pageantry and writes: "There is no elaborate ceremonial, but it is a unique scene, and so very English, that it is worthy of mention as being a small part of the whole tapestry of our national pageantry and also of our way of life" (1979:103). What makes it so very English, so evocative of a way of life, is the horse. Barr and York corroborate the significance of the horse as the English totem: "The horse is the . . . sacred animal. . . . Everything to do with horses: stables, grooms, jockeys, harnesses, stirrups and spurs, snaffles, takes on a symbolic life of its own." The sanctity of the horse and its milieu, the country life, is reflected in those "marvelous Hermes scarves" which are "a kind of montage of *everything that's good.*" They are "patterned with horse insignia and enough whips and straps to excite memories of prep school" (Barr and York 1982:23, 35).

Paget never specifies what he means by Ascot being "so very English," a small but significant part "of our way of life." The importance of the occasion transcends the ritual display of the horse. Ascot, after all, is not just a horse race; it is one means by which humanity is divided into the common and the elite. This division is as essential to English life as are the warp and woof to that of a tapestry.

Social class is roughly apparent from where one views the races: the fields, the grandstand, the Royal Enclosure, or the Queen's Lawn. The

Different categories of social persons are evident at Ascot. Sartorially correct individuals in the Royal Enclosure, on the right, contrast with the more motley, though hardly poor, assemblage in the Grandstand. *Photo by Dafydd Jones.*

surrounding fields are the most common. Next on the pyramid is the grandstand, though it is separated from the fields by a considerable gulf. It contains 284 private boxes which rent for as much as 630 pounds per year. The Royal Enclosure is definitely exclusive, as are the car parks where it is "hampers out, gloves off and into the aspic" (McKerron 1982:53) for debutantes and men who seem as if they had just stepped out of a Moss Brothers commercial. (Moss Brothers, familiarly referred to as Moss Bross, is to clothes-hire trade what Lloyds' of London is to the insurance business [Petschek 1981:45]). These picnickers view the races from the Royal Enclosure, admission to which is regulated by the Queen's Ascot representative at St. James's Palace (the Marquess of Abergavenny). Not just anyone can apply for admission, however. A new applicant must be sponsored by someone already on the "list" (Laird 1976:229). The Enclosure, however, is not the last word in social honor. In front of it is the Queen's Lawn, to which access is by the Queen's personal invitation. The most privileged of all are the Queen's house

party, who "attend the theatre, play games at the castle [Windsor], race each other in the early morning down the course (a practice in abeyance for some years now), and drive in state in the afternoon. Women curtsey. Men raise their toppers and give a cheer" (Duncan 1969:283). The royal house party watch the races from the Royal Box with the Queen and Royal Family. The distribution of categories of persons at Ascot makes evident British social hierarchy.

## The Opening of Parliament

The Opening of Parliament is the most splendiferous of the annual royal events. Although the Opening now happens in November most often, it can still occur anytime there is a change of governments. Ten years ago the Opening was usually in October. It is a fitting conclusion to the ceremonial year. On this occasion, the Queen wears the Imperial Crown and Crimson Robe of State to read the Most Gracious Speech from the Throne. This speech, written by the Cabinet, concludes, "I pray that the blessings of Almighty God may rest upon your Counsels." Although this ceremony ostensibly sets forth the government's programs and policies for the coming year, it really is an enactment of "The King in Parliament," the slogan *par excellence* of constitutional monarchy.

The Opening incorporates many elements of the Coronation and as such is an annual replay of that grand occasion. For example, the Queen rides in state from Buckingham Palace, as she did for the Coronation (though not in the same carriage), with a Sovereign's Escort through streets lined with other troops to Westminster. She does not, however, wear the Imperial Crown for the procession through the streets. The Crown, the Cap of Maintenance, and the Sword of State are brought, on the morning of the Opening, from the Jewel House at The Tower of London to Buckingham Palace. Riding in Queen Alexandra's State Coach, with their own escort, the Regalia precede the Queen to Parliament. Here again we see the distinction between sovereign and sovereignty symbolically maintained. Unlike the Coronation, the Queen is not ceremoniously invested with the Regalia. There is no need to reinvest the Queen with these symbols of her sovereignty. Since the time of the Coronation they have been part of her persona despite the separation of her person and her office. Once in Parliament she puts on the Regalia in private, withdrawing to the Robing Room in the House of Lords. From the Robing Room, the Queen is escorted to the dais by an elaborate procession of Heralds and the Great Officers of State. So reminiscent of the Coronation is this procession that it is not uncommon to see photographs of it mislabeled (e.g., Edgar 1979:133).

When the Queen is seated on the Throne, the Lord Chancellor hands the speech to the Queen. Before it is read, the "faithful commons" must be summoned. At this point the Opening of Parliament assumes certain inimical overtones.

Constitutionalists today consider "Parliament" to mean the Crown, Lords, and Commons, even though government work conducted in "Parliament" is generally understood to be the House of Commons. The Opening of today's Parliament recalls that in the Middle Ages the House of Lords was undeniably the dominant body. This erstwhile dominance of the Lords can still be seen in the pageantry that precedes the Speech from the Throne. The Gentleman Usher of the Black Rod, the Sovereign's messenger, is sent to summon the lower house, whose "Sergeant-at-Arms there carefully slams the door in his face" (Paget 1979:45). (Slams the door in his face!?) Black Rod must then knock three times before the door is finally opened. Once the Queen's command to attend has been conveyed, the Commons proceed to the House of Lords "deliberately chatting casually as they approach just to show that they stand in no awe of the 'other place'" (Paget 1979:45). They are not allowed to enter and must stand outside thronged at the bar (like beggars at the gate?) to hear the speech. When the speech is concluded, the Queen returns first to the Robing Room and then to Buckingham Palace.

The calendric events take us, then, through the year, beginning with the Christmas Broadcast and ending with the Opening of Parliament. Intertwined with the Christian Ordo, that is, the list of feasts and offices for each day of the year as determined by the Church, they hasten the year from the dead of winter to the promise of spring and Easter, through the glorious events of the English summer, and back to a traditional harvest festival (though a bitter one indeed) of Remembrance Sunday. The Opening of Parliament, reenacting the Coronation, reassures with the notion of time as an endless return.

## The Fabric of History

The grand occasions are colorful and appealing spectacles—after all, everyone loves a parade. As we have seen, they generally conform to the formula: procession, ceremony, return procession. But this formula is an oversimplification. It ignores many of the symbols and emblems that imbue these events with much of their appeal. And that appeal derives from the sense that history is recreated.

Take, for example, the crowns with which the Sovereign is invested. Crowns are forever being broken up and remodeled. What lends them sanctity, tying them to the history of the realm, is their jewels. The Imperial State Crown, which the Sovereign wears to read the Speech from the Throne, was made as recently as 1838. It is crafted of platinum and contains 2,700 diamonds as well as hundreds of other precious and historically significant stones. Among these are Elizabeth I's pearl earrings; the Star of Africa, cut from the Cullinan diamond (originally given to Edward VII by Boer leader General Smuts in 1905 and thus a recent addition to the Crown Jewels); and the Black Prince's Ruby. (This Black Prince, so-called because of his black suit of armor, was the oldest son of Edward III. He died in 1376, a year before his father, from a wound suffered in the Hundred Years War. The ruby was given the Prince by Pedro the Cruel of Castille. Henry V wore it in his helmut at Agincourt in 1415. In the sixteenth century Henry VIII added it to the Crown Jewels.)

This Crown, then, is a mnemonic device for some 600 years of British history. Other such devices exploited by the grand occasions are the places where these ceremonies take place. The site of Westminster Abbey was important even in pre-Norman Saxon England. The adjoining Westminster Hall, where sovereigns lie in state, was a favorite residence of English kings till Tudor times. The Colour is trooped at the site of another royal residence, that of the Palace of Whitehall, a favorite home of Charles II until it burned down. Horseguards Parade Ground is all that remains of that palace. Just as Westminster (both the Abbey and the Palace) celebrates that portion of English history stretching from the Saxon to the Tudor, so does the Birthday Parade celebrate another: that of the Restoration of the Monarchy and the creation of Great Britain. The most important symbolic entities of this occasion are the Regiments of the Household Brigade.

Among this Brigade, the Grenadiers and the Coldstream Guards rival each other for seniority. The Grenadiers, the descendants of two regiments formed by Charles II, were granted the privilege of carrying the Sovereign's body because of their unswerving loyalty during his exile (Windsor 1947:268). The loyalty of the Coldstream Guards to the monarch was not so unswerving, however. This regiment descends from one formed by Cromwell in 1650. It was made an "Extraordinary Guard" in 1660 for the Restoration.

The regiments of the Household Cavalry also date from the late seventeenth century. The three other regiments of Foot Guards are more recent. But their significance lies not with their time of origin so much as it does with their place of origin. The addition of Scots, Irish, and Welsh Guards to the English regiments creates a tableau, so to speak, of Great Britain, compounded as it is of England, Wales, Scotland, and, today, Northern Ireland.

The individual symbolic elements (jewels, sites, and soldiers) are woven into an immensely rich and aesthetic fabric. This fabric is draped about the shoulders of the Queen, transforming her not only into an effigy of kingship but also into a personification of British history.

## The Continuity of the Realm

The grand occasions render, as Durkheim would say, the mythical past of the clan present to the mind (1967:419). That rendering is possible partially because they distort time. Thus, the importance of archaic modes of transportation and fancy dress. The Palace of Westminster or the jewels of the Imperial Crown would not lose one whit of their historical significance if the Queen were to go to Parliament in a car rather than a horse-drawn carriage. But the Irish State Coach adds to the magic of the occasion. Similarly, many other elements used on such occasions lack any historical rationale. Why, for instance, do the pages, who carry the Queen's train at the Opening and at the Garter Service, wear eighteenth-century court dress? Why are they not dressed as Tudor courtiers, or loyalist cavaliers? Ironically, it makes better symbolic sense that their costumes are out of sync. The anachronism of the costumes dissociates chronological time from the occasion.

Moreover, those deliberately archaic and sacred elements used to symbolize the social order simultaneously insinuate the morality of that order. Timelessness and goodness are often identified in the human mind. The archaic confounds the authority of the present regime with the authority of tradition; it has been sanctified by time. "Men celebrate [these rituals] to remain faithful to the past" (Durkheim 1967:415).

Clearly, the grand occasions are meant to be historical. What is not so clear is that they also celebrate, covertly, hierarchy. The hierarchical aspect is obscured by the mystique of the Queen, that is, her ability to attract and move deeply those who come to watch, but it is possible to discern a series of ranks even within the audience. The spectators at royal occasions resolve themselves into a series of concentric circles. These circles are described by apparel, time of arrival, and proximity to the "stage." For example, the crowds who line the route of the Birthday Parade often camp overnight on the pavement. They dress as if they are backpacking, which of course, they are. They arrive hours ahead of time, remain far from the action and for all their pains get only a quick glimpse.

Not everyone is so disadvantaged. Take again, for example, the Trooping of the Colour. Along the northern side of the parade ground are bleachers for which it is possible to get tickets. These can be gotten by applying between January 1 and March 1 to the Brigade Major, The Household Division, Horseguards, Whitehall. Tickets are awarded by ballot. Now, anyone can apply for these tickets, but the point is that one has to know about them, and that is a form of privilege. Those who win these tickets do not have to suffer to see the show. Instead, they enter the parade ground about a half hour before and are able to watch sitting. The men wear suits and the women hats, gloves, and the characteristic ensembles of the upper middle classes.

This pattern of circles of proximity and privilege is evident on all royal occasions. Inversions are rare, but the announcement of Prince Charles's engagement was marked by one. Lady Diana's father and stepmother were actually outside the Palace. A reporter, recognizing them, asked, "What are you doing on the pavement *outside* the Palace? I thought you would be *inside*." The Earl replied, "I've been posing for photographers" (Honeycomb 1981:15).

Once one is aware of the importance of hierarchy on these occasions, the aristocratic element is unmistakable. The horse, for example, is responsible for much of the timeless quality of a royal occasion and is also the nearly perfect emblem of the aristocrat. Not only are horses expensive to keep, they are also dangerous, being big, dumb, and skittish. To handle them with grace (not to mention safety) is an art, requiring skills not easily acquired. Moreover, the element of danger is an asset. Horsemanship is evidence of the aristocrat's insouciance in the face of danger, an exhibition of the "grace to lay aside the fear of man" (see Appendix A, p. 169). Those riding closest to the Queen are aristocrats. Their trustworthiness, manifested in their horsemanship, is signalled by their proximity to the Queen. An inexperienced horseman riding close to the Queen would surely endanger her.

Royal public occasions are the *sine qua non* of the modern British monarchy. A major obligation of the Royal Family is that they must be seen. What they are seen doing provides insights into certain aspects of the belief system that is the underpinning of British society. These insights are possible because ritual symbols make statements about the social reality. But even this cursory view of royal ceremonial reveals that symbols make statements that are logically inconsistent. On the one hand, the Queen's forays beyond the Palace confirm the importance of the bonds that unite Sovereign and subjects. On the other, certain conventions proclaim that social distances must be maintained between certain categories of persons. The distinctions between King and Kingship proclaim that the rule of law prevails. Maundy Thursday and Remembrance Sunday remind us that social life is premised upon fellowship and sacrifice. Yet, countervening these messages are those elements of privilege confirming the importance of hierarchy, an aspect of social life far more seductive since it depends to a great extent upon informal judgments of moral value.

# III

~W~

# A Royal Scoreboard

## Who's Who on the Balcony

The Queen of England never appears alone in public. It is unthinkable that she should do so. Her most constant companions are the members of the Royal Family. They are her entourage and her ornamental setting. They escort her and assist her on the occasion of grand events. (On the occasion of a lesser event the Queen is most frequently accompanied by courtiers.) They accompany her on her travels abroad. Their presence intensifies the Queen's majesty. Never is that majesty more intense than at the conclusion of a royal rite of passage, when the entire Royal Family appear on the balcony of Buckingham Palace.

The Royal Family not only intensify the Queen's dignity, they also disperse it, for they are her surrogates. They undertake similar constellations of activities that orbit those of the Queen. Thus, they radiate the Queen's majesty beyond the limits of her person and reflect it back upon her. "By being shared, the King's superiority becomes more, not less" (Simmel 1950:207–8).

The Queen's majesty needs other individuals to radiate and enhance it. Yet it would be diluted if too many individuals were called to the Queen's side. The Queen may not appear alone, but she cannot appear with *all* her relatives either. A balance must be struck between the need to consolidate and the need to extend her majesty. That balance is reflected in the configuration of individuals—the Royal Family—who appear on the balcony with the Queen.

Fleming wrote that to be "royal" one must stand in the "correct biosocial relationship to the sovereign" (1973:232). The correctness of those relationships (for there are more than one) is predominantly determined by the rules of descent, primogeniture, and marriage. The balcony of Buckingham Palace is a metaphor for membership in the Royal Family; any person who regularly appears there is a member in good standing. They are those individuals who are a distinctive enclave within a much larger group of people who are related to the Queen.

As we shall see, the balcony is also a mnemonic for the social relations within which monarchy exists. One often infers from contemporary accounts that the monarchy is merely tacked on to an essentially republican society, but this is not so. Just as the Royal Family and the balcony are settings for the Queen, so is the hierarchy of British society the setting for the monarchy.

## The House of Windsor

Many of those who appear are as familiar as the Queen herself, for example, Prince Charles, the Queen Mother, the Princess of Wales. Others—the Duchess of Kent, Marina Ogilvy—are less familiar and their right of access to the balcony obscure.

The individuals on the balcony are the House of Windsor, that is, they are descendants of George V. King George and Queen Mary had five children who survived to adulthood. A sixth, Prince John, the youngest, died when he was fourteen. The four surviving sons were Edward (called David), Prince of Wales, later Edward VIII, and later still, Duke of Windsor; Albert, Duke of York, later George VI; Henry, Duke of Gloucester; and George, Duke of Kent. Their daughter, Mary, became the Princess Royal in 1931—an honorific that may be bestowed upon the Sovereign's oldest daughter—married Henry, Viscount Lascelles, later 6th Earl of Harewood, and assumed the title of Countess of Harewood.

The offspring of George V, in turn, had nine children of their own. The Duke of Windsor died without issue. Albert (George VI) had two daughters, Elizabeth and Margaret Rose. The Princess Royal had two sons, George, the 7th Earl of Harewood, and the Hon. Gerald Lascelles. The Duke of Gloucester also had two sons. Prince William died in a plane crash in 1972; Prince Richard succeeded to the title in 1974. Prince George, the Duke of Kent, who also died in a plane crash in World War

II, was survived by three children, Edward, Alexandra, and Michael. Prince Edward became the Duke of Kent when he was seven. Princess Alexandra of Kent married the younger son of the Earl of Airlie, the Hon. Angus Ogilvy. Prince Michael of Kent, barely two months old when his father died, married an Austrian baroness, recently divorced from a British businessman.

Six grandchildren of George V still appear regularly. These can be divided into the lineal descendants of George VI (Elizabeth II, Princess Margaret, and their immediate families) who are closer to the Throne, and the collaterals (the descendants of George V's younger sons, among whom are Princess Alexandra and Prince Michael, as well as the Dukes of Kent and Gloucester) who are pushed farther from the Throne with each birth of the Queen's grandchildren. In this division can also be seen the precipitous downward mobility of younger sons. No descent, however, is more precipitous than that of the children of princesses. Take the

The Royal Family gather on the balcony after the Birthday Parade. They are not a homogenous group—some have been born royal, others noble, or even commoner. Nevertheless, their congregation there confirms the special relationship that exists between royalty and the aristocracy. From left to right are Prince Philip, the Queen, Princess Michael, the Duke of Gloucester, Prince Charles, the Princess of Wales, (Prince Michael not visible behind Diana), the Queen Mother, and the Duchess of Gloucester. The children are Peter Phillips, Lord Frederick Windsor, and the Gloucesters' two daughters. *UPI/Bettmann Newsphotos.*

Lascelles, the sons of the late Princess Royal and Lord Harewood. They do not appear at all. This is probably because their claim to royal status is through their mother (always tenuous) and because of their own disinclination to appear. The sons of the Princess Royal, George and Gerald, are the bohemian members, however peripheral they may be, of the Royal Family. The older, the 7th Earl of Harewood, has been managing director of the English National Opera (formerly the Sadler's Wells Opera) since 1972. The Hon. Gerald Lascelles has written extensively about jazz. The Lascelles brothers are interesting, not by virtue of their independent musical careers, but rather by their matrimonial irregularities and penchant for producing illegitimate children. Lord Harewood and Patricia Tuckwell, a musician, had a son, Mark, before the Earl was divorced from his wife, the former Marion Stein. Similarly, Gerald Lascelles and Elizabeth Calvin had a son, Martin, in 1962; they were not able to marry until 1978.

The oldest son of the Earl of Harewood has followed in his footsteps. In 1979, David, Viscount Lascelles, married the mother (the daughter of a carpenter) of his two children—a daughter born in 1975 and a son in 1978. In 1980, the Viscountess gave birth to another son who will eventually inherit the title, taking precedence over his once illegitimate older brother (Reynolds 1982:71). No doubt some pretty intense sibling rivalry will exist between these two brothers; a rare case of ultimogeniture, that is, the system wherein the younger son inherits.

Just as the stigma of illegitimacy bars the oldest son of Viscount Lascelles from inheriting his father's title, so does it eliminate him from the succession, as his Uncle Mark and Cousin Martin are eliminated.

The children of Princess Anne further illustrate the tenuous hold on royalty that the children of princesses have. For some unfathomable reason the Princess and her husband, Mark Phillips, refused a title for him when they married. Thus, their children Peter and Zara have no titles whatsoever, and so are the most "common" members of the Royal Family. Yet, when plain Peter Phillips was born, he was fifth in line to the Throne, taking precedence over cousins with much more lordly and regal titles like HRH Prince Edward, Duke of Kent.

The children of Princess Anne are not the only ambiguous figures in the Royal Family. In 1978, Prince Michael of Kent risked his place on the balcony when he married the divorcee, Baroness Marie-Christine Reibnitz, a Catholic to boot. As a condition for obtaining the Queen's permission to marry (by the Royal Marriages Act, all members of the Royal Family must obtain the Sovereign's consent if they are to marry with parliamentary approval), Prince Michael had to relinquish his rights to the Throne. At the time he was sixteen in line.

Interestingly, his children, baptized in the Church of England, did not forfeit their rights. The union of Prince and Princess Michael of Kent is a peculiar variation of a morganatic marriage. A morganatic marriage is one in which one partner (usually the wife) is so vastly inferior in rank to the other that the children born to them are legitimate, but unable to inherit the superior parent's rank. In the Kent marriage, the inferior partner—the Catholic divorcée—caused the superior one to lose his place in the succession, but their children are still in line to the Throne as if there had been nothing irregular about their parents' marriage.

## The Line of Succession

Many, though not all, individuals on the balcony are in line to the Throne. Conversely, there are many in the succession who do not appear; the limited space of the balcony can accommodate only the top contenders. Elizabeth II is Queen because she is legitimate and the older child of King George VI. In time, Prince Charles will succeed his mother. Charles's claim to the Throne would seem to be an instance of matrilineal, rather than patrilineal, inheritance. But Elizabeth II is a Queen Regnant and as such is not really a "woman," socially speaking. Queen Regnants are ambiguous and androgynous creatures. They can bequeath their rank to their children as would a man in a patrilineal system (see figure on page 40). Prince William's right to the throne is clearly patrilineal. The birth of Prince Henry (Harry) has secured the succession.

If all the descendants of George V were to disappear, however, the succession would go to those of George's sister, the Duchess of Fife (the oldest daughter of Edward VII). Failing these, the succession would move to the Royal House of Norway. Maud, the youngest daughter of Edward VII, married her cousin, Prince Charles of Denmark, who was elected to the Throne of Norway in 1905 (see Reynolds 1982 for a thorough discussion of the line of succession).

## Many Ways To Be Royal

Walzer wrote that there is no single way to define the King (1974:8). Similarly, there is no single way to be royal. Because new members are recruited to the Royal Family either by birth or marriage we can discern different categories of royal persons. Some have been born royal and will die royal (e.g., the Queen, Princess Margaret, Prince Charles). Others, born "Common," will die royal (e.g., The Queen Mother and the Prin-

The Line of Succession to the Throne of England

HRH The Prince Charles*
HRH Prince William of Wales
HRH Prince Henry of Wales
HRH The Prince Andrew, Duke of York
    (any children born to the Duke and Duchess of York)
HRH The Prince Edward
HRH The Princess Anne
    Peter Phillips
    Zara Phillips
HRH The Princess Margaret
    Lord Linley
    Lady Sarah Armstrong-Jones
HRH Prince Richard, Duke of Gloucester
    Earl of Ulster
    Lady Davinia Windsor
    Lady Rose Windsor
HRH Prince Edward, Duke of Kent
    Earl of St. Andrews
    Lord Nicholas Windsor
    Lady Helen Windsor
Lord Frederick ⎤ the children of HRH Prince Michael of Kent
Lady Gabriela ⎦
HRH Princess Alexandra of Kent (Mrs. Angus Ogilvy)**
    James Ogilvy
    Marina Ogilvy
Earl of Harewood
    His children (excluding Mark)
Hon. Gerald Lascelles
    His son Henry (but not Martin)

---

*"The" in Prince Charles's title indicates that he is the son of a Sovereign.
**The lack of a "the" as in Princess Alexandra's title signifies that she is a grandchild of a Sovereign.

cess of Wales). Royalness is either ascribed through the possession of royal blood, or achieved by marrying a royal person as did, for example, Sarah Ferguson.

The two Queens on the balcony, Her Majesty, The Queen, Elizabeth II, and Her Majesty, Queen Elizabeth, exemplify achieved and ascribed royalness most dramatically. One married her queenliness, and the other was born to it. Elizabeth II is a Queen Regnant, that is, Sovereign in her own right. Her mother is a Queen Consort, the wife of a king. Incidentally, the Queen should never be identified as "Queen Elizabeth," though she often is in the American news media. The Queen Mother reputedly dislikes the title Queen Mother. Her Household and those in the know correctly call her Queen Elizabeth. In this book I have called her the Queen Mother for the sake of clarity.

The Queen Mother has no royal blood. Her son-in-law, Prince Philip, on the other hand, has a great deal of it, even more than the Queen. His father was a nephew of Queen Alexandra; his mother, a descendant of Queen Victoria. Both his parents bore princely titles while only the Queen's father was royal. Even though Prince Philip has more royal blood than either of the two Queens, he is only High, while they are Majestic. Majesty derives from the Coronation where sovereigns (both Kings and Queen Regnants) as well as Queen Consorts are anointed with the Sacred Chrism, and crowned. (Prince Philip was neither anointed nor crowned during the Coronation but was the first of the Lords Temporal to swear his oath of fealty.) Thus, the Queen Mother is more majestic than all save one on the balcony, though she has no royal blood to speak of.

As we have seen, individuals can acquire royalness either by birth or marriage. But royalness can also dissipate, as it were. On the balcony are some who can only be described as "royalish." Although they were born to unions in which one parent was royal, they are unable to inherit that parent's rank. In some instances they are unable to inherit because their mother is the royal parent, namely, Princess Margaret's children, Lord Linley and Lady Sarah. But even individuals whose fathers are royal are still not royal themselves. The Earl of St. Andrews, for example, has a royal father—the Duke of Kent—but neither he nor his siblings are royal (though they are currently members of the Royal Family).

The key to understanding this anomaly lies in the nature of royal blood—the mystical fluid that conveys the election of God, sanctifying the succession (Kantorowicz 1957:331). A popular assumption is that once royal always royal. This is not true. Royal blood is a volatile and evanescent substance that vaporizes by the third generation, and with it dissipates an individual's right to a princely title. After the third generation in the male line (sooner in the female line), the blood royal stabilizes as the merely blue; erstwhile royalty blend imperceptibly with the aristocracy.

This process is evident in the Royal Dukedoms of Kent and Gloucester. The present Dukes, Prince Edward and Prince Richard, are grandsons of George V. Their sons, the Earl of St. Andrews and the Earl of Ulster, are only great-grandsons of a Sovereign and so have slipped beyond the three-generation limit. Thus, when these two Earls succeed their fathers, they will be Dukes, but no longer royal ones.

In the reign of Charles III and Queen Diana the noble Dukes of Kent and Gloucester will probably not appear on the balcony. Their places will have been usurped by the royal families of the Duke of York and Prince Edward who has yet to receive his royal dukedom. The Kents and Gloucesters will be living comfortably in comparative obscurity somewhere in the country. Although the practice of conferring royal dukedoms on younger sons of the Sovereign antedates the current practice of limiting princely titles to three generations, its advantage is clear. It transforms descendants of Kings into scions of the aristocracy.

Was British royal blood always so volatile? No. A hundred years ago, had there existed the convention of the balcony, no individual who appeared would have been anything but royal. For several centuries, British royalty had been strictly endogamous, that is, they married only other royalty. They persisted in the practice even if their spouses had to be dredged up from some flyspeck of a principality on the continent. In those days, one was born royal, died royal, and in the interim married royal, producing invariably royal children.

Nineteenth-century royalty, however, was very different from that of the twentieth. It was, in essence, one large, relatively close-knit, international family. Dynastic marriages shuffled royal personnel across the face of Europe, one consequence being that royalty to an extent existed apart from the societies over which they reigned. They were not rooted in the soil as is the House of Windsor.

Toward the end of the nineteenth century, the British Royal Family began to sever its ties with continental royalty. Whether this was a matter of deliberate policy or not is unclear. But this change from royal endogamy to exogamous unions with aristocrats contributed to the strong national identity that the Royal Family enjoys today. These changes will be examined more closely in the next chapter.

To sum up, then, the balcony makes clear who is a member of the House of Windsor and thus capable of magnifying and extending the Queen's majesty. Behind the individuals appearing there we can also glimpse the abstract rules that bestow (and retract) royal status. This all seems to be very forthright. Nevertheless, the balcony is a prime instance of the ability of royal symbols to appear to be saying one thing but can also be seen as saying something entirely different.

The periodic assembly of the Royal Family has become a primary occasion on which to display the Sovereign to her people, who often wait for hours in the Mall for a glimpse of the Queen. This need to exhibit the monarch is an ancient one. It underscores the contractual nature of kingship whose legitimacy in part depends upon the recognition of that contract by the people. Indeed, the Coronation commences with the recognition and the consent of those gathered in the Abbey.

Despite the contractual elements of kingship, it is hardly a relation-

ship of equals. The inherent inequality is signified by the high elevation, above the populace, of the Sovereign on the balcony. Although the
Queen is shown to all who have managed to squeeze into the Mall, she
is essentially unapproachable.

The balcony, thus, becomes a device that smuggles notions of social
superiority—and by insinuation, inferiority—into a world supposedly
inhabited by legal equals (Hobsbawm 1983:10). It represents the small
tip of a largely submerged relationship that involves in part the exchange
of wives, a significant method of recruitment to the Royal Family.
Spouses, however, are not exchanged in a vacuum. People meet and so-
cialize with one another, and occasionally fall in love and marry because
they share interests premised upon shared material circumstances. Prince
Andrew and Sarah Ferguson, after all, "met on the polo fields. But then,
doesn't everyone?" observed Sarah's mother, Susan Barrantes. Thus the
exchanges of personnel that bind the aristocracy and royalty take place
within a larger social context—one mostly hidden from the public, that
is, the people who mass below the balcony. Balcony appearances are a
public confirmation of the exclusive, privileged, and largely hidden relationship. But even hidden relationships must occasionally become apparent. Significantly the only individuals, besides the Royal Family, who
are allowed on the balcony are the royal in-laws and members of the royal
wedding party. The intensity of the Queen's majesty on the balcony con-
sequently both denies and legitimizes that hidden but essential relationship.

# IV

⌒⌒⌒

# The Anglicization of
# the Monarchy and
# the Reign of George V

What could be more English than the British monarchy? Nothing perhaps. But it was not always so. The reign of George V from 1910 to 1936
was the watershed of the modern monarchy. It was during this twenty-
five-year period that the ancient and ceremonious traditions of the *English* monarchy were invented. This "anglicization" involved two inter-
related processes. The first was the transformation of the Germanic
House of Hanover into that of Windsor. The second was the incorporation of ceremonies suggestive of "merrie olde England" into the public
life of royalty. These struck a sentimental chord among the populace and
reinforced the newly fashioned Englishness of the Royal Family.

## The House of Hanover in Britain

The monarchy had been German since George I of Hanover succeeded
his distant cousin, Queen Anne, in 1714. This succession had been ensured thirteen years earlier with the Act of Settlement. Those who had
framed this act had not been as interested in putting a German on the
Throne as they had been in keeping a Catholic off it. The Catholics that
they had been especially mindful of were the son and grandson of James
II. This impolitic King James had had two families. His first included

two Protestant daughters—Mary and Anne—who, in time, both ascended the Throne. After their mother, the former Lady Anne Hyde, died, James married a Catholic princess, Mary of Modena, whose son, James Francis Edward, was denied the crown because of the incredible folly of his father. (This Prince James, also known as the Old Pretender, was the father of Bonnie Prince Charlie, who, despite his romanticization in Scottish legend, inherited the familial foolishness of the Stuarts.) Neither Mary nor Anne produced a child who lived very long. Thus, when Queen Anne died, the Crown reverted to the heirs of Sophie, the Protestant granddaughter of James I. Princess Sophie, married to the Elector of Hanover, would have become Queen of England herself had she not died just two months before her cousin Anne. Her son George became the first Hanoverian King of England.

When Victoria ascended the Throne in 1837 her family had been in England for more than 120 years. Yet they had retained their German identity mainly by marrying Germans and speaking German amongst themselves. Even Victoria—Englishborn and brought up speaking English—perpetuated the Teutonic image by marrying her German cousin, Albert of Saxe-Coburg.

Had not the First World War broken out (not to mention the Second), the British Royal Family might very well have remained Germanic, keeping close family ties with the Continent. But the Great War did occur and English indignation at the excesses of the "bloody Hun" spawned a wave of anti-German feeling. So virulent were these sentiments that even sausages and sauerkraut could no longer appear in shop windows labelled as such; instead they had to be displayed as "good English viands" (Marwick 1965:37).

By 1917, people were calling for the abdication of the "German King." H. G. Wells, among them, wrote that England was struggling along "under an alien and uninspiring court," to which George V replied, "I may be uninspiring, but I'll be dam[n]ed if I'm alien" (Talbot 1980:61). Under such circumstances, it was prudent for the Royal Family to shed its Teutonic plumage. The King became an English gentleman, obliterating any evidence of the German Prince. Thus, some 200 years after George I of Hanover came to England it behooved his descendants to become English at last. This Anglicization of the monarchy did more than change its ethnic identity or save its skin. It also made the Royal Family seem timeless and firmly rooted in the moral landscape, enabling them to shield so effectively the system of class privilege.

The first step was to change the surname of the Royal House from Hanover to Windsor. This was not as easy as it sounds.

The King was not sure that strictly he *had* a surname. He had never used one—understandably, because no royal surname operated in

Britain. He belonged to a branch of an old German family of course, and his Queen was a Teck, but even the Royal College of Heralds [sic] said they were not certain what his Majesty's own name was. Not "Guelph," they thought, and not "Wipper" or "Wettin"—which were names associated geographically and dynastically with the Guelphic Saxe-Coburg family, and in any case were unfortunate labels if given English pronunciation. (Talbot 1980:61).

Courtiers scratched their heads trying to come up with names that were both euphonic and suggestive of great Englishness. Tudor-Stewart and Fitzroy were among those considered and rejected. (Fitzroy was an odd choice since "Fitz" can mean "bastard son of." The illegitimate son of Henry VIII was known as Henry Fitzroy, that is, the King's Bastard.)

Finally, George V's Private Secretary, Lord Stamfordham, in a moment of genius, hit upon the name Windsor. As Hough wrote, "a name that no modern public relations firm could have improved upon: Windsor, so English, so safe, so steady, so immediately traditional, as solid as the Castle" (1981:38).

Windsor has been royal since Saxon times. Christopher Hibbert describes the way Windsor might have looked a thousand years ago, when it was nestled deep in the countryside. (One also gets a sense from this description of the importance of the countryside in English mythic traditions, a theme examined in a later chapter.) Around the castle,

> farther than the eye could stretch, lay a vast expanse of uncultivated country of heath and forest where wild oxen and boars, red and fallow deer, foxes, wolves, and hares, roamed and ran, bred and multiplied beneath skies alive with the movement of birds. The Saxon Kings had hunted then, chasing wild boars with bows and arrows, returning at night to a royal manor house in the parish of Wyndleshore (now Old Windsor) down by the river. (Hibbert 1964:6).

Windsor, then, was the perfect name for the Royal Family, suggestive as it was of a thousand years of history and a fierce, untouched countryside.

## The House of Windsor

The adoption of the new name was not the only change made. In July 1917 George V issued the proclamation that made public the new royal name:

> Our House and Family shall be styled and known as the House and Family of Windsor and that all British based descendants in the male line of our Grandmother Queen Victoria of blessed and glorious memory were immediately to relinquish "all German Titles and Dignities." (Talbot 1980:62)

The Royal Family henceforth eschewed foreign titles and dignities and adopted the strict practice of English primogeniture in the inheritance of their new princely styles and titles. They also forsook, by and large, foreign marriage alliances. The genius, or perhaps the great good fortune, of the monarchy was that it was able to fob off as age-old traditions these abrupt departures from established royal practice.

Not only was the King's immediate family deteutonized, but so were his more distant British-based relatives. To compensate these individuals for their loss of princely rank, George V raised them to the peerage. Thus, the princely Battenburgs became the noble Mountbattens, prompting one Prince Louis (later Mountbatten of Burma) to quip: arrived Prince Hyde, departed Lord Jekyll. Mountbatten's father, the former Prince Louis, became the first Marquess of Milford Haven. Similarly, Queen Mary's older brother, the erstwhile Duke of Teck, was made the Marquess of Cambridge. The Duke of Teck, like Queen Mary, was the grandchild of the Duke of Cambridge, the youngest son of George III, Adolphus Frederick. By making his brother-in-law the Marquess of Cambridge, the King was resuscitating a family honor.

Queen Mary's younger brother, Prince Alexander of Teck, became the Earl of Athlone. This ennoblement of the King's relatives ensured them places of honor in British society. I know of no individual who began 1917 as Prince or Princess and ended it as plain Miss, Mrs., or Mr. Windsor.

The price of this ennoblement, however, was that the King's near and distant relatives had to abide by the rules of English primogeniture wherein only the eldest son (and in some cases the oldest daughter, if she has no brothers) inherits the title. The English system differs from that of the continent where all the sons and daughters of, say, a count, are counts and countesses. Continental inheritance results in a great proliferation of titles which debases them in a way. In contrast, English primogeniture casts out younger sons to fend for themselves. This preserves the currency of the title; it also conserves the estate upon which a family's prominence has been predicated. This is what George V did in 1917, four months after he had proclaimed the new name of Windsor for the Royal Family, when he restricted the use of princely titles to the children of the Sovereign, the children of the Sovereign's sons, and the grandchildren of the Prince of Wales. He preserved the worth of royal styles and he conserved the royal estate upon which his family depended.

As heartless as it may seem, the strictness of English primogeniture has had a fortuitous consequence. It has kept the English aristocracy from congealing into a rigid caste (as happened on the continent). Aristocratic younger sons blend with those below. Their lack of distinctive titles gives no clue to their origins. Similarly, younger royal children began, after 1917, to blend with the aristocracy, that is, the stratum beneath themselves.

This change in the inheritance of royal styles coincided with an equally abrupt one in royal marriage patterns. Before World War I, British royalty had married mostly other royals (and in comparative privacy). After the war, royal weddings went public, being celebrated in Westminster Abbey; but more importantly, non-royals suddenly became acceptable as spouses for royals.

It was not always so. One of Queen Victoria's daughters, Louise, married an aristocrat, as did one of Victoria's granddaughters, also called Louise. In 1871, the first Princess Louise married Lord Lorne, the son and heir of the Duke of Argyll. Her choice of husbands had been a cause of consternation in her family, especially over the disparity of rank between bride and groom. Queen Victoria, however, took it upon herself to prepare her son, the future Edward VII, for the eventuality of having a subject for a brother-in-law. But Fritz Ponsonby, the Queen's Private Secretary, felt that Victoria herself was rather apprehensive about the prospect: "[She] is not accustomed to intimacy with a subject" (Longford 1964:368).

Whatever discomfiture Victoria may have felt, she apparently did an adequate job of preparing her son for intimacy with a subject. And it was a good thing, too, since Edward VII himself would soon have a subject for a son-in-law. In 1889, Edward's daughter Louise married a Lord Fife (who was made a Duke on his wedding day). Although something of a precedent had been set seventeen years earlier by her aunt, many people still "thought it was wrong for a Princess to marry anyone less than a Prince" (St. Aubyn 1979:115).

Victoria
```
        ┌──────────────────┬──────────────────────┐
Edward VII          Louise = Lord Lorne        Arthur (Duke of
Louise =                 (1871)                Connaught)
Lord Fife                                      Patricia =
(1889)                                         Alexander Ramsay
                                               (1919)
```

The Early Royal-Aristocrat Alliances

The next time, however, a royal Princess married "down" no such reservations seemed to have been expressed. In 1919, Princess Patricia, daughter of Victoria's favorite son, Arthur, married Commander, the Honourable Alexander Ramsay, younger son of the 13th Earl of Dalhousie. Not only was this an immensely popular union (no doubt deriving from this particular Princess's enormous popularity), it also set a precedent for the public celebration of royal weddings—a point to which I shall return shortly.

## Once a Princess, Not Always a Princess

The Princesses Louise may have married down but they remained princesses, nonetheless. Not so Princess Patricia of Connaught: after her marriage she was no longer a princess. Subsequently, she became Lady Patricia Ramsay. This apparently was her own decision:

> In accordance with the express wish of HRH Princess Patricia of Connaught and with the concurrence of HRH the Duke of Connaught, the King has approved that subsequent to her Royal Highness's marriage she relinquishes the above title, styling and rank, and assumes the name of Lady Patricia Ramsay. (in Warwick 1980:34)

Notice that she did not become Princess Patricia, Mrs. Alexander Ramsay, as has the present Queen's daughter, HRH The Princess Anne, Mrs. Mark Phillips, and Anne's first cousin, HRH Princess Alexandra, Mrs. Angus Ogilvy. All three women, Patricia, Alexandra, and Anne, are the daughters of royal Dukes: Connaught, Kent, and Edinburgh, respectively. Thus, the differences in their choice of titles are significant. Moreover, Patricia was the only one to have used the title correct for a daughter of a Duke. In England, a nobleman's daughter who marries outside the peerage retains the rank and precedent she enjoyed as her father's daughter; she does not become *plain* Mrs. someone, though she does normally assume her husband's surname. Thus, Princess Alexandra should really be Lady Alexandra Ogilvy, and Princess Anne, Lady Anne Phillips—the style adopted by Princess Patricia. Though Anne and Alexandra appear to be more egalitarian, they nonetheless proclaim their royal rank.

Yet the question of why Princess Patricia abandoned her royal estate remains. Neither her aunt nor cousin—the Princesses Louise—ceased being Princesses; nor have her more distant cousins Alexandra and Anne. One would assume that once a Princess always a Princess. But we must remember that Patricia wed less than two years after 1917, which had seen a number of hitherto princely individuals stripped of their rank. Princess Patricia by deciding to be known as Lady Patricia emphasized her father's noble rank (a Duke) rather than his royal one (a Prince), and underscored the acceptability of aristocrats as royal marriage spouses.

The switch from relatively strict royal endogamy to exogamous union with subjects was a significant aspect of the Anglicization process. Following the example of their cousin Patricia, the children of George V married aristocrats. In 1920, Princess Mary married Viscount Lascelles. In 1923 Prince Albert (later George VI) married Lady Elizabeth Bowes-Lyon. Prince Henry married Lady Alice Montagu-Douglas-Scott in 1935, and the Duke of Windsor married a twice-divorced American in 1937. (The only child of George V to marry royally was Prince George, who married Princess Marina of Greece.) Such unions freed British royalty from alliances that might compromise their Englishness. One can only wonder how Victoria would have reacted to the First World War had she been alive. The Kaiser was, after all, her first grandchild. (It was somewhat miraculous when Princess Elizabeth married Prince Philip a scant two years after the Second World War that no one mentioned that the groom's sisters were married to former Nazi officers.) More importantly, union with the indigenous aristocracy identified the Royal Family with the mythic bedrock of English virtues. The genealogies of the noble houses, into which royal children began to marry, were and are intertwined with the history of the realm. Furthermore, these noble genealogies, unlike those of the Royal Family, lack the unfortunate German interlude of the erstwhile House of Hanover.

The newfound Englishness of the Royal Family was underscored in yet another way: the metamorphosis of Queen Mary. She was becoming the quintessential English Queen. At the time, few would have guessed that the obscure Princess May (as Queen Mary was known in her childhood) would become the very model of an English Queen Consort. Indeed, it is easy to forget that she had been a very odd choice for royal bride even though she was the daughter of Queen Victoria's cousin, Princess Mary Adelaide of Cambridge, a granddaughter of George III. This daughter of the Duke of Cambridge was something of an embarrassment to Queen Victoria and the rest of the Royal Family. She was grossly overweight, a fact that even the rigid corseting of the times could not hide,* and seems to have been something of a card. Two biographies of

---

*This corseting has been described by at least one young Englishwoman: "I was placed at the age of fifteen at a fashionable school in London, and there it was the custom for the waists of the pupils to be reduced one inch per month until they were what the lady principal considered small enough. When I left school at seventeen, my waist measured only thirteen inches, it having been formerly twenty-three inches in circumference. Every morning one of the maids used to come to assist us to dress, and a governess superintended

Queen Mary, those of Woodward and Pope-Hennessy, described Mary Adelaide as being "expansive," and a woman with "dash." Royal biographies are hagiographic in nature and thus routinely omit incidents that might embarrass the Royal Family. "Dash" and "expansive," two adjectives not normally employed to describe Victorian women, are clearly euphemisms for what must have been rather outlandish behavior. Woodward goes on to describe Mary Adelaide as "so stirring and energetic, so popular, so immensely kind and generous a mother [that her daughter] the shy and retiring and anything but expansive Princess [May] suffered inevitably some eclipse" (1923:26).

Woodward obligingly includes a passage which gives us a hint as to the nature of the interactions of energetic mother and modest daughter: "But what to do with a daughter who has no small talk? Only talk more oneself. This the Duchess [Mary Adelaide] did remarkably well. . . . Princess May never did develop the art of small talk and simulation" (1923:29). One can imagine the mortification May must have felt in the presence of her mother. A family friend who observed mother and daughter together regarded May's self-effacing nature a blessing: "Really, there was not room in the family for more than one with such 'dash'" (Woodward 1923:28).

Queen Mary never did acquire the ability to communicate comfortably with others (let alone make small talk). This lack was all the more poignant when it came to her own children with whom she was invariably cold and distant. "Queen Mary's exceptionally reserved and undemonstrative temperament made it impossible for her to give her children the love and affection which are taken for granted in happier homes" (Donaldson 1975:25). In some ways, then, the character of Mary Adelaide, the Duke of Windsor's maternal grandmother, may have contributed to the Abdication Crisis. Bryan and Murphy, among others, conclude that the lack of maternal sympathy was responsible for a "personality deficiency" in the Duke, making him particularly susceptible to the wiles of the domineering Wallis Simpson (1979:98).

Mary Adelaide's dash and obesity may or may not have had something to do with her difficulty in finding a husband. Queen Victoria re-

---

to see that our corsets were drawn as tight as possible. After the first few minutes every morning I felt no pain, and the only ill effects apparently were occasional headaches and loss of appetite. . . . Very few of my fellow-pupils appeared to suffer, except the pain caused by the extreme tightness of the stays. In one case where the girl was stout and largely built, two strong maids were obliged to use their utmost force to make her waist the size ordered by the lady principal—viz., seventeen inches—and though she fainted twice while the stays were being made to meet, she wore them without seeming injury to her health, and before she left school she had a waist measuring fourteen inches, yet she never suffered a day's illness." (This passage was taken from correspondences in *The Englishwoman's Domestic Magazine*, May 1867, and was quoted by the F.I.T. Catalogue.)

ferred to her as "'poor Mary' because of her vast proportions and prolonged unmarried state" (Longford 1964:371). In 1867, however, Princess Mary became engaged (to everyone's relief) to a penniless German
princeling, Prince Francis of Teck. He had washed up in England and
had apparently been pressed into marriage by "poor Mary's" anxious
relatives. The marriage, a union of mutual convenience, seems to have
worked rather well. The Tecks spent their days living beyond their
means, and visiting (i.e., sponging off) their friends and relatives. At one
point, Queen Victoria even sent them to live abroad because Mary Adelaide was 70,000 pounds in debt. (In the 1890's, 160 pounds was enough
for a middle-class family to live on comfortably, while 300 pounds per
annum enabled a family to keep a carriage.) Mary Adelaide may have
been extravagant but she also was surprisingly frugal, saving bits of
string. She even tore off and kept unused portions of note paper (Woodward 1923:26).

Colorful though the Tecks may have been, they were definitely the
poor relations of the Royal Family. Their daughter would hardly seem
to have been an appropriate match for the Heir to the Throne. But two
things were going for Princess May that put her into the running for the
Consortship. The first was that in spite of her mother, or maybe because
of her, May had a strength of character which impressed Queen Victoria.

> Queen Victoria invited Princess May to stay and suddenly her cau-
> tious approval broke into ecstasy: May was nice, quiet, cheerful, sen-
> sible, good mannered, very fond of Germany, very cosmopolitan
> and grown very pretty. (Longford 1964:513)

The second was that, as bad as the Tecks were, the Heir to the Throne
was probably worse. He was "Eddy," that is, Prince Albert Victor, Duke
of Clarence and Avondale, son of the Prince of Wales. May was chosen
as his fiancée because it was hoped that she would have a good effect on
this prince, who might have been retarded. "Rumors credited Eddy with
every vice and folly. . . . It was even whispered that the Prince was Jack
the Ripper. He was also reputed to have been compromised with Lord
Arthur Somerset, his father's Superintendent of Stables, in a homosexual
bordello in Cleveland Street" (St. Aubyn 1979:105). Mercifully, Eddy
died of influenza in 1892. Fortunately, Princess May's sterling qualities
were not lost to the monarchy. She presently became engaged to his
brother, the future George V. They married in 1893 and lived in the shadows cast first by Queen Victoria, then Edward VII, and, later still, those
of World War I. It was only after the war that King George and Queen
Mary came into their own, fashioning in their own image the modern
British monarchy.

## Monuments and Ceremonies: Mythic Creations

The Royal Family did not become English in a vacuum. Their Anglicization coincided with a new emphasis upon the ceremonial in British public life. This ceremonial was manifested in two main ways: the elaboration of royal pageantry and a new taste for monumental architecture that transformed the face of London. Although pageantry and architecture might seem to be different orders of phenomena, they are both media of expression wherein a society can make statements about itself, especially conceits of its own greatness. They are ways that enable a nation to contemplate itself—if not always the way it is, then the way it wishes it were. Massive architecture and colorful spectacles are mythic creations. They may not be *charters* of belief, but they can act as mnemonics of that belief. Thus we find in the early twentieth century both pageantry and monumental architecture serving as settings for the presentation of the newly English Windsors.

Let us look first at the increasing importance of royal pageantry in the post–World War I period, that is, in the reign of George V. We are so accustomed to thinking that these are *ancient* ceremonies that we forget that the ceremonial monarchy as we know it did not exist before the 1920s.

Modern royal occasions give the impression that they consist of rites and ceremonies faithfully reenacted, if not from time immemorial, then certainly from, say, the reign of Henry VIII. Thus, it comes as a surprise to learn that the "ancient traditions of monarchy" (Cannadine) are a modern invention.

For most of the nineteenth century, the British were not particularly interested in ceremony, and their Queen actively disliked it. Victoria considered that "'public religious displays' were apt to degenerate into 'merely show'" Longford 1964:390). Her antipathy to pageantry was reflected by her infrequent attendance at Parliament. The State Opening was then the Sovereign's major ceremonial obligation. Yet Queen Victoria frequently refused to come to Parliament for the occasion! In the twenty years between 1865 and 1884, the Queen came to Parliament only six times. The last Opening that she attended was in 1886, a whole fourteen years before she died. Frank Hardie wrote that Victoria's attendance at Parliament "was a fairly accurate barometer of her feelings towards the ministry of the day" (1935:appendix).

Victoria detested Gladstone and thus rarely attended during his ministries. This breach of custom was regarded by Gladstone as nothing less than the "dereliction of public duty" (Lee 1927:22). He grappled with the

Queen over this issue throughout his tenure in the Prime Ministership. For example, in February 1870, the Queen refused to open Parliament because she "would catch cold wearing a low cut dress in her carriage." But two years later, when Gladstone suggested she swathe herself in ermine, "she laughed scornfully: the House of Lords is too hot" (Longford 1964:376). Martin suggested that "Gladstone could have revived republicanism if he had revealed a tithe of what he had suffered from the Queen."

It was only at the end of her reign that there began to appear "those great public pageants which have become so familiar and so 'traditional'" (Cannadine 1977:439). In 1887, a year after Victoria's last Opening of Parliament, the Queen's Golden Jubilee (i.e., fifty years on the Throne) was celebrated. Even then Victoria's dislike of "religious public displays" was evident in her refusal to wear the Imperial Crown and Robes, or ride in the State Coach.

The British Queen was not much interested in public ceremony, and the British themselves were not much good at staging it. In the 1860s, Lord Robert Cecil wrote, prompted by his observation of the Queen's Opening Parliament,

> Some nations have a gift for ceremonial. . . . Everybody falls naturally into his proper place, throws himself without effort into the spirit of the little drama he is enacting, and instinctively represses all appearance of constraint or distracted attention. . . . In England the case is exactly the reverse. We can afford to be more splendid than most; but some malignant spell broods over all our most solemn ceremonials, inserts into them some feature which makes them all ridiculous . . . Something always breaks down. (Cannadine 1983:101–2)

Indeed, at the Coronation of Queen Victoria, the organist had his pocket picked, two bishops argued throughout over the Order of Service, and the Archbishop painfully jammed the Coronation Ring on the Queen's wrong finger. At one point, Victoria, thinking the ceremony at an end, left only to be recalled unceremoniously. Moreover, the Queen was appalled to find the altar in St. Edward's Chapel afterwards covered with sandwich wrappings and empty wine flasks left there by the peers of her realm.

Toward the end of Victoria's reign, between 1887 and 1897 (the years of her Golden and Diamond Jubilees), royal pageantry began to assume greater importance (cf. Cannadine 1983). The broad outlines of much subsequent ceremony were evident in the Golden Jubilee (Lant 1980:iii). Following that spectacle was a spate of similar ceremonies: the Diamond

Jubilee (1897), Victoria's funeral (1901), the Coronation (1902) and Funeral (1910) of Edward VII; and George V's Coronation (1911) and the Delhi Durbar (1912). (Scenes of the Delhi Durbar accompanied the opening credits in the 1980s PBS television presentation of "The Jewel in the Crown.") Lant and Cannadine both see an unbroken continuum between the great spectacles of Victoria's last years and today's royal ceremony. The Victorian Jubilees, the Sovereigns' Funerals, the 1902 and 1911 Coronations, and especially the Durbar were great imperial displays whose model had clearly been the Roman Triumph. They had been assertions of power, their purpose, to impress the outside world.

To be sure, contemporary British pageantry is still staged to impress the outside world; indeed some 20 million Americans were lured from their beds in 1981 to witness the Prince of Wales's wedding. Nevertheless, today's pageantry contains elements not evident in the imperial displays that marked the fin de siècle. To find these we must turn to the 1911 Investiture of that Prince of Wales who later became the Duke of Windsor.

That Investiture lacked the triumphant processions through London, the center of the Empire. Instead it was held in far-off provincial Wales, in Caernarvon Castle where the first Prince of Wales (Edward II) had been born in 1284. According to legend, Edward I had promised the Welsh, after conquering them, that he would provide them with a Prince who could not speak a word of English. Naturally, they expected a Welshman to govern them; instead they were presented with the King's newborn son, Edward II. Until 1911, Princes of Wales had been invested either in Westminster Abbey or in *English* provincial towns. But in 1911, Lloyd George, hoping to make the royal ceremony a *Welsh* pageant, proposed investing the Prince in Wales itself. As it turned out, the occasion was neither Welsh nor English. Instead it was British celebrating the thirteenth-century union of England and Wales. For the first time, British court spectacle began to exploit the specifically medieval rather than the classical. Classical motifs and allusions had been the *lingua franca* of court spectacle since the Renaissance, equally intelligible to the Burgundian, English, and Italian courts. But the new emphasis upon the medieval, apparent in the 1911 Investiture, marked a turning inward. Or, rather, it marked a shift from an internationally understood idiom to a more parochial, specifically anglicized, idiom.

One, of course, wonders who was responsible for the creation of the ceremonial monarchy that appeared almost fully formed during the reign of George V. It is easy to cite the genius of the monarchy for creating its own instantaneous traditions, but this leaves unanswered the question of who precisely was responsible.

Cannadine attributes the renascence of royal ceremonial during the very latter part of Victoria's reign to three individuals: the courtier, Lord Escher; the future Edward VII; and the composer, Sir Edward Elgar. Cannadine explains their contributions in terms of their love of pageantry. Edward VII, for one, "was eager to 'show himself to his subjects, clothed in his attributes of Sovereignty'" (1983:135). While Escher's "charm, tact, historical sense, flair for organization and love for ceremonial" provided the stage upon which Edward could make "a better show" than his nephew Kaiser Wilhelm II, Elgar, for his part, provided "the ideal martial, musical background to the great royal ceremonies" out of his "genuine love of colour, pageantry, precision and splendour" (Cannadine 1983:136).

It may very well be true that all three men loved a good show, but the love-of-ceremony explanation does not really illuminate much about the strategies that resulted first in the imperial processions of the late Victorian and Edwardian eras, and later the more parochial displays of the inter-war period. Moreover, Cannadine does not seem to have noticed that Georgian ceremony was quite different from the Edwardian. An area for future research would be an investigation of who exactly figured out that reviving and revamping royal rituals would enhance the popular appeal of the monarchy. Was it the Palace or successive governments who found it in their interest to preserve a social system of which they approved? Again questions like these might prove particularly fertile research fields to plow.

Cannadine is no doubt right in identifying Edward VII, Elgar, and Escher as being responsible for organizing displays that could compete with those of the Kaiser. But this does not explain the continuing elaboration of ritual in the reign of George V; nor does it explain the shift from the imperial to the medieval. Who, for example, decided that George V should distribute the Maundy Money in 1932, the same year he made the first Christmas Broadcast? These questions, requiring the skills of a historian, are worth examining.

Whoever was responsible, World War I interrupted the development of this new style of royal ceremony. But once the war was over, royal pageantry continued to use medieval elements, such as the choice of Westminster Abbey as the setting for the wedding of Princess Patricia in 1919. The following year, 1920, the Abbey became the burial place of the Unknown Soldier. This also was a royal event since the King as chief mourner walked behind the gun carriage bearing the coffin in the procession that filed past the Cenotaph.

Before the war, the annual royal events had been the Opening of Parliament, Trooping the Colour, and Ascot. Immediately after the war,

the Cenotaph wreath-laying was added to this roster as an annual com-
memorative of the Armistice and the burial of the Unknown Soldier.
There was another flurry of royal activities in 1932 when King George
distributed the Maundy Money and inaugurated the custom of the Sovereign addressing his people over the airwaves. Moreover, George V also
instigated the practice of the Sovereign wearing the Imperial Crown to
the Opening of Parliament in imitation of medieval kings at their *parles*.

## Monumental Architecture

We are used to thinking of London as the setting *par excellence* of splendid
royal ceremony. Thus, it is surprising to learn that in the nineteenth century the city was quite inadequate for that purpose. In this, London was
quite different from contemporary cities such as Paris, St. Petersburg,
Vienna, Washington, D.C., or even Dublin (which had been laid out
most magnificently as the "Second City of the British Empire"). "In
these great capitals, the grand buildings—splendid thoroughfares were
monuments to the power of the state or the influence of the monarch"
(Cannadine 1983:113). But the "First City of the British Empire" lacked
these; its higgledy-piggledy development "was a statement against absolutism, a proud expression of the energies and values of a free people"
(Cannadine 1983:113).

Ironically, this indifference to having a grand city can be seen as a
sure sign of the confidence the British had in themselves throughout
most of the nineteenth century. But towards the end of the century, that
confidence began to wane. Monumental architecture (and pageantry)
bolstered "self-esteem in the most visible, ostentatious manner" (Cannadine 1983:126).

I do not mean to imply that until the early twentieth century there
was no construction. Like all cities, London was constantly being built
up and torn down. But in the early twentieth century the British began
to feel the need for "grand buildings and splendid thoroughfares" as tes-
taments to the power and the glory of their Empire. For the purposes of
this book, the most significant piece of rebuilding involved the monumental ensemble focusing on Buckingham Palace.

The Mall, "the avenue which sweeps from Trafalgar Square to Buckingham Palace," was widened and resurfaced (Service 1979:243). At one
end, the Admiralty Arch was built in the baroque style. At the other
end, a new, classical facade changed the appearance of Buckingham Palace. In front of the Palace the Memorial to Queen Victoria was raised.
"Whatever the faults of its individual parts, the overall scheme of trium-

phal arch [i.e., the Admiralty Arch], boulevard [the Mall], rond point [Victoria Memorial] and palace front, is a highly distinguished achievement of the move to give London a center worthy of an imperial capital" (Service 1979:243).

This triumphal ceremonial way (still using the classical idiom) not only made London a worthy capital, it also underscored the centrality of the monarchy.

The Mall connected the home of the monarch to some of the most historically significant sites in London—Trafalgar Square; and beyond that, Horseguards, a remnant of the Old Palace of Whitehall; and farther yet, Westminster, the palace of Danish, Saxon, and Norman kings and the River Thames flowing to the sea, past Hampton Court and the Tower of London. Sir Aston Webb, the architect engaged to oversee the refacing of the Palace, had replaced the Caen stonework used by Blore (the 1847 architect) with gray Portland stone, the material favored by Christopher Wren (Smith 1930:56). Thus, the Palace was also connected with Wren's masterpiece, St. Paul's Cathedral.

The very heart of this new imperial London was the area described by the Houses of Parliament on the east and Buckingham Palace on the west, connected by an impressive artery of authority. Regardless of the sentiments that had promoted this rebuilding, an inescapable effect was the emphasis that the monarchy was rooted in the center of things.

The 1919 wedding of Princess Patricia placed royal public ceremony upon the monumental stage recently created in the heart of London. The bride drove in an open carriage from Clarence House down the Mall to Westminster. Although this does not seem to be particularly remarkable today, at the time it was a singular reaching out to the people, involving the public in the private events of royal persons. Until then, royal rites of passage had been comparatively private occasions.

This is not to say that the public knew nothing about them. For instance, Warwick quotes an anonymous columnist who mixed with the crowds that gathered near the Palace in hopes of glimpsing the carriages on the occasion of the wedding of George V and Queen Mary in 1893.

> I mixed on wedding day with the unwashed in St. James's Park. Heavens! how unsavory is hot humanity. The sun poured down, the people steamed up. . . . I clung to the railings before the palace, kept a handkerchief offering incense to my nose, and for reward saw everything. (Warwick 1980:28)

It's not clear what this reporter for *The Spectator* meant by "everything." It is doubtful that he could have seen much in a crowd of people. Queen Victoria's carriage, moreover, had only to go from Buckingham

Buckingham Palace (above) as it looked before the new classical facade was added in 1912 and (below) in 1913 with its new facade. *Photo by Alastair Service from his book,* London 1900.

Palace to St. James's Palace, a veritable hop, skip, and jump away. Although it sounds like a contradiction to say that royal rites of passage were "private," yet great crowds turned out to celebrate. The closest approximation that we have today to the conduct of "private" royal events are royal christenings. The date is announced in advance, and masses of people throng outside the Palace to see the limousines of parents and godparents arrive. But no part of the ceremony is orchestrated with an eye to accommodating the public.

When Princess Patricia married, a different attitude toward the public was evident from the one that prevailed in 1893. The vastly extended procession from Clarence House to the Abbey not only drew attention to the newly triumphant proportions of the Mall, it also accommodated a great many more people than had the wedding of Patricia's cousins, George and Mary. Her procession included the public in the festivities, fostering the illusion that those who turned out to cheer the bride were somehow participating in the private life of this particular Princess.

Royal pageantry and monumental architecture drew attention to the monarchy; it also sought to present it as an integral part of the timeless, and thus moral, English order of things. This notion, however, could not be communicated solely by parades and Portland stone. The Royal Family had had also to shed their alien German identity; they had to be anglicized. Thus, they changed their name to Windsor, inherited their princely titles according to the rules of English primogeniture, and married into the indigenous aristocracy—the guardians and embodiments of tradition. This anglicization was but a means to an end. That end was the transformation of the monarchy into an autochthonic institution, that is, one that had sprung from the very bedrock of the moral landscape.

The new surname, the resurgent royal public spectacle, and the new ceremonial complex at the heart of London all proclaimed that the monarchy had come from the ancestors. The effectiveness of these tactics is evident in the following quote:

> Thus she was twenty-five when she became Elizabeth II, sixty-third monarch of the British line—a list that can be traced back to Egbert of Wessex, the regional warlord who brought the whole of England under his rule in 827, and that has included all sorts: weaklings and heroes, saints and murderers, dunderheads and people of genius. It is the oldest reigning royal house in Europe. . . . The monarchy . . . provides schoolchildren with a splendid framework for remembering their history. (Bailey 1977a:42–43).

Evans-Pritchard, in pleading that anthropology not ignore a people's history, suggested that attention be paid to "[the] mnemonics [that] are employed as points of reference in tradition." He noted that "history is often attached to places rather than to people." British history *is* attached to places—Westminster, Wessex, Wales all conjure up the heroic past. But history is also attached to people, especially royal ones. As Bailey's observations make clear, the Sovereign is literally history incarnate. The celebration of "Queen and Country" is a way of "remaining faithful to the past." But this could not be had not the monarchy undergone the elaborate process of anglicization in the early twentieth century.

# V

⁕

# The Dichotomy
# of the Royal Face

Royalty show two faces to the world: one ordinary, the other extraordinary. The Royal Family possess vast country estates, racing stables,
strings of polo ponies, and one of the world's great art collections.
Nevertheless, they manage to present themselves as ordinary people.
This peculiar posture of modern royalty contributes to the oft-quoted
observation that the British monarchy is a "middle-class" institution.
The advantage of this image in a democratic society is obvious. Broad
segments of the British public are able to identify with, or at least take
an interest in, these seemingly "classless" persons (Perrott). Thus, the
incongruous British Throne endures.

The ability of the Royal Family to appear simultaneously ordinary
and extraordinary derives from the conjoining of the King's two bodies.
Modern royalty, however, have tampered with the union of these two
natures. Earlier kings denied, as far as was humanly possible, that they
were anything less than extraordinary beings. In contrast, modern British royalty have made the ordinary a royal virtue. There is something
endearing about seeing the Queen or Queen Mother inelegantly sitting
on the ground at horse events.

The presentation of one or another of the King's bodies is determined to a great extent by the clothes with which a monarch chooses to

deck that body. Accordingly, kings have rarely been indifferent to the power inherent in clothing. Indeed, what a king wears can even be an instrument of rule, dazzling his subjects, increasing his majesty in their eyes and thus securing him in his right to rule. In the past, the style set by the King could bankrupt his potential rivals—the nobility. Take, for example, the Court of Louis XIV:

> For a courtier it was quite essential to be in fashion. . . . The King set the example. He wore magnificent clothes. So courtiers ruined themselves buying ribbons, jewellery and wigs. At least they could not be accused of niggardliness. This was another aspect of the King's policy. Crushed by his debts, a courtier had to beg for a pension, an annuity, or a gift. He was more than ever chained to the King's chariot. (Levron 1968:105)

In contrast with the regal finery of the past, until the advent of the Princess of Wales, the clothes worn by the House of Windsor have rarely "dazzled" anyone. Indeed, they tended to have the opposite effect. The Queen's hats, dresses, and general "dowdiness" are often objects of derision, as is her predilection for powder blue. Although her clothes do not generally dazzle, they are nonetheless very expensive. This is true of the whole Royal Family: as a rule they appear to avoid sumptuous dress. This apparent avoidance is an inversion of the traditional approach to royal dress which usually sought the utmost in opulence. Nevertheless, the dress of the House of Windsor has had much the same effect as the lavish silks and satins of, say, the Tudors. Their conservative suits and pastels have also secured them in their right to the Throne by making them appear in touch with the sentiments of their subjects.

One such sentiment is an "underlying puritanism in the British character which [makes] for reluctance to spend money on fancy clothes" (K. Fraser 1981:194). To do so would be to identify oneself with the "flashy new rich." Thus Victoria advised her oldest son never to "wear anything extravagant or slang, not because we don't like it but because it would prove a want of self-respect."

From this we can see that clothes transform the perception of raw physical substance into the socially perceived person. Clothes do make the man. They are not merely utilitarian instruments of warmth, protection, or modesty; they also serve as devices for the expression of moral notions such as what it means to be human. They enable individuals to communicate their social status and the social categories to which they belong. What is so fascinating about the Queen's clothes is that they are able to communicate such contradictory notions. For example, the anoraks (parkas) that she wears at horse events may seem quite ordinary, yet they are greatly favored by aristocrats (cf. Barr and York 1982:30). Indeed, the very setting confirms their toniness. The Queen's avoidance of the very fashionable does not alienate her from her subjects. She does not exude the competitive ultra-chic that, say, Nancy Reagan does.

There is another advantage to be found in anti-fashion. Fashion is a temporal phenomenon. It changes constantly. If we cannot perceive differences, we have no awareness of the passage of time. Changing fashions make us acutely aware of that passage. What is the height of fashion today may very likely be embarrassingly ridiculous tomorrow. The Queen's clothes communicate a certain timelessness that is an aspect, not of her natural body rooted in time, but of her body politic which is beyond time.

Diana, unlike the Queen, notoriously enjoys clothes. But there is another aspect to her wardrobe that shows her to be sartorially in step with her mother-in-law: her clothes are not on the cutting edge of fashion either, as the Italian press pointed out on the Waleses' trip to Venice in 1985. Although she dresses with verve, Diana's clothes are classics that could be worn from year to year without ever being in or out of style. And like the Queen's, her clothes can also come under attack, as they did when Diana visited America in 1985.

> "And for the clothes, well, they won't go down in fashion history (though perhaps those hats will). Diana looks ill-at-ease in her rigid suits and finky lace dresses. There's an inconsistency here that takes Diana from "Dynasty" to dowdy in one day. . . . Why can't her British designers figure out how to dress a beautiful and enchanting young woman with the glamor and chic she deserves?"
>
> Anne Pilmer of the mass-circulation Woman's Weekly was even less complimentary. She called Paul Costelloe's purple hacking suit with a black velvet collar "the worst outfit she has dared wear on this tour. It is utterly dreadful, the kind of thing your mother wouldn't wear. And as for the purple stockings—yuuck! She has a perfect model's body and can wear clothes beautifully, so why doesn't she show us what she can wear?"
>
> Though virtually everyone in the U.S. was impressed with Diana's English rose bloom, her chronic stoop set back posture 50 years. The princess greeted America with downcast eyes and downtrodden shoulders. In fact, the Di Slouch is now as well-known as the shy-Di smile. Even when Long, Tall Di isn't with compact Charles, for whose benefit the slouch was invented, the princess just can't seem to stand up straight. (In W 11/29–12/6/85)

These snide comments are nothing compared with the savaging Sarah Ferguson received, essentially because of her "fuller" figure.

Surprisingly, the avoidance of extravagant dress appeals not only to the middle classes but to the upper ones as well. Shabby (though well-made) clothes are considered virtuous by the aristocracy.

> Although as a rule a gentleman will wear well-cut suits when appearing in public, in his own home he can be seen wearing clothes that would not grace a scare-crow and that long ago should have been given to the rag and bone man, as they would be considered quite unacceptable by the poor. (Nelson 1976:73)

> Both my father and grandfather [i.e., the 11th and 12th Dukes of Bedford] were the least clothes conscious men I have ever known. I was allowed to go round with clothes that were either bulging with tucks to be grown into or with my arms and legs sticking out of a suit that was too old and too small. . . . [My grandfather] never used a wardrobe. In one of the four dressing rooms opening off his bedroom at Woburn [the ancestral home of the Dukes of Bedford] he had four long, plain, wooden trestle tables. His sixty or seventy suits were folded across them like clothing at a jumble sale. (J. Bedford 1959:23)

But this reluctance to spend money on clothing (evident in the upper-class "cult of studied shabbiness") is part of a larger British virtue: simplicity. The importance of simplicity to all classes perhaps explains why it is so difficult to get a decent meal in Britain; why the upper classes tend to affect a certain Philistinism; and why aristocrats would so heartily pursue pastimes such as hunting, shooting, and fishing—which more than anything else insure that by the end of the day they will be very cold, wet, and muddy. All these discomforts confirm them in their belief that they are really simple and hardy country folk. Thus what we refer to as the ordinary in modern royalty could more aptly be called simplicity.

Keeping this in mind we can address the anomaly of the Princess of Wales's obviously extravagant wardrobe. The princess is extravagant, but she has other virtues which compensate for it. The most obvious was her naturalness (i.e., simplicity) which originally endeared her to her people. "'What a long time to sit!' she exclaimed, after her first official engagement. 'I've got pins and needles in my bottom'" (Lacey 1982:125). Her naturalness may now be a thing of the past, but her glamor has become a source of national pride.

Although ancient kings dressed up and modern ones dress down, the importance of clothes in the perception of the kingly persona has remained constant. How we perceive kings depends upon the interactions of their bodies politic and natural, mediated by the clothes they wear. For example, throughout her reign Elizabeth I's splendid gowns enhanced her royal estate and dignity by obscuring her aging body natural. The Windsors, on the other hand, have secured their royal estate by emphasizing their simplicity, signaling their fitness to reign in the age of the ordinary man.

Clothes are moral constructs, communicating notions of good and bad taste, among other things; so are categories of persons, including sovereigns. Let us examine, then, the interdependence of clothes and the perception of the monarch.

The recent history of the monarchy—from Victoria to the present—has been characterized by oscillations of the pious and the imperious. The young Victoria, learning of her eventual succession, proclaimed, "I will be good." This, Longford asserts, was her "secret." Her "belief in and striving after improvement—was also the very fibre of Queen Victoria's being" (1964:576–77). Victoria's essence is the secret of the success of modern royalty. They strive to be good and are generally admired for it.

Victoria, however, was followed on the throne by her imperious son, Edward VII, whose motto very well might have been, "I will be bad." Having eventually escaped the pedagogical tyranny inflicted upon him by his well-meaning parents, Edward spent his adulthood indulging his every whim. Edward's son, George V, reverted to the monarchial style of his grandmother that stressed simple domestic virtues. These two styles of monarchy—the austere and the self-indulgent—collided in what is known as the Abdication Crisis.

## Domesticity as a Royal Virtue

Hocart wrote in the aftermath of that Abdication that the sovereign must be a pattern of character, an ideally moral figure (1970a:119). He could never have expressed such sentiments had not Queen Victoria and Prince Albert recast the sovereign as that ideal figure. Today we tend to regard the emphasis that Albert and Victoria placed upon morality, especially the conjugal, as quaint. The association, however, of domesticity and royalty was a radical departure in the style of monarchy. In a sense, they put the Royal Family on the Throne. Until the accession of Victoria, the House of Hanover would never have been able to put their families on the Throne, even if the idea had occurred to them.

George I had hated his son, the future George II, as well as his son's mother, who never became Queen of England because she was imprisoned in Germany for having committed adultery with a Count Koningsmark. George II, in turn, hated his son, Frederick, Prince of Wales, who died (before becoming King) in the arms of his dancing master. George II was succeeded by his grandson, George III, who continued the family tradition of despising his son and heir, the future George IV. George IV was an unregretted King (as a *Times* editorial described him at his death) whose major interests had been "gambling, dress, extravagant and ostentatious buildings and women" (Murray 1974:36). George IV's legitimate wife was Caroline of Brunswick, the German Princess, who was famous not only for her amatory excesses but also for rarely bathing. George IV, however, broke one family tradition by dearly loving his heir, his daughter Charlotte who never became Queen because she died in childbirth. (George IV also had had an illegitimate wife, a Mrs. Fitzherbert, who bore him a number of children. The nature of his affections towards these children does not seem to have been recorded.)

George IV was succeeded by his brother, William IV, Duke of Clarence, called "The Sailor King," a peculiar appellation since he hated the navy. William IV also had a common law wife—a Mrs. Jordan—with whom he had ten children—the FitzClarences. When Princess Charlotte died, her uncle, the future William IV, made a legitimate marriage with Adelaide of Saxe-Meiningen in the hopes of producing an acceptable heir to the Throne. But Queen Adelaide failed to produce that heir, paving the way for the accession of William's niece, Victoria. Jane Murray describes the situation Victoria, King William and Queen Adelaide found themselves in as a rather awkward one with "the Queen still hoping to produce a living child, the court swarming with FitzClarences who had only one thing the matter with them, and the young princess waiting modestly at one side" (1974:33). Today it would be unacceptable that a Prince as close to the Throne as young William IV would have a common law wife and a passel of bastards.

Given the scandalous familial relations of the Hanovers, the importance that Victoria and Albert placed upon their own family was remarkable. The early decades of the Queen's reign coincided with the advent of photography, the growth of illustrated journalism, and the rapid expansion of the print market, all making the Royal Family very visible. Victoria and Albert exploited this (no doubt unintentionally) by commissioning a great many family portraits that commemorated births, christenings, and marriages. Formal royal portraits were hardly new; but what distinguished Victoria's and Albert's approach was the often relaxed manner in which they and their children were portrayed. As Ormond wrote, "The artist was also invited behind the scenes to record informal incidents of family life in a manner unthinkable a generation or two earlier. Domesticity had become a royal virtue, linking the monarchy with the aspirations of ordinary men and women" (1978:34).

This "embourgeoisement" of the monarchy not only reflected the

Queen Victoria, the
Widow-Queen, steadfastly
wore her white widow's
cap and mourning clothes
as a mark of uxorial
constancy. *Keystone Press
Agency Ltd.*

royal couple's tastes and needs (both had been deprived of family life as children), it also fortuitously coincided with the embourgeoisement of British society as a whole. The nation was becoming "more serious, more religious, more domestic, and more responsible" (Girouard 1978: 270). Even the aristocracy felt the need to change its licentious ways to accommodate emerging middle-class morality. As G.K. Chesterton put it, "The great lords yielded on prudery as they had yielded on free trade" (Arnstein 1973:241).

The premature death of the Prince Consort halfway through her reign transformed Victoria from devoted wife and mother into the grieving widow she remained for the rest of her life. Henceforth it was impossible to dissociate mourning from the sacred person of the Queen, who steadfastly wore "white cap, black bombazine dress filled in with white *lisse* at sleeves and neck, [and] black silk stockings with white soles" (Longford 1964:573).

Domesticity had been the theme of the earlier years of her reign; uxorial constancy became the virtue of the later ones. Even at her Jubilees, Victoria remained faithful to the memory of her husband. She insisted, to the consternation of her family, upon wearing her mourning clothes and widow's bonnet instead of State Robes and Crown.

Victoria's retreat from public life was initially unpopular. In 1864, posters appeared outside Buckingham Palace that read, "These commanding premises to be let or sold in consequence of the late occupant's declining business" (Longford 1964:321). In retrospect, however, it can be seen that her withdrawal was a chrysalis of sorts from which emerged a transformed monarchy more mysterious and more popular than ever before. What was most beguiling about this new monarchy, glimpsed during the Jubilees, was the utter simplicity of the little Queen from whom radiated all the imperial splendor of the mighty British Empire.

> The image of this dumpy figure in mourning black, cooped up in her castle, mistress of a vast empire, mother and grandmother of Europe's royalty, immeasurably the most important woman in the world, caught the imagination of the people. (Ziegler 1978:22–23)

"Even her seclusion in the end added another dimension to . . . her 'mythic glory,' making her all the more remarkable for being so seldom seen" (Longford 1964:576). And when she was seen, the incongruity of her attire also added to the mystery of the monarchy. There she was: just like everybody else yet totally different from everybody else.

Queen Victoria, however, does not seem to have been the only royal lady to have adopted an "anti-fashion" mode of dress. Loelia, Duchess of Westminster, wrote: "Indeed at some date in the nineties a sudden paralysis seems to have struck the wardrobes of the Royal Families of Europe: All Queens and Princesses with a few notable exceptions dressed in a style that was peculiar to themselves. Boned up to the neck and with hair like a very neat bird's nest and of course in black—with so many relations they were always in mourning for somebody or other—they seemed a race apart. And one can't deny that this royal uniform did hedge them with a kind of divinity" (Westminster 1961:70).

When Victoria died, she was succeeded by her son, Edward VII, who resembled his dissolute Hanoverian ancestors far more than he did his earnest Saxe-Coburg parents. Like George IV, he was extravagant in dress as well as being a philanderer and a gourmandizer.

Had this Hanoverian style of monarchy prevailed, the Victorian one might have proved to have been nothing more than a passing aberration. But as it turned out, the Edwardian era lasted only nine years; the King died in 1910. Soon after his death, the twentieth century arrived with a vengeance. A ghastly war was quickly followed by the collapse of most European Thrones, the frightening General Strike (1926), and finally a devastating worldwide depression. Under these circumstances, a monarchy in the mode of the House of Hanover, or Romanoff, might very well have been short-lived. George V and Queen Mary were acutely aware of this, and, like Queen Victoria, strove to be good. In public

Queen Mary with the Princesses Elizabeth and Margaret Rose. Although this picture was taken in 1939, Queen Mary could easily have stepped out of a time warp. *Fox Photos Ltd.*

they "exuded duty, dignity, courage, honesty, common sense and hard work—all the virtues the British believed they [themselves] possessed in abundance" (Lacey 1977:7).

These virtues as well as the durability of the Throne were signified most of all by Queen Mary's manner of dress, which quite suddenly ceased to change with the times. Until she died in 1953, Queen Mary resolutely wore a style fashionable around the time of the First World War. And there was a message in this, as Prudence Glynn writes:

> [Queen Mary's dress was as] immutable as the seasons, a very rock of princely clothing, while all around her throne exploded. Her long dresses, her parrot-headed brollies and her buttonstrap shoes became in her life-time the symbols of something admirable and enduring in the British monarchy, but they bore no relation to what everyone else was skipping around in. (1978:114)

## The Abdication: The Failure of Character

The rogue factor, as Lacey put it, in the monarchy so carefully constructed by George V and Queen Mary was their Heir Apparent, Edward, The Prince of Wales. When the Prince first entered public life, it was widely believed that he would blaze "a new trail for twentieth century monarchy to follow" (Lacey 1977:39). But Edward proved to be self-indulgent and irresponsible in a manner reminiscent of the sons of George III. Duty was the password of his father's monarchy. Queen Mary wrote to her wayward son after the Abdication, "After all, all my life I have put my Country before everything else, and I simply cannot change now" (Lacey 1977:67).

There is very little that can be added to the literature of the Abdication Crisis. The story still compels because nothing reveals the nature of a pattern quite like the failure of that pattern. What is particularly interesting, however, is the extent to which that failure was revealed by the clothes worn by the principal players in this agonistic struggle in which the nature of British kingship was contested. Was the King above the law, his only obligation to please himself; or was the King the embodiment of the law, no matter how tiresome or distasteful some of those obligations might be? Although royal dress was hardly the issue, it is interesting how often the characters (or sides) were described or identified in terms of their attire.

The tale unfolds against the impressive and regal backdrop newly created by King George and Queen Mary in her long Edwardian dress. George V placed great importance upon clothes. Believing "that the customs and fashion of his youth were immutable, . . . he attached a moral significance to such things as dress or speech" (Donaldson 1975:21). The Prince of Wales, fully aware of his father's distaste for the flashy new, galled him no end by dressing like a "cad." He mixed up his uniforms and insisted upon loud tweeds in often startling combinations. As we know, Wallis Simpson was later a perennial inclusion on the best-dressed list.

When Edward VIII sought to marry Wallis Simpson, never had such a furor been raised over a King's marriage since Henry VIII connived to marry Anne Boleyn. Like Anne Boleyn, Mrs. Simpson was offensive to many at court. Her brassy repartee jarred those of high birth (Lacey 1977:56).

> The important thing was, [Wallis] was always full of vitality, "pep" we called it then. She shone at parties! She could dance up a storm and match drinks with anyone. . . . She was a born raconteur, and with an inexhaustible fund of risque stories. (Bryan and Murphy 1975:38)

In short, she had no idea "how to behave in the circle to which she so nakedly aspired" (Lacey 1977:56). The real objection to Mrs. Simpson was, I think, that she did not fit the mold cast by Queen Mary. Almost overnight Queen Mary had become the archetypical English Queen. Matching drinks, telling racy stories and dancing up a storm were not activities easily associated with the tightly corseted figure of Queen Mary. Thus many had difficulty paying Wallis Simpson the homage due a Queen. A good summation of her failure was offered by Prudence Glynn.

> Even if further evidence were needed that Bessie Wallis Warfield Spencer Simpson would have been quite unsuitable as Queen of England it could be supplied by the fact that she was obsessively chic. There is hardly a reference to her in any memoir which does not contain the details of what she was wearing. (Glynn 1978:111)

Whatever Wallis Simpson's failures may have been, they were nothing compared to those of Edward VIII. Quite simply, he was unsuited to be King. The tragedy of his story is rooted in his immense popularity and promise as Prince of Wales. But he never matured. As Donaldson wrote, this symbol of authority childishly divided the world into himself and kindred spirits on one side and authority and friends of authority on the other (1975:113). Donaldson relates his immaturity to the clothes he wore (or to those he did not).

> One of the oddest things about him . . . is that he was singularly uninformed about all those shibboleths which go to make up what has been so conveniently and compactly labelled for later generations by the single letter "U" [upper class]. The Prince was in some ways surprisingly "non-U." This was most noticeable in the clothes he wore. It was not merely that the upper classes agreed with his father in disliking the loudness of his tweeds and the cut of his clothes: the Prince wore his top hat on the side of his head out hunting, a thing even schoolboys at Eton or Harrow knew was done only by cads. . . . These things were all taken with the utmost seriousness then, not for themselves but for what they told people about one another in a class society which was deeply divisive and made possible only by the complete acceptance of the superiority of one class over another. (Donaldson 1975:119)

Lacey also saw Edward's character flaws in terms of his clothes. In 1936, the King chartered a sailing ship, the *Nahlin,* with which to sail the Dalmatian Coast of the Mediterranean in the company of a few select friends and Mrs. Simpson (still married to a Mr. Simpson notably absent from the cruise). By doing this, the King not only paraded his mistress for the whole world to see, he also did it as skimpily clad as possible. Robert Lacey summed up the King's folly:

> He defied the sartorial as well as the ethical conventions of the period by taking every opportunity to strip down to the bare minimum of clothing. It would have been considered somewhat eccentric for any upper-class Englishman to sail through the Corinth canal dressed in nothing more than shorts and a pair of binoculars in 1936, but for the King of England to be photographed thus in the presence of the leering hoi polloi shouting and standing on the banks close enough to touch him, was like hearing that men had landed from Mars. (Lacey 1977:61)

The Abdication of Edward VIII has probably been invaluable for the monarchy: it rid it of a man temperamentally unfitted to be King. In addition, it helped further the fiction of a middle-class monarchy. Popular interpretation of the fracas had it that they would not let Mrs. Simpson be Queen because her past was offensive to the Royal Family and the "Establishment." This sentiment was also echoed by Hocart. "For a King to place on the throne a woman whose first husband is still living is unthinkable; it would be a breach of the close connection between queenship and chastity" (Hocart 1970a:119).

The irony of the Abdication drama is that it is so often seen as a morality play of sorts in which the essentially democratic and heroic Edward VIII was forced off the Throne by a hidebound and snobbish Royal Family and Establishment. The truth of the matter is that Edward was really reverting to another, more autocratic, mode of monarchy wherein the King reigns at his own pleasure. This was a betrayal of the monarchy that his parents had so assiduously fashioned. King George and Queen Mary by their very sobriety and dignity of bearing proclaimed that the King was not above the law, but rather was its very embodiment.

The British monarchy survives because it corresponds to certain fundamental British values, not the least of which is the incongruous love of both hierarchy and democracy. This chapter has dwelt largely upon the supposed "ordinariness" of the House of Windsor. King George and Queen Mary may have come to symbolize all those attributes that the ordinary Briton would have liked to have thought characterized himself, but there was really never any question that a parity existed between the King and Queen and that ordinary fellow. Queen Mary's dress may not have kept up with fashion but it was hardly within the means of most people.

This dichotomy is also evident in the face of their granddaughter,

Elizabeth II. By day the Queen dresses in a way that could almost let her pass as one of us. This "camouflage" consists of much that the Queen puts on—at least for her diurnal engagements. Why the Queen should dress so horribly is an intriguing question. The best explanation I have encountered is a piece of market research that segments women according to their attitudes toward their apparel. The author, Maggie Fine, divides women into seven groups that reflect central sentiments towards clothes. Among these are such easily recognizable types as the "Clothes Junkies," "Classic Individualists," and "Defensive Dressers." The last group that Fine describes are the "Don't Cares." The Queen clearly belongs in this segment, which consists of those women who are simply uninterested in clothes. "They don't care whether the world around them makes judgments about them via clothes. They tend to dress quite functionally. . . . They don't choose clothes to be different or to express their individuality."

Even though the Queen has appeared in some awful outfits, the supposed ordinariness of her attire is belied by her extraordinary daytime jewels. The Queen "has at her disposal more costly jewels than any [other] woman in the world" (Edwards 1977:59). The Queen wears her more "modest" jewelry during the day. She always wears two or three strands of pearls (which the New York Times once hyperbolically described as being the size of marbles) and earrings to match. On the lapel of her coat she wears one of twenty-four broaches. They are so enormous that they could easily be mistaken for paste. Her gloves hide her comparatively simple wedding and engagement rings.

In addition to her jewelry are other accessories: her hat, gloves, and handbag. It used to be that any woman with pretensions to gentility would never go to "town" without gloves. Today, those gloves underscore the formality that sets royalty apart, figuratively and literally. The Queen's gloves ensure that she never has to touch another human being. Barbra Streisand, presented to the Queen at the premier of "Funny Girl," asked, "Why do women have to wear gloves to meet you and men don't?" The Queen, apparently taken somewhat aback, replied, "I'll have to think about that—I suppose it's traditional" (New York Times [3/19/75] 38:4). The International Herald Tribune advised that gloves are de rigueur for women at Ascot.

> The gloves have a purpose it seems—in case the Queen, strolling around the Royal Enclosure, should suddenly want to shake hands. Actually when she walks around, the polite British thing to do is to look in the other direction. (The International Herald Tribune, 6/21/79)

The Queen's miner's overalls seem to say that social differences are not important. The deference shown by the real miners, who are properly grimy and are keeping their distance, says they are. *Central Press Photos Ltd.*

The Queen always has on gloves when she touches a person, but they are often removed when she pats a horse or dog. In a memorable scene from the film "The Royal Family," the Queen feeds her horse carrots in the courtyard of Buckingham Palace after the Birthday Parade. The carrots are handed her on a silver tray. She holds her gloves in her left hand as she feeds the slobbering mount with her right. The Queen does not seem to mind equine saliva on her hand. Apparently she is not squeamish, and the presence of gloves cannot be explained entirely in terms of any fastidiousness on the part of the Queen.

The Queen's hats also denote the formality that attends her public appearances. The Queen almost always appears with her head covered either with a head scarf, hat, or tiara. The covering of the Queen's head is also a manifestation of the deliberate archaism of much that royalty does. Forty years ago it was unthinkable to go hatless. "Before World

War II it was considered almost improper for a woman to be seen in public with her head uncovered" (Glynn 1978:89).

The Queen's head scarves are a different matter.

> . . . if a female ghost from Mayfair of the twenties were to revisit the London of today I think the thing that would surprise her most would be to see the streets full of women without hats—worse still, women wearing head-scarves. Imagine the Queen of England appearing in public with a handkerchief over her head like the poorest sort of continental peasant! (Westminster 1961:96)

Perhaps the most intriguing royal accessory is the Queen's handbag. The "capacious size of her handbags remains a mystery, for she never has to pay out ready cash, doesn't need the front door key, doesn't smoke, doesn't need a shopping list, doesn't have to pay the grocer's bill out of pocket, and appears to go for hours without renewing her makeup" (Edwards 1977:97). This is not to say that her purse serves no purpose. When the Queen is on home ground, it can be used as a signaling device. At Investitures, the ceremony ends when the Queen retrieves her purse from behind the dais. Buckingham Palace luncheons are over when the Queen removes her purse from the hook under the table. It also gives her something to do with her left arm. All of her pocketbooks have large straps so that they may be looped over her arm and forgotten, leaving the left hand free to hold the bouquet. Women can look quite ungainly in public with their left arms hanging limply at their sides.

Another explanation is perhaps psychological. In public many women feel undressed and vulnerable without purses. The Queen may very well use her handbag as a psychological prop to maintain a certain distance between herself and others. One has only to look at the many photos of the Queen in which her left, purse-holding arm is held across the front of her body as a kind of defense. Her right hand is, of course, free to shake other hands.

The Queen's evening clothes are an entirely different matter from her daywear. Her gowns are elaborately embroidered with beads and seed pearls so that they cannot be easily copied and mass produced. But more important is the sheer weight of the jewelry—measured in pounds, not carats—that she wears by night. Her tiaras, necklaces, and earrings proclaim her elevated status.

Despite the supposed simplicity of the Queen—the emphasis on her family life, her devotion to her corgis,* her dumpy dresses, her serious

---

* "In our ten minutes she talked, as I am told she always does, about her corgis. (Two fat corgis, roughly the same colour as the carpet, were lying at her feet.) She remarked how

approach to her duty—it fools almost no one. A public opinion poll conducted by Lord Montagu of Beaulieu found that most people *are* aware of the aristocratic nature of the monarchy. For example, to the question of whether the Queen and the nobility are close, that is, whether the Queen has most of her private friends among the peers, a surprising sixty-eight percent answered yes, twenty-eight percent no, and eight percent did not know (1970:197). One had only to note the ease and familiarity with which Lord Spencer chatted with the Queen during the return to Buckingham Palace from St. Paul's after the marriage of their children to know that there was one aristocratic fast friend.

It is possible to see in the two, very different faces that the Queen presents to the world the reconciliation of the irreconcilable values of democracy and hierarchy. The Queen is like most of us; the Queen is different from all of us. This incongruity infuses the monarchy with an unmistakable vitality.

The dichotomy of the royal face—like the fiction of the King's two bodies—reflects a larger problem, namely, the incongruity of the ideal and the real; the lack of fit between the sublime kingly office and the flesh and blood individual who occupies that office. Sovereignty is an institution and as such can be defined in ideal terms. But sovereigns are merely humans who, no matter how good they endeavor to be, can never fit the ideal.

The King as King, for example, commits no folly. Yet we know very well that kings have always committed a great deal of folly. Paradoxically, these foibles of the individuals who have occupied the kingly office have not compromised the dignity of that office. Rather, they seem to enhance it. Edward VII, for instance, was by most accounts a self-indulgent and narrow man. Yet his renowned gluttony and philandering did not offend his subjects; rather, they endeared the King to his people. "Good Ole Ted," they cried as he drove by.

Similarly, the lack of smartness in the Queen's clothes does not detract from the mystery of her queenliness; rather, it intensifies it. The absolute incongruity of a Queen who does not know how to dress is as beguiling today as was the glorious Queen-Empress who was at heart nothing more than a simple little figure in mourning black.

This ability of the Queen and the Royal Family to charm and enchant us derives from their symbolic nature. They are both persons and symbols; and because they are persons they cannot be used as can inanimate symbols. But this intractableness does not distract from their symbol-

---

often people fell over the dogs. I asked what good they were and she said they were Welsh dogs used for rounding up cattle by biting their legs" (Crossman 1975:52).

ism. It intensifies it, for the power of symbols emanates from their ability to reconcile the irreconcilable. The dichotomy of the royal face is a constant reminder of those irreconcilables that are mysteriously resolved in the person of the Queen.

# VI

~~~

# The Country Life

Eight months of every year Royals are accessible to the public, participating in one or another of the grand events, traveling about the kingdom meeting subjects engaged in the activities of the work-a-day world. Their schedules are grueling timetables, leaving little leeway for such common human failings as a headache, toothache, or having gotten up on the wrong side of the bed.

But as Robert Lacey cautioned, let us not exaggerate their toiling, for they spend at least another four months of the year ensconced in the privacy of one or another of the royal estates. January is spent at Sandringham in Norfolk, Easter and most of April at Windsor Castle, and August to mid-October at Balmoral Castle in Scotland. In their leisure, they progress around the kingdom as did Kings in olden days.

Even though Royals would seem to be off-stage during this interval, they are not. Country life is a kind of morality play, which appears to be an enactment of Englishness: country life is the quintessential English life. It embodies the ways that English people ought to live, even though relatively few can actually manage to do so. The Royal Family are prime players in this cycle of national drama. The seasonality of the blood sports—shooting, hunting, and fishing—identifies them with the ebb and flow of nature in whose waxing and waning can be glimpsed the eternal rhythms of the fields and forests.

Such fluctuations transcend the man–made schedules characteristic of modern life, making the country a mythic domain. Its timelessness is part of its appeal, a welcomed respite from the hurly-burly of urban routines. Like the anachronistic costumes of the grand occasions, grouse moors and woodlands confound the perception of the passage of time. Thus, it is in the country that royal persons also merge with the moral landscape. As symbols they assume elements of their meaning. But, as we shall see, the country setting itself reveals differences between what these symbols seem to be communicating and what is being insinuated.

That England has retained as much open space as it has borders on the miraculous. It is a very densely populated place (610 persons per square mile, compared with India's 510 and the United States's 64). This density is not a twentieth-century phenomenon. Since the nineteenth century, Britain has been one of the most industrialized and urbanized countries in the world. Yet the belief persists that it is an essentially rural nation (one has only to look at British travel posters to confirm this). Photographs of the Royal Family tramping across their estates or watching horse shows on one or another bucolic estate help keep alive the fiction of an essentially rural England.

Most Britons, as described by Paul Theroux in *The Kingdom by the Sea*, live in dreary little towns and cities where unemployment is rampant, yet one would assume from those travel posters or Burberry ads that the British live either in stately homes or in quaint half-timbered villages. This fiction of the country life is not one that has been fobbed off solely on foreigners. The British themselves seem to believe it.

> For a population which is among the most highly urbanized in the world, the English have a strong attachment to the countryside, and towards a traditional social structure which they rightly or wrongly think still characterizes it. (Weinberg 1967:5)

Crucial to the belief in a rural England is the upper-class institution of country life or country weekend. Like the private phase of the royal year, it too centers upon one or another of the British blood sports, each in its appointed time. Indeed, royal privacy and aristocratic country life are pieces of the same cloth.

Let us look, then, at these sports which give form and definition to country life.

## Shootin', Huntin', and Fishin'

Shooting in England most resembles what in America is called hunting. (Hunting in England means that of the fox; but more of that later.) An

English shoot is a formal, highly choreographed event. The "guns," as participants in a shoot are called, do not wander at random through fields shooting at whatever bounds from cover. Rather, six to ten guns (the usual number) stand in a line, each by a numbered peg. The numbers are assigned by lot and are varied throughout the day, assuring that each gun gets a chance of standing in the middle of the line where the shooting is best. The birds are driven toward the line of fire by a team of ten to twenty beaters. (The 2nd Duke of Westminster normally used eighty beaters and retrievers for his shoots.) Since the beaters are walking toward the line of fire, they are most in danger from inexperienced or overzealous guns (see the film "The Shooting Party"). Thus shooting etiquette demands that guns not be fired horizontally but rather at an inclined angle. Legal considerations also demand that guns be fired over the heads of oncoming beaters rather than at their chests.

One of the best descriptions of a shoot was provided by Norman Mursell, gameskeeper for the Dukes of Westminster:

> As soon as His Grace got to his peg Fred blew a whistle and an answering whistle could be heard in the distance; it was Dick starting the beaters off in the wood. Within minutes shooting started, and it built up to a barrage as the pheasants came out of the wood in a steady stream. I was of course fascinated by all the birds and all the shooting, but by now His Grace himself had started shooting and Fred was fully occupied, handing him a loaded gun and reloading the one he had just fired. The pheasants were falling like autumn leaves, and to me it was a never-to-be-forgotten occasion. I stood and watched Fred changing guns with the Duke with incredible speed, and never was His Grace waiting for a gun, or a target for that matter. The shooting went on for quite half an hour, one continual bang, bang, bang, building up at times almost to deafening point. In the moments of comparative silence the tap, tap, tap of the beaters' sticks could be heard in the distance, and sometimes a muffled voice. The red and white of the beaters' garb eventually appeared through the bushes and the stand came to an end.
>
> Now more men appeared from behind where the guns had been standing. They all had dogs, some two or three. The duty of the "dog men" was to make sure that all the pheasants were quickly dispatched. No doubt some of the birds had only been wounded but the bulk of those I had seen fall had been killed cleanly, through the heads. (Mursell 1981:11–12)

At the end of the day's shooting, each gun is given a brace of birds regardless of how many he has shot. The rest are sold to defray the cost of raising the birds. Duncan writes that in 1970 a brace of pheasant shot at Sandringham sold for 36 shillings, 6 pence (1970:130). Given that 72,000 pheasants were killed that year, the estate garnered some 65,000 pounds. Yet that was probably only a drop in the bucket. Twelve years later, York and Barr estimated that a single pheasant cost 10 pounds "in keepering, feeding, beating, shooting" (1982:149). Thus, 72,000 pheasant shot at Sandringham would cost about 720,000 pounds to raise. (Before World War II, the adage was: up goes half a crown, bang goes six pence, down comes seven shillings and six pence.)

To shoot one has to know what one may kill and when.

Shooting in Britain is governed by ancient and complex game laws under which you cannot shoot pheasant or grouse on Sundays but you may shoot geese and duck in most English counties, though not on Christmas Day. (Heald and Mohs 1979:210)

Shooting begins with the "glorious twelfth," that is, the Twelfth of August, when the grouse season opens. Balmoral with its excellent grouse moors is home to the Royal Family from August into October. Grouse are the most highly prized game birds because of the high speeds at which they fly and corkscrew and the consequent great difficulty in killing them, to say nothing of killing them cleanly. The partridge season opens September 15, the pheasant season October 1; both close February 1.

The shooting season finally comes to an end in the early spring with wild fowling on tidal waters. In the United States, duck hunting is often a blue-collar sport. Not so in Britain, where it is eminently a gentleman's sport.

One of the forms of shooting most suitable for gentlemen is going after wild duck in a gun punt. Prince Philip has indulged in this dangerous pastime, which fulfills all the most admirable demands of a gentleman's sport. It is hazardous to the hunter, who is often in danger of being drowned or frozen to death. Even if he does not perish from exposure, the odds of so much as getting a shot off are heavily weighed against him. (Nelson 1976:112)

"The monarchy and its associates have always put their seal of approval on shooting" (Nelson 1976:111). George V drove his biographer, Harold Nicolson, to distraction because for seventeen years he seems to have done nothing "but kill animals and stick in stamps." George V and his father may have espoused different styles of monarchy, but they were united in their devotion to shooting. Edward VII had all the clocks at Sandringham House set a half hour ahead lest his guests cause him to be late getting to the field. So strong is the association of the Royal Family with shooting that Anthony Bailey wrote of Prince Philip: in one respect he qualified badly for the British Royal Family—he was a poor shot. The first time he went out with his father-in-law, he missed forty out of fifty (Bailey 1977b:58). (Similarly, Diana Spencer qualified badly for the Royal Family by her aversion to horses.)

The association that royalty enjoys with shooting may have proved to be too much of a good thing, as Crossman found from talking to a lady-in-waiting at Balmoral.

> Hurrying back so as not to be late for tea with the Queen, I asked the lady in waiting how the Royal Family spent their time and whether they liked Balmoral. "Oh yes," she said, "they like it very much." . . ."Does she like shooting?" "No, she does a little deer-stalking but she doesn't really like it. Prince Philip, of course, likes the shooting." "And how do they spend their time?" I said. "Oh," she said, "they're kept terribly busy. It's a tremendous burden keeping the stags down and culling the grouse. They have to go out every day early in the morning and there's a regular routine of guests arriving for shooting. It's very hard work indeed." I began to realize how pleasure can become a chore. At Balmoral the elaborate pleasure of grouse-shooting has now become a mechanical routine into which royalty has to fit whether it likes it or not.
>
> As we got back to the house the landrovers had just returned from the grouse-shooting; they had 170 brace [i.e., 340 birds]. We went into tea with the Queen while they were disposing of their booty. (1976:45)

## Fox Hunting

Although shooting may be regarded as the pinnacle of all sporting activities, its essentially restrictive and private nature—one participates in a shoot only at the personal invitation of a landowner—has insured that it has remained a relatively arcane pursuit. Fox hunters, in contrast, "assemble at open meets, most of them announced publicly in advance. Attendance does not [always] depend upon invitation, membership, or land ownership, and even strangers may show up to ride" (Howe 1981:285). This last point is not strictly true, since most hunts allow strangers to ride with them only at the invitation of a member. There are, however, some hunts which do welcome visitors without a specific invitation. These are indicated in *Bailey's Hunting Directory*.

Once assembled, the field follows the fox through open country, cutting across the land of different owners. Additional individuals are able to enjoy the hunt by watching the hunters assemble, or by following the field on foot or in cars. All of these aspects of hunting have helped make it most evocative of the country way of life. Indeed, fox hunting has been mythologized, idealized into a national institution. "Few things seem more English or more aristocratic than fox-hunting. As the almost obligatory hunting prints on the oak and pseudo-oak panelled walls of countless restaurants, clubs and hotels testify, the power of the sport to evoke images of a particular way of life is very strong" (Itzkowitz 1977:1).

Approximately thirty thousand people hunt during the twenty-week season which ends in late March or early April. Throughout Britain there are many hunt clubs, but among the most prestigious and exclusive are the Pytchley (which meets at Althorp Hall), the Quorn, the Belvior (pronounced "beaver"), the Cottesmore, and the Beaufort, to name a few. Hunt clubs meet on a regular basis—anywhere from two days a week to as many as six days a week.

Despite hunting's apotheosis into an idealized national pastime, it is not universally admired, frequently drawing the ire of such groups as the National Society for the Abolition of Cruel Sports. Members of this society and their sympathizers often show up to harass riders, verbally abusing them and misleading the hounds with aniseed (concurring with Oscar Wilde's assessment of hunting as "the unspeakable in full pursuit of the uneatable").

Sometimes even more drastic protests are contemplated. In 1986, two men plotted to dig up the body of the Duke of Beaufort, a hunting enthusiast. They intended to cut off his head and mail it to Princess Anne, another avid fox hunter. Instead, they were convicted and jailed for desecrating the Duke's grave.

It's easy to understand the antipathy that hunting arouses. Even those who hunt can be ambivalent as this passage from *The Pursuit of Love* indicates:

> The next day we all went out hunting. The Radletts loved animals, they loved foxes, they risked dreadful beatings in order to unstop their earths, they read and cried and rejoiced over Reynard the Fox, in summer they got up at four to go and see the cubs playing in the pale-green light of the woods; nevertheless, more than anything in the world, they loved hunting. It was in their blood and bones and in my blood and bones, and nothing could eradicate it, though we knew it for a kind of original sin. For three hours that day I forgot

everything except my body and my pony's body; the rushing, the scrambling, the splashing, struggling up the hills, sliding down them again, the tugging, the bucketing, the earth and the sky. I forgot everything, I could hardly have told you my name. That must be the great hold that hunting has over people, especially stupid people; it enforces an absolute concentration, both mental and physical. (Mitford 1945:30)

A single fox is pitted against a pack of hounds (never "dogs") rarely numbering fewer than fifty or sixty animals. Hounds under five are preferred because they give better sport and kill more foxes (Sutherland 1965:250). The fox is clearly outnumbered. In addition to the hounds, a field of riders may include up to two hundred individuals. Moreover, it is not unusual, the night before a hunt, to stop up a fox's burrows, or earths, forcing him to find a covert (pronounced "cover") elsewhere.

Under the guidance of the huntsman, the hounds must find a fox's scent, flush him from his covert, and chase him, with the riders in full pursuit. When the hounds catch the fox, they tear him to bits. The huntsman beats the hounds off the carcass and smears any novice rider with its blood.

The rationale for hunting is that it rids the countryside of vermin, namely, foxes; thus, riding to hounds is not only a pleasure but is also seen as an obligation—an aspect of *noblesse oblige*. This does not really follow, however. Debrett's *Etiquette and Modern Manners* advises that on a shoot, killing foxes "is a delicate point and varies from shoot to shoot, depending on the interest in fox-hunting among the guns and their relationship with the local hunt" (1981:364–65).

Because of the strong sentiments that fox hunting arouses (despite its ability to evoke a way of life), the Royal Family's association with it is rather oblique. Princess Anne hunts openly. Prince Charles is more circumspect, joining the field after it has moved off from its assembly point. He does this ostensibly lest photojournalists and the curious disrupt the assembly needlessly. The Queen would probably love to hunt but does not out of deference to those who find the pursuit and slaughter of a canine repugnant.

Part of the appeal of fox hunting lies in its association with the horse, that emblematic animal of the aristocracy. The Queen and Queen Mother raise and race horses. Prince Charles tried his hand, or rather his seat, at steeplechasing. He has been more successful at polo. Prince Philip, having had to give up polo, now competes in four-in-hand carriage races. Princess Anne has been an internationally competitive equestrienne.

# Fishing

Fishing differs from hunting and shooting in that it is a solitary pursuit. Unlike shooting and hunting, there are two kinds of fishermen: coarse fishermen and anglers. The social distinctiveness of the latter derives from the social distinctiveness of the quarry: salmon and trout are considered to be "the aristocrats of the lochs and rivers." One distinction of the angler is that he does not try to make the bait as attractive as possible as do ordinary fishermen. Angling is pursued for its form rather than for the results, as this rather long passage from Nelson indicates:

> In true gentlemanly fashion, the gentleman rates most highly the most difficult and complicated form of angling. A gentleman never takes a trout with a worm, although he may go after salmon with a live or imitation prawn. He may not spin for trout although he may do so for salmon. The most honourable way to go after both trout and salmon is with an imitation fly, preferably one you have tied yourself. Trout are more difficult than salmon to catch in this manner, because you have to convince the trout that the imitation fly you are offering him is either the same as the one on which he naturally feeds or such a delicacy that it is worth trying for flavour. The salmon, on the other hand, is thought to slash at the imitation fly because its presence in the water irritates him or he is in a bad temper.
>
> While it is permissible to fish for trout with an imitation fly floating beneath the surface of the water ("fishing wet"), dry-fly fishing, which requires that the fly float on the surface, is by far the most honourable way for a gentleman to fish. This is because it is by far the most difficult method and requires the greatest skill. Some owners of rivers refuse to allow their guests to offer the fish a wet fly and insist that one may only fish dry on their water.
>
> Flies, before they hatch, cling to weeds and stones on the river bed. At this stage of their development they are known as nymphs. Trout consider nymphs very tasty, and love to nose them out or eat them as they float up to the surface, where they will hatch out as flies. It is comparatively easy to catch trout by presenting them with an imitation nymph, and some gentlemen who have grown bored at the way the trout have disregarded their imitation flies all day, preferring to feed on the luscious nymphs, have been tempted stealthily to offer them an imitation nymph. When doing this, one should take care that neither the water bailiff nor the owner is watching. Gentlemen have been sent home for nymphing, and never asked again.

Nymphing is never an occupation for gentlemen. (Nelson 1976: 113–14)

Country sports are elite pastimes not the least because they cost a lot. The expenses involved in hunting, shooting, and even fishing put them beyond the reach of all but a very privileged few.

Shooting, for example, is considered to be "the highest pinnacle of all gentlemanly sporting activities" (Sutherland 1978:35). It requires a lifetime of practice, starting with an apprenticeship in early childhood. Upper-class children have ample opportunity to observe the sport and learn its rules from the perspective of the beaters, loaders, and retrievers whom they assist when their parents and relatives shoot. Such apprenticeships are essential lest one threatens one's fellow sportsmen with extermination. Shooting, moreover, requires vast acreage for the breeding of the birds who will be slaughtered in the fall. (One reviewer advised that shooting does not require "vast" acreage since he had had "many admirable days' shooting on estates of 300 ± acres." In a country where there is roughly one person per acre, a 300-acre estate still seems to be a substantial one.)

Hunting, too, is quite expensive, though not as prohibitively costly as shooting. One does not need as much land. (Hunts are clubs that individuals may join, this, of course, being easier said than done.) The costs are not insignificant, however. A hunter (i.e., the horse) can easily cost several thousands, and a serious huntsman needs more than one horse. Stabling charges can run several thousand dollars a year. Membership fees are another $1,000 or so a year (Nelson 1976:109). In addition, proper attire, correct to the smallest detail, is required. Tailor-made habits can cost 500 pounds with top hats alone going for some 80 pounds. For example, Debrett's advises that the stock (i.e., the hunting tie) is "always fixed with a plain gold pin" (1981:375).

Even fishing, the solitary pursuit of the aristocrats of the lochs, costs a great deal. In Britain one cannot throw a line into any stream one comes across. The rights to trout and salmon streams are owned, leased, and jealously guarded. "Between them [sic] the gentlemen of the country own almost all the trout and salmon fishing and certainly all the best water" (Nelson 1976:112). What little fishing they do not own is owned by syndicates of businessmen. The cost of these rights is staggering.

Trout-fishing rights on the best English chalk streams [for instance, the Test, Itchen, and Kennet] were selling for 35,000 pounds per mile (both banks). By the beginning of 1975 they were down to 20,000 pounds a mile. The cost of salmon rights on grade-one salmon rivers such as the Wye, Test, Usk and Exe have been reduced from the equivalent of 1,000 pounds per salmon to about 600 pounds per salmon. (Nelson 1976:112)

Knowing the costs involved in the apparently simple pastime of fishing casts photos of the Royal Family in their waders in an entirely different light.

Not all country pursuits are as bloody as shooting or hunting. Gardening—concerned with nurturing rather than killing—is an equally respectable rural pastime, and is equally essential to the notion of Englishness. The importance of the garden could be seen, for example, in the proliferation of English gardens throughout the alien lands of the British Empire.

> The Briton fresh from Britain . . . as soon as he moved into a new bungalow, or set down the family baggage on a new small holding, almost always got hold of some seeds or cuttings to make himself a garden. . . . Love of their own country was very strong among this people; nostalgia and homesickness were among their weaknesses. It was roses these transient imperialists pined for, stocks and honeysuckle, lavender hedges and spring daffodils. Up their little gardens sprang, hopeful around each bungalow. (Morris 1968:332)

The Empire may have passed but the English garden endures. Like fishing, gardening cuts across class divisions; and like fishing, it reaffirms those divisions. The aesthetic of the true English garden derives from those of the upper class. Since the eighteenth century that aesthetic has been to enhance nature rather than regimenting it as did the formal gardens of France and Italy (Hinde 1983:7).

Upper-class gardeners like to give nature its head, much as an experienced rider controls an unruly horse by allowing it to take the bit in its mouth, running wild for a while. Vita Sackville-West, creator of some very famous gardens at Sissinghurst Castle, was opposed to tidiness. "Let self-seeded plants grow where they naturally fell; let wild flowers sometimes be allowed to invade the garden; if roses stray over a path, the visitor must duck" (Nicolson 1983:11).

The social distinctiveness of upper-class gardens derives from both their arcane and rustic aesthetics and their costs. Proper gardening, like any of the blood sports, is expensive. It requires a certain amount of land and more often than not the assistance of a gardening staff. But more important than land or the money necessary for the creation, upkeep, and maintenance of a garden is the time required to care for it. Great gardens are not static creations planted in a single spring. Instead, they are organic entities that take decades, if not longer, to evolve. Vita Sack-

The Queen Mother in waders casts for trout. The undue privilege of this pastime is underscored by the invaluable pearl necklace she wears to muck about in streams. *Central Press Photo Ltd.*

ville-West, for one, labored on her garden from 1930 until she died in 1962.

Gardens take time because their goal is to enhance nature ("nature unobtrusively coaxed into order" [Morris 1968:329]) rather than letting her run wild. This requires laborious planning which must take into account seasonality, color, and the lay-out of the garden, so that plants and flowers complement one another throughout the year.

## The Moral Universe of the Field

The country is not just a place "out there" where the pavement and streetlights end. Nor is it merely a set of ecological relations. Rather, it is a source of metaphors and images that the British use to think of themselves. The ideal type remains the country squire. The country is a setting for the display of certain fundamental British values: courage and grace in the face of danger; an allegiance to the rules; pleasure derived from the aesthetic of a game well played; and trust in one's comrades.

English country pursuits are really agonistic struggles between the cultural and the natural. Ironically, this is probably nowhere more apparent than in gardening. Ruthlessness was Vita Sackville-West's first principle for subjugating nature to the will of the gardener. If something displeases, eradicate it.

The same ruthlessness is apparent in shooting and hunting, though there it is eclipsed somewhat by the importance of knowing and observing the rules. Anglers must not choose the most appealing bait—that would make landing a fish too easy. Similarly, fox hunting is more concerned with the etiquette that choreographs hounds, horses, and riders than it is with actually killing the fox. It is more important to follow the first fox flushed than go after a second one that might be more easily chopped (i.e., torn to pieces by hounds). One exception is shooting, where prestige depends upon the ability to kill as many birds as fast as possible. Nevertheless, points are lost if the birds are not killed cleanly through the head.

It is this primacy of etiquette that infuses country sports with the qualities of a morality play. The essential orderliness of the cultural triumphs over the chaos of the natural. To guide a large and skittish horse over a fence in step with the rest of the field; to kill a grouse corkscrewing some eighty miles an hour over one's head; or even to coax patiently and methodically a garden into the semblance of wild abandon is to impose the will of man upon nature. Thus to hunt, shoot, or to garden demands a commitment to a high standard of behavior, a chivalrous code of conduct, as it were.

Despite the often avid participation of women, British field sports still extol the manly virtues. The mannishness of country women is almost a standing joke: "English Ladies as a class are almost indecently energetic and competent. As the men are settling down for a quiet siesta after a good luncheon, it is always some Amazon who bursts into the room crying: 'Who's for tennis?', or, no matter what the weather, gird themselves in an assortment of deer-stalker hats, anoraks and wellies and drag everyone off on a five-mile trek. [As a result] most Ladies, as the years advance, develop complexions of deep-sea fishermen with a taste for the bottle" (Sutherland 1979a:35). The character of Audrey in "To The Manor Born" was the archetypical country/county woman.

The country, as knightly tournaments and holy crusades once were, is an arena in which honor can be won or lost. Indeed, there has always been an overlap between the battle and the hunting fields. One was preparation for the other. For example, Simon Blow reports a certain ambivalence towards the outbreak of World War I: "For the hunting men it was going to be sad indeed to miss the opening of a new season but here at last was their opportunity to show that courage prepared in the field" (1983:50).

And country sports do demand courage. Aside from the costs involved, country pursuits (with the exception of gardening and fishing) are remarkable for the dangers they pose. Shooting is probably the most dangerous of all since a gun has no other purpose than to kill, and it will regardless of what it is pointed at (Debrett's 1981:367). In the excitement of a drive an inexperienced gun, trying to take aim, can easily swing his shotgun in the direction of his fellows or the oncoming beaters. The danger is compounded by the social acceptance of "aiming juices." Debrett's *Etiquette and Modern Manners* advises, "It is quite correct to take a pocket flask on a day's shooting: cherry brandy, sloe gin, whisky and water, and a concoction known as 'Rusty Nail' . . . being popular aiming juices" (Debrett's 1981:367).

As dangerous as shooting is, it is not the only perilous sport. One can also break one's neck riding, either to hounds or in the show ring. A passage from Margot Asquith's biography suggests some of the danger involved. (She also demonstrates a commendable aristocratic indifference to that danger.) "I ride better than most people. . . . I have broken both collarbones, my nose, my ribs, and my knee-cap; I have dislocated my jaw, fractured my skull and had five concussions of the brain; but . . . I have not lost my nerve" (Asquith 1962:214). (One wonders what those whom she considered to be inferior riders looked like after a few hours in, or out of, the saddle.)

The danger of blood sports is not incidental; rather, it is the point. Honor accrues to those who are able to play the game fairly, heedless of the risk involved. Howe sees in this the "tension or contradiction between ascription and achievement that is common to hereditary aristocracies. While upper-class ideologies stress that social class is a matter of birth and thus unchanging, at the same time they wish to promote the idea that the accomplishments and behavior of the upper classes justify their position and that they deserve to be where they are" (1981:290). Country sports are ordeals that confirm upper-class participants in their privilege.

Moreover, Howe observed that "hunters in many societies, both primitive and modern, implicitly identify themselves with at least some of the animals they pursue, and by killing them, they symbolically transfer certain of their qualities to themselves. A similar kind of identification holds in war, with the concept of noble *adversary* whose sterling qualities confirm one's own" (1981:293). This makes the fox, whose verminous confirm one's own" (1981:293). This makes the fox, whose verminous state is used to rationalize its pursuit, an unusual quarry, especially in light of hunting's social cachet. "Hunters are not at all eager to transfer the fox's qualities to themselves" (1981:295). Howe feels that foxes are since the more noble quarry—wild boar and deer—vanished long ago (1981:296–97).

But the qualities of the fox (or the trout, or the pheasant) are irrelevant to an extent. What is important is that they represent nature. In overcoming them, the sportsman triumphs over them and symbolically absorbs the ferocity and worthiness of nature. Because of this the English are the best they can be in the country.

This absorption of nature's qualities is vividly confirmed by the spectacle of some 200 or so hunters riding pell-mell across what's left of open countryside, hurtling over fences and walls. Howe writes that the lower and lower-middle classes who "are drawn by the excitement and spectacle of the chase" are *ipso facto* passively consenting to the social hierarchy which permits the upper classes to hunt. But this cuts both ways. By hunting (or shooting, or fishing, or gardening) the aristocrat acquires nature's qualities both for himself and also vicariously for those who follow on foot, display hunting prints, wear country tweeds, or plant garish suburban flower beds.

Given the importance of the country in the "imaginative universe" of many Britons, it is surprising to learn that all land in Britain belongs to someone or another; there are few expanses of public or unowned land as exist in the United States. The country is coterminous with one or another private estate. Although country pastimes are identified with an idealized English life embraced by all classes, they are accessible to only the most privileged.

Given, then, the privileged nature of country life, the question remains: how can royal persons, displayed against that particular backdrop, be seen as embodying so many aspects of British life in general?

Part of this is due to the apparent simplicity of country life:

> Jumping in and out of landrovers with great wet Labradors is [the Queen's] idea of a perfect afternoon, trudging across ploughed fields in Wellington boots. [Like shooting and fishing, these] tastes and pastimes do not appear unduly privileged or out of touch, though when examined closely, their cost and scale can be seen to put them impossibly out of the reach of all but a tiny minority of her people. (Lacey 1977:299)

Part is due also to the mythic quality of the country. Indeed it is as mythic as is the heroic past. Royal public occasions identify royalty with ancient and venerable traditions. The private lives of royalty identify them with the timeless and noble terrain that is the country. They shoot, hunt (mostly on the sly), fish, and garden—activities tied to the timeless rhythms of the countryside. Foxes burrowing deep in the earth, trout and salmon lurking beneath icy rivers and lochs, game birds nesting in woodlands and moors—all of these creatures are rooted in the landscape. Both the past and the country are mythic realms within which the Royal Family are equally at home. The private country life of the Queen is synonymous with the public life of the Kingdom. To be more precise, it symbolizes the way English life ought to be. The Queen's pastimes are national pastimes even if only a small portion of the nation can pursue them.

# VII

## The Minor Event

### A Descent into the Ordinary

The most regular employment of the Queen and her family is to visit all over the United Kingdom (Howard 1977:29). These seemingly inconsequential calls to such ordinary places as schools, mines, hospitals, student residences, and factories are the increments of an interminable modern royal progress. Each stop along this route is a minor royal event. On these occasions the Queen is brought face to face with many of her most ordinary subjects.

This class of royal event can probably be traced to Prince Albert. Coming from Germany, the earnest Albert wished to learn as much as possible about his adopted country. "Albert was the first royal prince to be well known to the working classes, to take an interest in them which was neither patronizing nor officious, and to speak to them in language which they could understand. . . . Albert went wherever the workers were to be found in large numbers—building sites, coal mines, factories but especially ports and dockyards, all drew him like a magnet" (Bennett 1977:155). Bennett adds that London society was baffled by Albert's interest in classes "from whom little but deference was expected." Be that as it may, Victoria's uncle, King Leopold, thought that such visits to manufacturing centers like Birmingham were "a useful counterbalance to the prevailing view of Birmingham manufacturers that royalty was useless" (Bennett 1977:113).

94

Minor royal events are brief, informal (no red carpets), and usually happen in the afternoon. They are highly repetitive (despite the great variety of places visited). The generally unremarkable nature of these institutions guarantees that this class of royal event attracts scant national attention, warranting little more than passing notice in the Court Circular. Though they garner little media coverage, neither the Palace, nor apparently the Queen, considers them unimportant. "On the connecting door between the offices of [her Principal and Deputy Private Secretaries] is a map of Britain which is slowly being covered with pins to denote the places [the Queen] has been on official visits" (Bailey 1977a:70).

## The General Format of a Minor Event

Neither the Queen nor the Palace decides that a visit will be made to this place or that. The Queen is always invited, though never directly. She must be petitioned through her Private Secretary. Those who know the proper form send a letter "suggesting" that the Queen "might" be interested in paying a visit "some time" in the future. Ostensibly the tone of the invitation is one of disinterest ("the Queen would enjoy seeing this"), but often the opposite is quite the case. A local visit may make poor newspaper copy, but a picture of the Queen *in situ* adds a certain cachet, for example, to a brochure appealing for funds.

The Queen receives innumerable invitations. She cannot honor them all. The Palace, then, makes the choices. If the proposed invitation is inappropriate, the Palace sends a polite decline. A courtier told me that royalty eschews association with organizations that are political, controversial, "cranky," or hint of financial instability. Instead, they favor those that are enduring, stable, and represent a balance of interests throughout the community.

If the request is appropriate, coming for instance from one of the hundreds of organizations of which the Queen is patron, the Private Secretary will discuss it with the Queen. If convenient, the Queen "graciously" accepts. Then begins the arduous and prolonged process of organizing the visit itself: what will the Queen see and how long will she see it; who will be presented and who will present the bouquet; what refreshment will be served and how will it be served? A tentative plan is drawn up and sent to the Palace for approval. Much of the planning is done over the phone. Eventually, a Palace official, often the Private Secretary himself, comes with stopwatch in hand to survey the site and go over the program, literally step-by-step.

On the day of the visit, the Queen leaves the Palace in one of the royal limousines. She is accompanied by a Lady-in-Waiting, an Equerry, her Private Secretary, and a detective. Her departure from the Palace is timed so that she will arrive exactly on schedule. When the limousine stops, the Queen gets out unaided. The Palace advises that the Queen does not like to be helped getting out of cars. She is not to be touched. At the curb the Queen is welcomed by her representative. (In the country her representative is the Lord Lieutenant of the county; in London, the Lord (or Lady) Mayor of the borough.)

Her representative is responsible for introducing the Queen to the host who will accompany her on her tour of the premises. En route she will be shown points of interest and will exchange a few words, memorable mostly for their banality, with representatives of the staff and others, whether these be workers, students, or patients. Ostensibly, the Queen wants to meet members of the "rank and file" rather than governors of the board. Along the way the Queen is given the first memento of her visit, a bouquet. The Palace advises that the Queen prefers a child's posy over florist concoctions, preferably presented by a child. In addition, the Queen is often given some other, usually quite expensive knickknack like a paperweight, a picture frame, or bookends, which find their way onto the many desks, shelves, and tabletops in the royal residences. (The gifts that the Royal Family have acquired during their visits can be seen in photographs of them sitting at their desks.)

The visit climaxes with the taking of tea. So sacred is this "communion" that even the official photographers, engaged to record the Queen's presence, are not allowed to take pictures. Photos of royalty while they are eating are generally proscribed. Before leaving, the Queen signs the Special Guest Register. A photograph of her signing the register is often a favorite souvenir of her visit. In addition, she might sign a formal photograph of herself that henceforth will be hung in a prominent place. With these formalities, the visit ends. The Queen and her party are escorted to the entrance, where the senior staff take their leave. Her Majesty's representatives see her to her car and take their leave at the curb—a royal visit, like all ritual sequences, begins and ends the same.

Later that day a thank-you note is sent to the Queen's Private Secretary asking him to convey to Her Majesty their "loyal duty and deep appreciation." The Private Secretary, at "the Queen's command," sends a similar letter expressing the Queen's pleasure at a "splendid afternoon which she enjoyed immensely."

There is a great deal more to a minor royal event than meets the eye from this short description. Essentially these occasions are public displays of courtesy. Like all public displays, they are highly competitive in nature. It is this underlying competitiveness that makes them so interesting, particularly since that competitiveness is assiduously denied.

A royal visit to ordinary places would seem to be a most egalitarian occasion. But this is not so. Rather, it underscores the inequities of the social system. When individuals seek to present themselves as more *comme il faut* than their fellows, they are striving for social honor. Minor events appear to give everyone an equal shot at such distinction, but the cruel fact remains that the higher one is in the social system the greater his share of that honor will be. In short, minor events are interesting because they allow us to watch the class system in action as powerful individuals (at least in terms of the institution visited) exploit their position to score points in the presence of the Queen.

Noel Coward observed that any occasion at which the Royal Family were present was "an unqualified exhibition of niceness." Minor events would seem also to conform to that definition. When the Queen drops by, everyone is most mannerly and deferential. Indeed, the sense of niceness that pervades such occasions derives from the emphasis placed upon the English virtues of etiquette and civility.

Underneath the veneer of the civility and calm that characterize the minor event lies a great deal of disruption. Ordinary routines are upset, if not entirely suspended, while the royal person is on the premises. Personnel and materiel (such as tables and chairs) are totally rearranged. Individuals are asked to line corridors and stairways. Rooms are emptied of their contents. A minor event confounds the ordinary social order of the host institution.

Most disruptive of all is the commingling of the ranks, that is, the drawing together of individuals from different strata of the institution. Institutions, as Goffman pointed out, are hierarchies in which there is a very definite split between "the small supervisory staff" at the top, and the "large maintained group, conveniently called inmates" at the bottom. Between the "capstone" and the vast pyramid below there is usually a great deal of social distance. Social distance is often expressed spatially; different ranks do not come into contact with one another. Indeed, social contact is commonly restricted to the extent that "even talk across boundaries may be conducted in a special tone of voice" (Goffman 1961:8).

But when the Queen comes to visit, the spatial distance between strata shrinks dramatically. Individuals from the highest echelons, rarely encountered on the premises, are seen moving freely among the "inmates" with a fictive intimacy. Even though the spatial distance between superior and inferior on these occasions has shrunk, the social distance has not. The social boundaries are as zealously guarded as ever. In fact, the courtesy that is so much on display in the Queen's presence is also called upon to protect those social boundaries.

Courtesy, or etiquette, is frequently defined as ways of showing concern for others. This is probably true as long as all present are of equal status. But when different categories of people are brought together, etiquette becomes something else entirely: it keeps the lowly in their place. Elias wrote that etiquette has always been a weapon to use against one's inferiors (1978:101). Marwick echoes this with his observation that "one of the purposes of a more invidious etiquette for centuries has been precisely to establish one's own social superiority (1980:311). A royal visit brings together different kinds of people so that all may greet the Queen.

But because different sorts are all jumbled together in ways not ordinarily countenanced, we find something else going on besides a good-natured greeting of the Queen. We see individuals sorting themselves into the socially superior and inferior. Out of the chaos and disruption the social order reestablishes itself.

The irony is that the very same etiquette that makes these occasions appear so cooperative is also responsible for their essential competitiveness. Some individuals have better manners than others. Not uncoincidentally, they are the same individuals who are responsible for organizing a royal visit, giving themselves ample opportunity to show off their superior manners to the Queen.

## The Queen's Visit to Worthmore House*

In the mid-1970s, the Queen made an hour-and-a-half visit to a London residence for overseas students of which she is a patron. The residence had recently been enlarged by the addition of a block of flats for married students. This addition was named Crossby Court in honor of a deceased benefactor of the trust that administers Worthmore House. The Governors of the trust thought the Queen might be interested in seeing the newly completed wing, and so tendered an invitation. The invitation was accepted but two years elapsed before the Queen was able to come.

This particular visit followed the prescribed format. The Queen, arriving exactly on time, was greeted at the curb by the Lady Mayor, the Town Clerk, and the Member of Parliament. They escorted her to the entrance of the residence where the chairman of the trust and senior staff were presented. In addition, Lady Worthmore and Lady Crossby, the widows of the founder and the benefactor, were presented. A number of the senior staff, presented at the entrance, joined the Queen and her ret-

---

*Because permission to publish the particulars of this occasion was not forthcoming, I have changed the names of the residence as well as persons involved.

inue, as did the Mayor, Town Clerk, and the Member of Parliament. This, then, was the select group which actually served as the Queen's hosts and companions for the duration of her stay.

As the "Programme" suggests (see Appendix A), there were two agenda. One was to inspect Crossby Court, the other to present the residents and staff to the Queen. Before crossing the parking lot to Crossby Hall, the Queen "reviewed" the lower staff—such as the secretaries, receptionists, porters, and kitchen workers. These individuals were pointed out to the Queen by one or another of the directors and wardens, as if they personally knew them. Ordinarily, the chairman of the trust would have no contact with those who ladle out soup in the cafeteria or who carry heavy parcels about the premises. Similarly, the senior staff who presented the ten foreign students in the dining room would not normally be on a first-name basis with those students. There is, of course, a limit to the number of individuals that can be presented in an hour and a half. Such limits are not, however, immediately apparent. Take, for example, the presentations in the dining room which took twenty-five minutes, a significant chunk of the ninety-minute visit. There were 150 residents in the room: 100 divided into five geographically defined groups and the other 50 dispersed around the room. Two from each group had been preselected to be introduced. Although twenty-five minutes seems to be a long time, this allots about four or five minutes per group. Even the lucky ten who were actually introduced had only a minute or so of the Queen's time.

In sharp contrast to this "assembly-line" intercourse was the privilege accorded the senior staff. Not only did they decide who should meet the Queen and who should not, they also made the actual introductions and, hovering about the Queen, insured that no one monopolized her time. Indeed, a number of the senior staff enjoyed a full hour and a half in close proximity to the Queen.

That such access to the Queen is treasured is evinced by the following passage of Cecil Beaton's diary, where he describes an occasion on which the Queen and others of the Royal Family attended the theatre in the first year of the Queen's reign:

> Such is the effect of Royalty that, although the play has been running for a hundred performances, the entire cast was nervous. Even the old professionals, like Ronnie Squire and Marie Lohr, were saying, "Oh, we'll be too keyed up to give good performances," and everyone was a bit too intent on putting their best foot forward. . . . Everyone behind the scenes was giving an extra spit and polish to their job. . . .

Throughout the performance the Regal Box was surreptitiously watched by half the audience, so that the play received scant attention. . . .

I wish I could make a better impression on the Queen . . . so much that I reproach myself for something inadequate within myself if she does not respond favorably. . . .

In the second interval the company was presented. Jolly jokes, graciousness: everyone had his proud moment. The final curtain. The cast bowed and curtsied to the Royal Box. Then the Royal party left. Cheers, hands waving to the gallery. The Queen Mother gets her special round of applause. Exit. Police in control. Sudden release of tension. Shouts, laughter, eyes wild, bouquets, flashlights. For the people responsible, an evening of great achievement. For the Royal Family, no doubt a pleasant enough excursion: one to be discussed very little on their return and forgotten completely in the busy events of tomorrow. (1973:112–15)

The disparity between those surrounding the Queen and those kept at bay was underscored by the clothes worn by the two groups. The senior staff were dressed as was the Queen, her Lady-in-Waiting, and Equerry; that is, the men wore dark suits, the women hats, gloves, pearls, and afternoon ensembles. This would not be remarkable except that the Palace advises prospective hosts that informal attire should be worn for a royal visit (presumably so that no financial hardship would be imposed). The residential lower staff were dressed so—skirts and blouses for the women; slacks, sweaters, and an occasional tie for the men.

Although a royal visit initially confounds the ordinary organizational order, it also results in the re-creation of that order. The hierarchy, in a sense, forms around the Queen. Those at the top, the capstone, enjoy the greatest access, while those at the bottom are kept away. These disparities are further communicated by the clothes that individuals choose to wear for the occasion. Although the fiction of a minor event is that it is an opportunity for the Sovereign to meet her people, we can see that she is not so much presented to them as she is *displayed*. Moreover, she is displayed in the midst of the most powerful individuals in the host institution. The proximity of such persons to the Queen allows them to bask in her reflected glory. They know how to dress and act in the presence of the Queen. This confirms and legitimizes their right to their high position.

Generally speaking, photographs of minor royal occasions are comparatively rare. Pictures of the Queen graciously inspecting yet another school do not make particularly good press. But I think there is another reason for their dearth. The fiction of a minor occasion is that it is an opportunity for the Queen to mingle with her people; yet, the Queen is effectively insulated from such contact by the veritable cocoon of upper echelon individuals that forms around her. Given the pride of place that the Ladies Worthmore and Lords Seagram enjoy on such occasions, one would assume that it would be easy to find photographs of royal visits showing the Queen firmly ensconced in the midst of such individuals. We expect to find pictures reflecting the social hierarchy which precipitates out on such occasions, that is, the Queen, her entourage, and the Ladies Crossby and Lords Seagram shown against a backdrop of resident students. But such photographic evidence of hierarchical or class differences is exceedingly rare. It seems that there is a conspiracy of sorts that prevents the publication of such pictures. The few pictures that I have seen that contrast the socially superior (i.e., the similarly attired Queen, royal retinue, and hosts) with the socially inferior (i.e., the contrastingly attired rank and file) involve children. On these occasions, the privileged individuals can be shown in proximity to the Queen because the distinctions between *hoi oligoi* and *hoi polloi* would not be easily recognized as those of class. Rather, they appear to be the differences of child and adult. Children are so deviant that all adults outrank them. No matter what the conscious reason for this convention (i.e., of not contrasting the privileged few with the anonymous many), the fact remains that the inequities of the social system are obscured.

Related to this phenomenon of the "invisible" privileged few is the general anonymity of those close to the Queen and Royal Family. Individuals who appear in photographs with them are rarely, if ever, identified. There is no way of knowing whether they are members of the Household, close personal friends, random strangers, or potential assassins. One must depend upon serendipity to identify them. For example, it is easy to learn the names of the Queen's Ladies-in-Waiting. Yet, to this day, I do not know what most look like even though I have followed the Royal Family for years. One exception is Lady Susan Hussey, more easily recognizable because she is one of Prince William's godmothers.

## An Asymmetrical Exchange: Graciousness and Gratitude

A royal visit is an exciting event. The Queen's presence makes the occasion a most memorable one. After all, "even the most tenuous brush with royalty is lovingly recorded" (Ziegler 1978:77).

Royal visits make apparent one of the Queen's key attributes: her graciousness.

"Grace" is an enormously complex word that carries a range of meanings. At one end of that range is the notion of divine assistance or intervention. Grace is a virtue coming (down) from God; it is supra-human. At the other end is the sense of a charming appearance and ease, especially suppleness of form and elegance of bearing which are the outward signs of an inner moral excellence. The Queen's graciousness becomes most apparent when she abandons her pinnacle and, descending, finds common ground with ordinary people.

It becomes apparent because to be gracious also implies overlooking or putting up with something. A royal visit may very well be a bore for the Queen. Yet she graciously condescends to grace such occasions with her presence. In return, the recipients of her graciousness are eternally grateful and express their gratitude. This asymmetrical exchange of graciousness and gratitude between the Sovereign and her subjects underscores the moral superiority of the Queen as well as her deviance.

Most people exchange gifts, thinking that presents are spontaneous, disinterested, and have no strings attached. Anthropologists have long recognized that the opposite is true. To accept a gift is to enter into a moral relationship where one is constrained to return not only a gift but one of higher value if possible. To fail to do so is to become subordinate or morally compromised.

These rules do not apply to the Queen, nor to royalty in general, who are in the enviable position of being able to give by receiving. They give nothing; yet they give everything. In order to understand this contradiction, let us look more closely at another aspect of the minor event: the costs involved.

Inviting the Queen to tea can involve enormous, though hidden, expense: Andrew Duncan provides numerous examples of the outlays involved in having the Queen stop by. For example, the Queen distributed Maundy Money in Selby Abbey in 1969. The town council spent £298 (approximately $894.00) on bunting alone, and another £125 ($375.00) on crush barriers. Moreover, the "normal police force of thirty was multiplied more than ten times to a total of 366, including twelve plain-clothes men in the Abbey, sitting among the choir and guests. At least twelve meetings took place to discuss security and other arrangements" (Duncan 1970:236).

The Queen once stayed in Dorchester for six hours. She was traveling by train. Seventy tons of coal had been lying about the railroad yard in twelve-foot piles. Coalmen worked round the clock to remove those unsightly piles lest the Queen be offended by the mess. In Brazil, the Queen was invited to a Commonwealth Community reception ("a microcosm of a 1930s world"). Three thousand pounds had been spent "preparing stands with crenelated blue and brown canvas awnings decorated with orchids, poinsettia, and tropical foliage, and laid with a new red carpet" (Duncan 1970:49). The Rio Yacht Club even had its harbor dredged for a royal visit at a cost of £10,000. Perhaps the harbor needed dredging. This is quite probable since impending royal visits are frequently inducements to local authorities, as well as to the Queen's prospective hosts, to make repairs or improvements that are overdue. Nevertheless, the modern royal progress of Elizabeth II resembles those of Elizabeth I, who methodically ruined her nobles by visiting them, with her large retinue, for extended periods of time.

## The Queen Gives Nothing

The enormous outlays of time, energy, and money involved in entertaining the Queen are never matched by similar outlays on her part. As we have seen, she is treated to tea, given bouquets, and small but costly mementos of her visit. Yet she brings nothing in return. She seems to leave a portrait of herself as a counterpresentation, but this is not really so. If her hosts wish to have such a picture, they must buy it themselves; Buckingham Palace obligingly provides a list of firms from which it can be purchased.

Bouquets are especially good tokens of appreciation since they are ephemeral and not easily priced (Beidelman: personal communication). One exception to the rule of no counterpresentations has been devised by the Princess of Wales. "She has worked out a beguiling routine with the carnations and roses that people press upon her. She slips them into the buttonholes of guests farther down the line, and this makes grown men blush like school boys" (Lacey 1982:23). The flowers circulate among the audience. The Princess, the medium through which that circulation takes place, garners the honor of both recipient and donor yet in no way depletes herself. As Lacey observed, she clearly enjoys being a princess.

It is not entirely true to say that the Queen leaves *nothing* behind her. She leaves her signature by autographing her portrait and signing the Special Guest Register. Although a sample of her writing costs her nothing, it should not be underrated. Anthony Holden, who wrote a biography of Prince Charles (apparently at the Prince's request, though it is not the "official" biography since "kings don't get official biographies until they're dead"), provides the following anecdote:

When I completed the manuscript, I showed it to [Prince Charles] with the understanding that I would not give up editorial control. He made a lot of margin notes on my scruffy copy. But when they came back, his suggested additions were all neatly typed. The royal handwriting is not given out. His changes are somewhere in the Royal Archives at Windsor. (*The New York Times Book Review* 10/28/79)

Handwriting, like the gift, is not inert. "Even when abandoned by the giver, it still forms part of himself" (Mauss 1967:9). In leaving her signature behind, the Queen bequeaths something of herself to her hosts. But that something is "invaluable" in sharp contrast to the valuable trees she has planted and the plaques she has unveiled. These, of course, have been provided by her hosts along with the bouquets and knick-knacks. This is a very asymmetrical form of exchange, and is all the more strange since "[to] give is to show one's superiority, to show that one is something more and higher, that one is *magister*. To accept without returning or repaying is to face subordination, to become a client and subservient, to become *minister*" (Mauss 1967:72). Yet there is little danger that the Queen of England will become subservient. This is a mark of her moral superiority. The Queen can take and take without ever being compromised, despised, or constrained to make counterpresentations. Instead, she is always *magister*. Clearly she is above the rules, that is, a deviant.

## Gifts

The Queen's peculiar moral superiority is evident in contexts other than factories or schools. First, the Queen does not generally give anything away to strangers. (Maundy Money and the wreath placed at the Cenotaph are exceptions.) The Queen, however, does exchange gifts with heads of state who are not so much strangers as they are fellow sovereigns. These exchanges take place during foreign visits. For example, Duncan described the exchange of personal gifts that took place during the Queen's visit to Brazil in 1969. President Artur da Costa e Silva gave the Queen a gold balanganda and Prince Philip a painting of birds. In return, the Queen and Prince Philip reciprocated with "an 18 inch silver centerpiece with acanthus leaf decoration, caryatid handles, pedestal fluted foot and engraved inscription to the President, and an 18 carat gold bracelet set with the royal cipher to Dona Yolanda from the Queen. Plus, of course, the reciprocal signed photographs in silver frames (Duncan 1970:37).

The gifts were of equal opulence: no one was overly generous; no one appeared niggardly. This cannot be said, however, of the exchange which took place when the Queen visited the Persian Gulf states in 1979. The Queen received staggeringly costly gifts while distributing in return what, in comparison, can only be described as mere tokens.

> The potentates seem to have exceeded their usual lavish standards for such gifts to fellow sovereigns, presenting the Queen and her husband with a royal ransom of jewels, objets d'art, carpets and gold coffee jugs, incense burners, handbags, swords, and a glittering knee length apron. (*The New York Times* 2/26/79:4:1)

The Emir of Qatar gave, among many other opulent things, a long necklace of gold discs studded with precious stones which jewel merchants in Qatar valued at $2 million. "This would exactly match Britain's balance of payments surplus for January," observed *The New York Times*.

And what did the Queen give in return? To one and all she gave silver trays engraved with the royal yacht and "an appropriate message." Some of the wives received, a bit incongruously, the *Times* reporter felt, a book on Bedouin jewelry. Although engraved sterling silver trays are far from cheap, the estimated cost being $30,000 apiece, they were positively cheesy compared to gifts like a diamond-encrusted gold statue of a horse and a $2 million necklace. The trays, no doubt, were graciously accepted by the emirs.

Not only were the Queen's presents chintzy, but, being all the same, they reflected little investment of the self in their selection. Together these features rendered the "exchange" between the emirs and the Queen a kind of potlatch. Giving costly gifts to the Queen of England is not unlike throwing vast wealth into the ocean from which nothing ever returns. As with the Kwakiutl, the rivalry was not so much between the chiefs and the sea, or the emirs and the Queen, as it was among the emirs to see who could outdo the others by destroying more wealth.

The Persian Gulf "potlatch" was the only time that the Queen came close to being "grateful." The Palace announced that the Queen was "gratified," letting it be known that she was "stunned." Perhaps the discomfiture of the Queen was due not entirely to the opulence of the gifts. Instead it is something inherent in exchange. The Queen, for matters of state, was obligated to accept. The vulgarity of the emirs' gifts underscored Mauss's curious observation that a gift is "*dangerous to accept*" (Mauss 1967:58). Significantly, the *Queen* was criticized for their gross ostentation.

Furthermore, did the emirs consider the Queen's failure to match their generosity a breach whose sanction, according to Mauss, is open or private warfare? Apparently not. By all accounts *they* were grateful for the opportunity to make presentations to such an august person as the Queen of England, the living incarnation of the most prestigious European monarchy. By giving the Queen such opulent presents they were validating the statuses of their emirates which, if not for the fortuitous possession of oil, would have remained the desolate backwaters they were in the early part of the century.

And what of the Queen? She received these embarrassingly opulent gifts graciously. She gives by receiving. She clearly has the gift of grace.

Minor events illustrate the Queen's grace in other ways. When the Queen meets ordinary people, she will naturally encounter many who are not as socially adroit as she is. Of course, the cards are all stacked in the Queen's favor. She has had over thirty years' practice; while for those she meets, greeting the Queen of England is usually a once-in-a-lifetime occasion. Being of such immense importance, it causes many to hem and haw, forget their lines, and generally be at a loss as to what to do. Because they are human, they err. The Queen, in contrast, always knows what to do, and is never at a loss. She does not err. This makes her suprahuman.

At first, it would appear that close contact with the stumblebums of the world might violate the Queen's dignity. Ironically, the blundering and general ineptitude of others do not threaten the Queen's dignity, they enhance it. They allow the Queen to overlook them, that is, to forgive, which is divine. And because the Queen does so graciously overlook such things her subjects are eternally grateful.

The Queen is most endearing on those few occasions when individuals have crossed some line of royal etiquette. Barbra Streisand, as noted earlier, violated the rule that one never speaks to royalty unless spoken to first. (Debrett's [1981] has noted that this rule has eased somewhat and that it is permissible for an individual to introduce a topic after the royal person has initiated the conversation.) Having been introduced to the Queen at the premier of *Funny Girl,* the actress discombobulated the Queen by asking her why women had to wear gloves in her presence. Although taken aback, the Queen was undeniably charming in her admission that she did not really know.

It should not be assumed from this anecdote, however, that the Queen takes lightly the matter of her own dignity, especially when she feels it is at risk. Duncan relates an incident that occurred on the Queen's visit to Brazil. The British Ambassador, introducing the Queen to a local musician, asked her if she had ever heard "the bagpipes played on the guitar?" The Queen "was not amused, an emotion always shown by ignoring the remark, while looking directly at its perpetrator" (Duncan 1970:57).

An even more vivid anecdote of the Queen's hold on her dignity was provided by John Groton, the former Prime Minister of Australia:

> "One of the greatest fun evenings I can remember," he said, was when he was cruising on the royal yacht *Britannia* with Queen Elizabeth II and members of her family along the Queensland coast in 1970. Someone suggested it would be "rather fun" to picnic on a little island in the Great Barrier Reef.
>
> People decided that everyone else ought to be thrown in the water. Prince Philip was thrown in and then Princess Anne. [And the Queen, too? Not quite.]
>
> "I was sitting beside the Queen. I was about to throw her in, but I looked at her and there was something in the way she looked back . . ." (*The New York Times* 5/3/72:43:3)

The Queen has other ways of protecting her dignity that can easily pass unnoticed. Take, for instance, handshakes. Lacey writes that "etiquette prescribes a special way of extending your fingers limply to be grasped by [the royal person]. And it is not polite for you to grasp her back" (1977:xx). When individuals are overly familiar with the Queen and grasp back, she shows her displeasure by averting her gaze. This sign of displeasure would be recognized by any public school boy who is taught to shake hands while "looking the person whose hand you are shaking steadily in the eyes" (Heald 1984:42).

This brings us back to my original point: minor events are interesting because they allow us to observe the class system in action. The institutional hierarchy, normally invisible, becomes modeled in space as members of the upper strata coagulate, as it were, around the Queen. But what does this have to do with the British class system in general? The individuals who enjoy the greatest access to the Queen are those with the best manners. They can be trusted to act properly in the presence of the sovereign, demonstrated by the absence of impertinent questions or overfamiliar handshakes. They signal their trustworthiness by their demeanor and most obviously by their dress which resembles that of the royal entourage. Thus, the institutional hierarchy is made manifest by a hierarchy of access, admission to which is regulated by social adroitness. Although most people try to be unfailingly polite to the Queen, some are better at it than others.

The people who spend the most time with the Queen are those who occupy not only the highest niches of, say, Worthmore House, but also of British society in general. Lord Seagram is only a life peer but his title identifies him with the hereditary nobility, the most prestigious group in all Britain. Thus, the configurations around the Queen—both those who are kept at a distance and those who are allowed to draw near—present a highly condensed model of British society which as in all societies is unfair.

# VIII

⟨≈⟩

# The Aristocracy

## By These Signs Ye Shall Know Them

The aristocracy is essential to the monarchy. Its role, however, is downplayed, if not negated. As we saw earlier, the hereditary aristocracy is the matrix in which royalty is embedded. New members are recruited from its ranks, and those sloughed off are returned to it. Royalty and aristocracy are natural allies for many reasons, not the least of which is that they do the same things.

Yet, royalty and the aristocracy would seem to be incompatible: royalty are highly visible; the aristocracy remains generally unseen. Invisibility has always been a form of protection. By staying out of the public eye and not flaunting their enormous privilege, the upper classes have been able, by and large, to hold on to what they've got. In the Age of the Common Man, it makes good sense to de-emphasize one's own material and social privileges. A number of factors protect their invisibility, but only two will be examined here. The first is the popular belief that the aristocracy has been brought to its knees by almost a century of high taxation and a pathetically low birthrate. Not only do these beliefs protect the elite, they also manage to make people feel a little sorry for the aristocrats. The taxed-out-of-existence canard is promoted by the aristocracy itself. This, of course, should not surprise us.

The source of the belief about the falling birthrate is harder to pinpoint. As an example of this assumption, let me cite Packard, who writes with confidence of the importance of Ascot to "the leading elements of Britain's dwindling landed aristocracy" (1981:89). The aristocracy, however, is hardly dwindling, with three or four children per family being not at all unusual. For example, if we were to take the top two (alphabetically ordered) peers in the top three ranks of the peerage (Dukes, Marquesses, and Earls), we would find the following: the Duke of Abercorn has two sons and one daughter; the Duke of Argyll has one son and one daughter; the Marquess of Aberdeen is unmarried (but his heir has one son and two daughters); the Marquess of Abergavenny has three daughters and two sons (with another son deceased); the Earl of Airlie has three sons and three daughters; and the Earl of Albemarle is nineteen years old and unmarried (his heir is his uncle who has two sons and one daughter). The aristocracy can hardly be said to be in danger of dying out.

The second factor that hedges its "invisibility" is the aristocracy's inhabitation of an extremely inaccessible corner of the social landscape. All kinds of barriers block its access. Among these must be counted the "current tyranny of democratic values that deny the obvious fact that some people are superior to others" (Beidelman: personal communication). Another barrier is that it is considered rather tasteless, indeed perverse, to be interested in class.

These attitudes have inhibited the investigation of class differences since at least the 1920s. "The received though paradoxical, academic view of class in Great Britain, as to the non-existence or non-importance of class [can be traced to the observance of] the dictates of good taste" (Marwick 1980:54). Marwick cites the 1927 edition of the *Survey of the Social Structure of England and Wales* whose authors assert "the belief in the existence of social classes . . . is the result of studying social theory of doubtful value and of neglecting social facts." Marwick adds that "the 'social theory of doubtful value' was, of course, Marxism."

This convenient denial of the existence of social classes, especially the uppermost ones, spares many from the awkwardness of examining those classes. So anxious are some to avoid that unpleasantness that one still hears echoes of the 1927 *Survey of the Social Structure of England and Wales*. "As a social class of really national significance, the upper class has nearly ceased to exist, though much is made of its snob appeal" (Cole 1955:69). This is a staggering assertion for an Englishman to make. Although much *is* made of its snob appeal (what anthropologists would call the distribution of social honor), the class has hardly lost its national significance, as we shall see.

## The Positional Study of Elites

The few social scientists who have not shied away from the study of elites, that is, those who have dared to venture into what Giddens calls "uncharted territory" have often done so by adopting the positional approach. This method focuses "upon those individuals who occupy formally defined positions of authority at the head of a social organization of institution" (Giddens 1974:4). This objective approach sidesteps many or the problems generated by the subjective nature of class given that one either occupies a formal position or does not.

The problem with the positional approach as it is applied to British elites is that the people for whom the greatest social prestige is reserved tend not to do anything at all in the conventional sense. (Of course, one should be wary of overplaying the notion of the indolent aristocrat. This is not always true. For example, the Earl of Cranbrook has a doctorate in zoology and specializes in the fauna of Southeast Asia; Lord David Cecil, son of the fourth Marquess of Salisbury, is Goldsmith's Professor of English Literature, Oxford.) In general, however, British aristocrats do not "do" anything, and so fall through the nets cast by sociologists who would study them; thus, they remain invisible. There is, however, one sociological study, brilliant in its use of a particular positional approach, which has captured the essence of the British upper class.

This is Ron Hall's "The Family Background of Etonians," which cleverly uses one of the most "definitive status symbols of the British aristocracy"—an Eton education. Although an Eton education is often an undeniable sign of upper-class membership, not every boy who attends comes from an aristocratic background. For example, there are seventy King's scholars who are admitted on the basis of their performance on a highly competitive examination. Hall, however, focused on the Etonian parent rather than the student. He did this because as smart as an Etonian education is (ranking with the Royal Yacht Squadron ensign, Brigade of Guards bowlers, and membership in the Jockey Club), it is not quite as great a distinction as being able to *give* one's son an Eton education.

Nevertheless, the use of an Eton education as a social indicator is open to an objection—it takes no account of any rise or fall in social status after schooldays are over. For an Old Etonian on the decline, the moment of truth comes when a place cannot be found for his son. And a *parvenu* can consider himself "arrived" on the day his son is offered a place. Clearly a more exact indicator of present social status is whether or not you are accepted as an Eton parent.

Two-thirds of Britain's dukes, marquesses, and earls went to school at Eton. So did the heads of most older baronial houses. About a half of all Etonians are armigerous [i.e., they enjoy the right to display heraldic coats of arms]. No other school has anything like so many old boys in high office. In the Cabinet, Etonians outnumber their nearest rivals, the Wykehamists [i.e., graduates of Winchester College], by seven to two. In the Court of Directors of the Bank of England, the proportion is even greater. About a quarter of all Tory MPs were educated at Eton. And Etonians have an absolute majority in that other bastion of established power—the Jockey Club. [And Etonians exercise an impressive monopoly over the Order of the Garter, the most prestigious knighthood of all.]

To attempt to classify parents of Etonians in terms of occupation is somewhat misleading, for the sample immediately reveals that Eton parents often do not have jobs in the conventional sense. Research indicates that one-third have no identifiable occupation, or are rentiers. Another third have been military officers, and continue to use their service rank after retirement, as befits an officer and gentleman. (The figure includes a few parents who may still be on active military service, and thus employed as career officers; for these, almost certainly, a military career will not be the sole or necessarily even the primary source of earnings.) An additional 7 per cent are "gentleman farmers," an accepted occupation for the squirarchy for generations. [Prince Andrew, wishing to maintain his anonymity while studying in France in 1972, wrote: "My name is Edward. My father is a gentleman farmer; and my mother does not work."] Six per cent are engaged in older professions, half as clergymen, scholars, barristers, etc., and the other half as senior civil servants, MPs, or cabinet ministers. Only one-fifth are in industry, commerce, or finance; this group is largely formed by directors of banks and financial institutions. . . .

The social distinctiveness of Eton parents is also shown by the types of residence in which they live. Only one-sixth of Eton parents have a house with a number on its door, and less than 1 per cent live in a home with a suburban type name. One half live in a residence styled "Manor," "Hall," "Court," or by a similar name, and 3 per cent live in a castle, abbey, or stately home. The remainder give a variety of country addresses. (R. Hall 1969:67–69)

Hall's description confirms the existence of the upper class. Etonian parents do not "do" anything because they do not need "to convert their inherited social advantage into powerful positions within society." They do not need to work because they are extremely secure.

The eighteenth edition of Burke's *Landed Gentry* has a profile of landed families. It is based upon one hundred landed families drawn at random. The public school distribution among the heads of these families is interesting. Nineteen of the lesser public schools including Haileybury and Gordonstoun (where the Princes Charles, Andrew, and Edward were sent) had educated one apiece. Charterhouse, Cheltenham, Fettes, Marlborough, the Oratory, Ripton, Sherborne, Stowe, and Uppingham claimed two apiece. Radley and Harrow each had had three, Wellington four, and the Royal Naval College at Dartmouth (which ceased to have a public school after 1951) had had five. Rugby and Winchester had each educated seven. But a whopping twenty-nine had gone to Eton.

According to Guttsman, the aristocracy or the upper class in Britain consists of people who enjoy the top one percentile of income. These people compose one percent or less of all British households (1963:321). To learn what the top income is, we have to go elsewhere. It can be a staggering amount. For example, the present Duke of Westminster succeeded to the title when he was a mere thirty years old. Along with the title went a fortune of a billion pounds which incidentally generates an estimated income of eleven thousand pounds an hour. Despite a century-long effort to level society, a great deal of wealth—25 percent—remains concentrated in the hands of one percent of the population.

## The Ownership of the Land

Much of that wealth is in the form of landownership. The total land mass of Britain is 56,000,000 acres. Six thousand acres belong to public bodies—the Forestry Commission, the Armed Forces, the National Trust, the National Coal Board, British Railroads, and airports. The Crown owns 275,000 acres, the Church of England 170,000 acres, the Duchy of Cornwall (the source of the Prince of Wales's income) 128,000 acres, and the Colleges of Oxford and Cambridge together own 275,000 acres. This second group totals almost a million acres, one-fiftieth of the land not owned by the public bodies, or, to be exact, 848,000 acres.

In addition to these landowners, another one-third of Britain is owned by 1,500 families, many of whom are titled. Perrott estimates that a third of the peerage, that is, about three hundred fifty lords, "still own enough land to provide a significant element in their income and outlook" (1968:149).

The possession of land confers a great deal of prestige. Yet it is almost impossible to learn who owns which lands. There have only been two comprehensive land surveys in the history of Britain: the Domesday Book of 1086 and the land survey of 1873, when the landed estates were at their peak in terms of acreage. The lack of a central registry is "an omission which is rather typical of the mystery surrounding property-ownership" (Perrott 1968:148).

Despite the secrecy, it is possible to get some information on landed estates. Nelson (1976:128) supplies the following list of a few titled landowners and their acreage:

| | |
|---|---|
| Duke of Buccleuch | 300,000 acres |
| Earl of Seafield | 193,000 |
| Lord Lovat | 160,000 |
| Countess of Sutherland | 150,000 |
| Duke of Westminster | 120,000 |
| Duke of Atholl | 120,000 |
| Col. Donald Cameron of Lothiel | 100,000 |
| Duke of Argyll | 90,000 |
| Earl of Cawdor | 90,000 |
| Duke of Devonshire | 70,000 |
| Earl of Lonsdale | 70,000 |
| Sir Alec Douglas-Home | 60,000 |
| Duke of Beaufort | 45,000 |
| Earl of Moray | 44,000 |
| Lord Feversham | 40,000 |

This list is not exhaustive and includes only a small portion of the titled landowners. A sense of the magnitude of their ownership can be grasped from the fact that fifty-six landowners in England and Wales own 900,000 acres and twenty-three Scottish lords own another 1,500,000 acres. All told, seventy-nine individuals own one-twentieth of the country.

It is difficult to say how this acreage translates into pounds, since the cost of land in Scotland and in the north of England averaged 3 to 10 pounds per acre in 1968, while in the South good arable land averaged 240 pounds per acre. The most valuable land of all is that which was once farmland in what is now London.

The fantastic wealth of the Grosvenors, the Dukes of Westminster, derives from a fortunate marriage in 1677 of their progenitor, Sir

Thomas Grosvenor, and the twelve-year-old Miss Mary Davies, who had inherited the Manor of Ebury which stretched from what is now Oxford Street to the Thames. The manor had once belonged to Westminster Abbey (Westminster 1961:173).

If it is difficult to ascertain how much land an individual owns, it is not likely that it will be easy to learn how much that land produces, aside from admission fees to the stately home and the sale of game birds. But let us look at the Duchy of Cornwall as a general guideline. The Duchy consists of 128,000 acres in the West Country. In 1980, the Duchy netted more than a million dollars. "The Duchy of Cornwall had record earnings in 1980, up almost 9% over 1979, and almost 400% over 1976" (Angelo 7/81:30). This rapid increase in profits has been attributed to efficient management and improved agricultural techniques.

In addition to wealth and landownership, upper-class membership has an educational component, as we have seen. The same 1 percent of the population also send their sons to the top twenty public (i.e., exclusive) schools, which educate about .5 percent of all British boys of that age bracket. Giddens writes of "the extraordinary near monopoly exercised by the public schools in general, the influence of the Clarendon schools in particular, and of Eton, especially, over elite recruitment [in Britain]" (1974:xii). The other .5 percent of the top 1 percent's children are girls who are educated at a number of exclusive boarding schools not as famous as those of their brothers. Among these are Benenden, where Princess Anne was educated, and Riddlesworth and West Heath, schools attended by Diana Spencer.

## The Stately-Home Business

The mistaken belief that the aristocracy is on its last legs is given credence by the stately home business. Aristocrats must be on the verge of ruin; why else would they endure the indignity of opening their homes to the public? "The noble warriors of old must turn into ignoble showmen of modern times in the fight to preserve their estates" (Sinclair 1969:153). Nelson estimates that in 1974 some seven million visitors saw some three hundred stately homes; this business pulls in between 20 and 25 million pounds per year, averaging about 80,000 pounds per year per stately home. (The figure does not take into account the wide discrepancy in entry fees which in 1974 ranged from five pence to a pound-and-a-half. Today the volume of business would be considerably higher.)

Stately homes are big business. Even Sandringham and Windsor permit tourists when the Royal Family are not in residence. There is also a great deal of sniping among the noble entrepreneurs. The Countess Manvers opened her home, Thoresby Park, "only to keep the roof on. . . . 'I don't believe in standing on my head to drag people in—not like the Bedfords at Woburn Abbey'" (Sinclair 1969:152). The Duke of Bedford owns, "I have thrust myself quite unashamedly in the public eye. I have been accused of being undignified. That is quite true, I am. If you take your dignity to a pawnbroker, he won't give you much for it" (1959:219). Lord Montagu of Beaulieu thinks that the Duke has turned Woburn into a zoo. The Duke thinks that Beaulieu is little more than a garage (Sinclair 1969:153).

As strange as it may seem, the stately-home business is *not* a twentieth-century phenomenon.

> In the eighteenth century there was the recognized minor Grand Tour of English country homes, and famous homes such as Holkham, Raynham, Blenheim, Wilton, Woburn, Chatsworth and Castle Howard were regularly opened to the public on fixed days. Wilton even published a catalogue, and the owner of Stourhead built an inn for visitors to take refreshments. (Montagu 1970:145)

The Duchess of Marlborough was appalled when Blenheim was overrun with tourists before it was even completed, and Lord Lyttleton complained in 1778 that hordes of sightseers kept him prisoner in his apartments, preventing him from enjoying his own estate during the finest part of the year (Montagu 1970:145). Indeed, Jane Austen's Miss Elizabeth Bennett encountered Mr. Darcy most awkwardly at his family's stately home in *Pride and Prejudice*.

Aristocrats have opened their homes to the public, and in the process have furthered the illusion of their own desperate straits. Witness the following remarks of the Duke of Bedford:

> Live like a duke—the phrase has become part of the English language, conjuring up visions of yachts, country mansions, retinues of servants, and the fat life in general . . . a happy round of coronets, grouse moors, and champagne. . . . [When my father shot himself] I became the head of a family whose estate was threatened with extinction. Now I am engaged in a desperate struggle to maintain our ancestral home intact with its priceless treasures. (J. Bedford 1959:13)

This *crie de coeur* comes from a man who owns thirty acres in Bloomsbury, a rather smart section of London. Although it is paltry in comparison with the Duke of Westminster's 300 acres in Mayfair and gravia, it was valued at twenty million pounds in 1968 (Perrott 1968:150). Regardless of what the Duke says, the wolf is hardly at his door.

This theme of the aristocrat on the brink seems to be accepted unquestioningly by those who write about the aristocracy. For example, Penny Junor, a biographer of the Princess of Wales, went to boarding school with Princess Anne. Presumably she would be in a position to know that the aristocracy is not about to go under. Yet she describes how Raine, Earl Spencer's second wife, saved the Spencer heritage. When Raine became Countess Spencer, she was

> installed as mistress of Althorp. . . . It has to be said to her credit, however, that the only reason the estate is a going concern today is because of Raine's business sense. There were crippling duties to pay after the 7th Earl died. Johnnie [the present Earl] wouldn't have known where to begin on his own. . . . Where there had been a full complement of servants in Jack Spencer's day there was now no more than the barest minimum: a cook, a housemaid, a butler, and a ladies' maid. (Junor 1982:83–86)

Such cheese paring and opening Althorp to visitors managed to have averted financial ruin. But stories of this kind subtly imply that Althorp's roof had all but fallen, the rooms devoid of their former splendor. Honeycombe gives us a slightly different picture of Althorp:

> The house, with its wonderful variety of pictures and furniture—it still contains one of the finest private art collections in Europe, including pictures by Titian, Holbein, Van Dyck, Lely, Reynolds, Gainsborough, Kneller, Nicholson, Sargent and John—is indeed a delight and still a home fit to receive a prince. Prince Charles has stayed there on shooting weekends more than once, sleeping in King William's Room, in a four poster bed occupied by King William of Orange in 1695. (Honeycombe 1981:48)

Countess Spencer may have ruthlessly pruned the staff, but the estate still continued to field the enormous costs of raising game birds so that Prince Charles could come for shooting weekends. Furthermore, one of the most prestigious hunts, the Pytchley, meets at Althorp (Itzkowitz 1977:75,83).

Discrepancies like these between the posture of financial ruin and the reality of incredible economic security recall the words of Michael Arlen, a popular novelist of the thirties. He described London night life where great sums were squandered, apparently, without a care in the world: "For years now one had been hearing how poor these people were, how they were overtaxed, how they could not live as they used, how they were being deprived almost of the necessities of life" (Donaldson 1975:118).

Despite rumors to the contrary, the British aristocracy continues to flourish, hardly noticed by social scientists. This should surprise no one; elites always have the wherewithal to protect their privacy. Nevertheless, the aristocracy are wealthy, an important measure of that wealth being landownership. Land is not merely a finite resource. In England it is a source of enormous prestige, the country being a mythic and heroic realm. The acreage of many landowners is impressive, especially when one considers that the population density of Great Britain averages roughly one person per acre. Lord Spencer owns 15,000 acres, not particularly an impressive number when compared to Buccleuch's 300,000, but significant enough. Either 15,000 people have been displaced by him and his family or are under his sway in one way or another. The village of Althorp is on Spencer lands; its inhabitants, along with the Earl's tenant farmers, pay him rents. Thus a kind of feudalism continues to this day.

# IX

## The English Court

In days gone by a king was unthinkable without his entourage, the court. Gathered round him were the most powerful individuals of the realm. The king tied these personages to himself with gifts, favors, and the promise of even greater power. The court formed a backdrop to the sovereign's daily life, witnessing his arising and his going to bed, the consummation of his marriage and the evacuation of his bowels. They accompanied him in public, magnifying his mystery, and kept him company in private.

Among this glittering assembly were also to be found ambitious members of the lesser gentry who used their place at court as a stepping-stone to greater things. Loyal service could be parlayed into hereditary honors for themselves and for their descendants. One has only to read the family history of the Spencers or the Russells to see that their good fortune accelerated after an ancestor found a place at court.

Today there does not seem to be an English court. To speak of the court or court life strikes the ear as arch. To be sure, ambassadors to Great Britain are still described as serving "at the Court of St. James's." But this seems to be just another endearing (and confusing) British anachronism since everybody knows that the Sovereign no longer lives at St. James's but rather at Buckingham Palace. Court life appears to have been done away with.

As recently as the 1930s, George V and Queen Mary enjoyed a court life which centered on the annual gathering of the court. To be presented at court was a great honor, and the *sine qua non* for a debutante making her entry into society. These were highly formal occasions: men wore uniforms or court dress, women tiaras and white ostrich feathers. Courts managed to continue into the reign of Elizabeth II but were abolished in 1958 as being too time-consuming (everybody and his brother were applying to be presented). They were also considered to be "an unfortunate anachronism" (Hibbert 1979:190), a rather curious explanation.

Appearances notwithstanding, there is still an English court. The Queen, like kings of yore, is surrounded by an entourage composed of some of the most socially powerful individuals in the land. One difference is that the court's existence is effectively denied. Another is that it is called "the Household," a designation that implies employment rather than esteem. Members of the Household do perform valued services but to regard them as mere employees would be a mistake.

Buckingham Palace is an immense operation, requiring 337 full-time and 126 part-time workers. These are divided into "three rigidly distinct casts: Household, Officials and Clerks, and Staff" (Packard 1981:85).

This chapter is concerned with the Household in which the court is embedded. (Some members of the Household cannot be considered courtiers.) The court are aristocrats. As we have seen, the criteria for upper-class membership are wealth, landownership (and the pursuit of those country sports associated with land), an Eton (or other public school) education, and that elusive quality, inherited social status. There is, however, another marker of elite status and that is royal service. Not surprisingly there is a great deal of overlap among these. Courtiers own land, have been educated at Eton, and in their later years are made Knights of the Garter or Thistle. Such knighthoods are among the surest confirmations of prestige in Britain.

Royal service, like titles and land, is something of a hereditary privilege. Some families have served the Royal Family for generations. To cite one example, the Queen's second Private Secretary, Sir Michael Adeane, now Lord Adeane, is the grandson of Lord Stamfordham, who had been Private Secretary to three sovereigns—Victoria, Edward VII, and finally George V, who wrote of him, "He taught me to be King." (This was the same Lord Stamfordham who suggested Windsor as the new name for the Royal Family.) Lord Adeane's Eton-educated son, the Honourable Edward Adeane, carried on the family tradition as the Prince of Wales's Private Secretary until 1985, when he left, according to Tina Brown (1985:118) because of Prince Charles's increasingly fey behavior.

The Adeanes are not an isolated case. For instance, the Queen

Mother has one Lady-in-Waiting, a Mrs. Campbell-Preston, whose grandmother, Lady Lyttleton, had been governess to Queen Victoria's children. The more one learns of the aristocratic world, especially where it abuts the royal one, the more one is struck by the smallness of that domain.

## The Royal Household

The senior members of the Household are, in order of precedence, the Lord Chamberlain (Earl of Airlie), the Lord Steward (the Duke of Northumberland), and the Master of the Horse (the Earl of Westmorland). Originally these offices were responsible for above stairs, below stairs, and out-of-doors.

The Lord Chamberlain is the thirteenth Earl of Airlie. The Earl, born in 1926, is the brother-in-law of Princess Alexandra. He went to Eton, served as a lieutenant in the Scots Guards in World War II, and was a member of the Royal Company of Archers, the Queen's personal bodyguard when she is in Scotland. His wife is one of the Queen's Ladies-in-Waiting. The Earl's grandmother was a Lady-in-Waiting to Queen Mary.

The tenth Duke of Northumberland, in his seventies, has been the Lord Steward since 1973. He is also the Lord-Lieutenant of Northumberland, where he owns 80,000 acres. The Lord-Lieutenant is the highest-ranking member in the social life of each county. Northumberland is the Queen's representative in the county (Howe 1981:297–98). He was made a Knight of the Garter in 1959. He was educated at Eton. His Duchess is a daughter of the eighth Duke of Buccleuch.

The fifteenth Earl of Westmorland succeeded the late Duke of Beaufort as Master of the Horse in 1978. Westmorland, a Lord-in-Waiting from 1955 to 1978, is Chairman of Sotheby's. He is a Knight Commander of the Royal Victorian Order.

Officially, the Lord Chamberlain, Lord Steward, and Master of the Horse are the highest-ranking members of the Household. In reality, the most important position at court is the Queen's Private Secretary, the individual who has more contact with her than any other member of her Household. The current Private Secretary is Sir Philip Moore, who once played cricket for Oxfordshire. Moore went to Cheltenham and Braesenose College, Oxford. He joined the RAF in 1940 and was a prisoner of war from 1942 to 1945. He is not as tony as the other members of the Household.

During her reign, the Queen has had four Private Secretaries: Sir Alan Lascelles (1952–53), a cousin of the fifth Earl of Harewood who married Princess Mary, George V's daughter; Sir Michael Adeane (1953–72); the Honourable Sir Martin Charteris (1972–77); and Sir Philip Moore. Adeane and Charteris both went to Eton; Sir Martin, the grandson of the Earl of Wemyss, is now Lord Charteris and the Provost of Eton (Hibbert 1979:156–57).

## The Ladies-in-Waiting

There is a distaff side to the Household as well. The women who serve the Queen come from the same background as do the men, and the Eton connection is again strong.

> The ladies-in-waiting all come from the same type of conservative background. They share the Queen's interests, her hobbies, and to some extent her attitudes. Their husbands, or their fathers, or both, nearly all went to Eton or Harrow and they inhabit a world where gentility is still largely uncorrupted. (Duncan 1970:153)

Duncan also writes that Ladies-in-Waiting

> are a bit more staid—county with a social conscience and a protective sense of history. . . . They are always dressed "sensibly," with clothes and hats less noticeable than the Queen's; and they have "sensible" faces, etched with a responsible prettiness that grows particularly well in the southern counties of England. (1970:151)

The Queen's seven Ladies-in-Waiting are divided into three ranks that reflect the social hierarchy; precedence among the Queen's ladies is obvious. The Mistress of the Robes, almost always a Duchess (currently of Grafton), is the leader. She is the female counterpart of the Lord Chamberlain, beside whom she walks at state functions (Hibbert 1979:177). The present Mistress of the Robes has been that since 1967, when she succeeded the Dowager Duchess of Devonshire. The Duchess of Grafton (her husband became eleventh Duke in 1970) was a Lady of the Bedchamber from 1953 to 1966. She was the daughter of a Captain Eric Smith (LLD), a cousin of Elizabeth Bowes-Lyon's father, the Earl of Strathmore. The Duchess was made Dame Grand Cross, Royal Victorian Order (the highest rank) in 1980. Her husband, who went to Eton, was made a Knight of the Garter in 1976.

The second rank of ladies-in-waiting is Lady of the Bedchamber. There are two. These are usually peeresses who are the wives of Earls or Marquesses. The current Ladies of the Bedchamber are the Marchioness of Abergavenny (whose husband owns a "scant" 1,000 acres in Kent, is a Knight of the Garter, went to Eton, and is Her Majesty's Representative at Ascot; that is, the Marquess is head of the Ascot Office, St. James's Palace, which decides who gets into Ascot and who does not. The other Lady of the Bedchamber is the Countess of Airlie. The Countess is an American. She was born Virginia Fortune Ryan, and comes from Newport, Rhode Island. There are currently four Women-of-the-Bedchamber, although in the past there had been more. Packard describes the Women-of-the-Bedchamber as "untitled but extremely well connected friends of the Queen" (1981:92). They are the Honourable Mary Morrison, Mrs. John Dugdale, Lady Susan Hussey, and Lady Abel Smith.

Lady Abel Smith is a niece of Queen Mary—which explains in part her inclusion in the Household. The Honourable Mary Morrison, born in 1937, is the only unmarried Lady-in-Waiting. She is the daughter of John Granville Morrison, who was made first Baron Margadale in 1960. John Morrison went to Eton and then to Magdalen College, Oxford. He was the grandson of the second Viscount Hambleden, and served in the Royal Company of Archers. Duncan describes the Morrisons as "a powerful Wiltshire political and landowning family" (1970:152).

Kathryn (Mrs. John) Dugdale is married to the son of a first Baronet. He too went to Eton and Christ Church, Oxford, and has been the Lord-Lieutenant of Salop since 1975. John Dugdale seems to have something of a sense of humor. In Who's Who he lists "sleeping" as his recreation instead of the almost predictable shooting, fishing, hunting, cricket, or polo. His wife's recreations are gardening, reading, and pottering.

Lady Susan Hussey is the fifth daughter of the twelfth Earl Waldegrave, a Knight of the Garter. Neither Lady Susan's father nor her husband, Marmaduke, went to Eton; they attended Winchester and Rugby, respectively. Her two brothers, Viscount Chewton and the Honourable William Arthur Waldegrave (MP for Bristol), did go to Eton, however. Marmaduke Hussey's social credentials are affirmed by his stint as an officer in The Grenadiers. He was appointed Chairman of the BBC's Board of Governors in 1986.

Susan Maxwell describes the lot of Anne Beckwith-Smith, the Princess of Wales's primary Lady-in-Waiting:

> Prestige, fun flower shows, fascinating world tours and the possibility of a brilliant marriage are about all Miss Beckwith-Smith gets from the post, nevertheless. Apart from her clothing allowance, she is unsalaried for a job which must at all times place the Princess above her own private life. She must find and pay for her own accommodation in London and risk disgrace and a right royal heave-

ho if an unguarded word about her mistress passes her lips and appears in print. Not that it would, of course. (Maxwell 1982:72)

Maxwell continues with Miss Beckwith-Smith's background—her father is Major Peter Beckwith-Smith, Clerk of Epsom, Sandown, and Lingfield race courses. What is left unsaid, of course, is that the requirements of the job mean that Ladies-in-Waiting must be of independent means.

Surprisingly, the Queen Mother uses more Ladies-in-Waiting than the Queen or the Princess of Wales, having twelve to her daughter's seven. The Mistress of her Robes is the Duchess of Abercorn; the two Ladies of the Bedchamber are the Dowager Viscountess Hambleden and the Dowager Countess of Scarbrough. In addition, there are four Women-of-the-Bedchamber and five Extra Women-of-the-Bedchamber (Packard 1981:78). Unlike the Queen's Ladies-in-Waiting, the Queen Mother's stay with her in Clarence House and share meals with her more frequently than do the Queen's ladies.

The duties of the Ladies-in-Waiting are real. They serve two-week "tours" (without pay) and help the Queen with her correspondence. They accompany her when she visits schools, factories, and other places of interest.

As these brief sketches indicate, the Queen's Household are drawn from the highest ranks of society. Service at court used to be an avenue for advancement. Today the Household is composed largely of individuals for whom it would be impossible to advance any more. They have been dealt some of the very best hands in life. This makes Maxwell's assertion that one perk of royal service is an advantageous marriage seem a bit naive. Women from this stratum do not need royal service to marry well; they have been *born* well.

These sketches also make clear that the court is not isolated from the rest of society. Those in royal circles are part of an elaborate network of personal relationships that extend into all areas of British public life. Lady Susan Hussey, to take one example, has a brother who is a member of Parliament and a husband who heads the British Broadcasting Corporation. Those who serve at court are very much a part of the power structure, which is all the more powerful because it is not accessible to all.

There is indeed an English court but it is not easily seen despite the prominence of those who serve it. This paradox derives from the very nature of any royal court. The word "court" refers both to the retinue with which the sovereign is seen in public and to the building in which the king and his entourage are ensconced. The court then both hides and shows off the king. As Walzer wrote, "In the depths of the royal palace

. . . the King acts out the public life of the realm" (1974:28). The public life of the realm cannot be dissociated from the life of the Queen. Her anniversaries are public events; the births of her children and grandchildren times of national rejoicing; her illnesses and ultimately her death, times of national crisis. Thus the Queen of England cannot have a private life! In this she is not alone, since sovereigns have rarely had private lives as generally understood. "Kings are not born, nor can they die in private; their illnesses are national crises; their celebrations, prayers, meals . . . are public occasions, spectacles in which the State itself is made visible and manifest" (Walzer 1974:28). Indeed, the death of a king is such a portentous event that it cannot be entrusted to the body natural and its own ineluctable rhythms. George V was given a shot of morphine to hasten his demise, ensuring a timely announcement of the King's passing in the London papers.

This is equally true of those close to the Throne. Six hundred million people saw the wedding of the Prince and Princess of Wales; of those, how many did not turn a carnal thought or two to the bedroom at Broadlands, the estate where they spent their wedding night? Similarly, when Diana first thought she was pregnant she left Balmoral for London to see her gynecologist. When the anticipated birthdate was announced and coordinated with the Princess's visit to the doctor, some publications even speculated on the time of Diana's missed period as well as the possible night of conception. When the whole world is made privy to the ebb and flow of one's menses, not to mention one's sex life, then one has very little privacy after all.

Having said that the Queen can have no private life, one is reminded how profoundly private the Queen's life really is. Friends and servants are given the boot for divulging the most innocuous detail. The foremost function of the court is to guard the Queen's privacy. Courtiers do not talk about the Queen.

> [The Queen's] private life is protected, as it should be, by a discretion that shames any other aspect of British public life. It is possible to sit for hours talking to one of her friends who will suddenly lean over conspiratorily as if to divulge the most intimate scandal or, at very least, a soupcon of criticism that will reveal a glimpse of her true character. You wait, giddy with anticipation. "Don't quote me." The suspense is unbearable. No, no, go on. "Please don't quote me. She is"—the words come slowly, pedantically—"an expert horsewoman, you know. And she's very interested in the breeding side. Racing is her only hobby, other than labradors." Surprise. Surprise. (Duncan 1970:100).

Sometimes guarding the Queen's privacy requires more than mere tight lips. The following incident was witnessed by Susan Crosland, who came with the Queen for her Bicentennial visit to the United States.

> The Royal Party was allowed ten minutes to retire and freshen up before the post-banquet reception. I lost two-and-a-half minutes when I stopped to talk with Tony [her husband]. My destination turned out to be a large, discreet, and rather elegant ladies' room, but as I approached it, all I knew was that two women in evening dress were wrestling in front of the outer door. One was the Lady-in-Waiting. The other, unknown to me, was enclosed in an emerald-green satin gown which undulated as they struggled.
> "You won't."
> "I must."
> The woman in emerald satin, it transpired, was an FBI agent assigned never to let the Queen out of her sight. The Lady-in-Waiting, the taller of the two, was strongly built. "You won't," she repeated, correctly.
> The Queen reappeared, serene, fanning her face with her banquet menu. "Frightfully hot in Philadelphia," she said before resuming duty. "Is it always like this in July?" (Crosland 1982:347)

The awesomeness of the Queen's privacy was never more apparent than when it was totally violated in July 1982. At that time, one Michael Fagan, a slightly deranged and unemployed Londoner, scaled the outer walls of Buckingham Palace and entered the building through a window very early in the morning. Incredibly, he had been able to wander about even though he had activated several alarms and a number of people had seen him. Eventually, he found his way to the Queen's bedroom where he had planned to commit suicide. Instead, he merely drew the curtains, awakening the Queen clad only in her nightgown. He sat at the front of her bed and, bleeding from a cut on his hand, told her that he loved her. The Queen tried to summon help several times but to no avail. She was finally rescued when a chambermaid entered and said, "Bloody hell, ma'am, what's he doing there?"

Fagan had been able to get into the Queen's room because the armed policeman who sits outside her door all night had just gone off duty. His replacement, a footman, had come and taken the royal corgis for their morning walk in the palace gardens. Prince Philip did not challenge Fagan's entrance because he does not share the Queen's bedroom but instead has an adjoining suite.

This incident fascinates because the daily routines of royal life, normally hidden in the depths of the Palace, had been exposed to public scrutiny. One hopes that the Queen did not have her hair in curlers. Fagan too seems to have been aware of the enormity of what he had seen. At a court appearance he angrily commanded his lawyer "not to mention anything about the Queen's bedroom." He said, "I don't want her brought into it" (*The New York Times* 7/20/82:1).

The palace intrusion was one instance where neither the Queen's court, nor her security arrangements were able to protect her safety or her privacy.

Generally speaking, Courtiers are the backdrop for the Queen. They are the impedimenta that the Queen brings with her when she visits schools, factories, or foreign countries. Their presence is rarely acknowledged. In 1983 the Queen and Prince Philip visited California. The press coverage of that trip was a prime example of the bizarre status enjoined upon the court. The entourage comprised forty people, yet their identities were not divulged, nor their activities given much notice.

The Queen was entertained at a luncheon given at the estate of Walter Annenberg, ex-Ambassador to the Court of St. James's. The press reported what the Queen ate, what she wore, and whom she sat next to. But of the royal entourage we learned only that they ate at an informal buffet on a sunporch, a separation implying social inferiority.

But this implication was most misleading, once the identities of the entourage became known. It was not so simple to learn them. Even the British Information Service in New York could not identify them. The Protocol Office at the British Embassy in Washington was more knowledgeable, explaining that whenever the Queen travels, she is accompanied by a Minister in Attendance; in this case, Francis Pimm, the Secretary of State. The Duchess of Grafton and Lady Susan Hussey were in waiting along with the Equerry-in-Waiting, the Hon. Adam Wise. Sir Philip Moore, the Private Secretary, came with the Assistant Private Secretary, Robert Fellowes, the Princess of Wales's brother-in-law. Michael Shea, the Queen's Press Secretary, was there, as was the Master of the Household, Sir Peter Ashmore. Rounding out the royal party were the Queen's surgeon and the British Ambassador to the United States, Sir Oliver Wright, and Lady Wright.

In light of the status of the members of the entourage, their anonymity was extraordinary. Perhaps *The New York Times,* among others, thought its readers would not be interested in the Duchess of Grafton or the Princess of Wales's brother-in-law. But this phenomenon is not particular to America. Even in Britain, the Household go unidentified in photos of the Royal Family.

Even though the court is given short shrift in the media, their closeness to the Queen and the Royal Family must not be underestimated. The degree of intimacy enjoyed by Courtiers, even when royals are off duty, was made clear by an unscheduled stop the Queen was forced to make in December 1981. Returning to Windsor after visiting Princess Anne at Gatcombe Park, the Queen was caught in a blizzard that made driving treacherous. Like many others she sought refuge in a nearby inn, the sixteenth-century Cross Hands Hotel, near Chipping Sodbury. But unlike the others, the Queen arrived with a retinue. The hotel was already packed with a hundred or so other motorists similarly stranded by the storm. The inn's owner, Roberto Cadei, later reported that a distinguished looking gentleman took him aside and said, "I wish to inform you that Her Majesty the Queen is outside. Could you accommodate her, too?" (*The New York Times* 10/24/82: Travel Section 35).

Miraculously, one room with a bath was still vacant. The owner shoveled a path to a back stairway so that the Queen could enter the hotel unobserved. Her entourage consisted of two chauffeurs, two detectives, a Lady-in-Waiting, and a "staff aide," no doubt the distinguished looking gentleman. The Queen stayed in the double room for some seven hours, unable to leave until almost midnight.

The Queen ate dinner in the Cadeis' private apartment, where she also made a number of phone calls. Mrs. Cadei said, "I must have been the only woman who ever received the Queen in her old blue jeans and a sweatshirt. We didn't have time to be nervous or fuss. I just made her a cup of tea and prepared the table for her to eat." The crockery and cutlery used by the Queen have been stowed away as souvenirs. The Queen's stopover has been good for business. The restaurant business at the hotel is up twenty-five percent; the rooms are always booked, "with particular demand for the 'Queen's room'" (*The New York Times* 10/24/82:35). Buckingham Palace announced that this was the only time that the Queen ever arrived unscheduled at a hotel.

This incident reminds us that time and tide, not to mention blizzards, wait for no one. It also shows us the degree of state in which the Queen moves even on occasions as prosaic as a Sunday afternoon visit to her daughter living nearby. Courtiers are very much a part of the private life of the Queen.

The British aristocracy is a group much obsessed with secrecy as are all elites. Like Freemasons, aristocrats have developed elaborate systems of signs—dress, speech, bodily postures—by which they recognize one another. "They might carry on in rags; still there would exist always a group affecting elegance and superiority, preserving their jargon, establishing their internal freemasonry, excluding the unwanted aspirant" (Sackville-West 1975:39).

The upper class still excludes unwanted aspirants. The alleged fluidity of English society is given the lie by the secret system that "evolved which separated those who were initiated from those who were not, i.e., the masses. . . . The inadvertent use of one incorrect word can reveal an intruder into society" (Brooks–Baker 1978:xv). Such secrecy enhances the consciousness, the moral solidarity, of the group: "For this reason, secret societies offer a very impressive schooling in the moral solidarity among men" (Simmel 1950:348).

Diana Spencer's discretion in handling the press was impressive. To reporters' incessant questions, she once answered: "You know I can't talk about the Prince. Not because anybody told me not to, but because I can't."

It is not surprising that the court is composed of aristocrats. They are individuals whose material circumstances enable them to lead lives similar to those of royals. But there is another characteristic that makes aristocrats perfect Courtiers and that is their habit of secrecy. Attendance at court places those who serve there in a most anomalous position. Normally exalted people are transformed into virtual nonentities while in the service of royalty. Court life demands the recruitment of socially prominent individuals even while it requires that they shed their prominence and recede from view. This paradox parallels those inherent in the very notion of a court that both displays and encloses the King. Their habit of secrecy insures that they will protect the Queen's privacy. Thus, there is an English court but we cannot always see it clearly. Its members do not wish to share their insights with others.

# X

## Royal Exchanges

We cannot always see the court because courtiers are disguised, they blend into the background. They are part of the baggage the Queen carries with her wherever she goes, whether that be to a factory, the Opening of Parliament or even visiting her daughter. Because courtiers blend with the scenery, "they are present during the interaction but in some respects do not take the role either of performer or audience" (Goffman 1959:151–52). This makes them non-persons. The presentation of normally exalted persons as virtual nonentities insinuates the greater glory of royalty. The Queen's magnification and elevation above the common herd are achieved, in part, by the transformation of normally powerful aristocrats into faceless nobodies. Their lowering raises royalty even higher.

Courtiers are often presented in the guise of servant, a convention that camouflages further their real role. The Queen's most intimate acquaintances are called "Ladies-in-Waiting," a sobriquet emphasizing the notion of attending as servant (as in "waiting on bended knee"). The master-servant relationship is the prototype of superior and inferior (Coser 1974:68). When she is "in waiting," the Duchess of Grafton is an inferior. This dissimulation helps detract from the unpleasant truth that some people have been born luckier than others.

To be sure, members of the Royal Household do provide services to their royal masters. But they must not be confused with the real servants who change sheets and take out the garbage. The foremost services provided by the Household are companionship and discretion, making this class of royal servant one of royal companion. To put it yet another way, the line between servant and companion is extremely thin when it comes to royalty. This is not to say that the relationship is devoid of all evidence of rank. The inferiority of the Household vis-à-vis royalty is apparent in the anonymity and social invisibility enjoined upon them.

Coser also observed that a characteristic of the servant role is that it is patterned, not after an occupational model, but rather after that of a family (1974:72). This too is evident in the connection of courtier and royalty. Servants have traditionally lived in the houses of their masters, making them *ipso facto* members of the household. Enforced intimacy blurs the line between superior and inferior. Neither can enjoy absolute privacy since all actions are open to scrutiny by the other. "In the traditional master-servant relationship, the master and his family always attempt—though they do not always succeed—to greedily absorb the personality of the servant" (Coser 1974:70).

Royalty are perhaps more successful than other masters in co-opting, if not absorbing, the personalities of their servants. The relationship of royal master and servant is, after all, more ambiguous than most. Courtiers must be most adroit in balancing deference and familiarity. As one of Prince Charles's polo-playing companions put it:

> "When he's out there he's out as a player. If he does anything wrong, he'll get a ballocking same as anybody else," says one fellow player. "All we do is put the word 'Sir' on the end. Get out of my f—king way, you imbecile . . . Sir." (Heald & Mohs 1979:205)

In contrast, deference clearly outweighed familiarity at the Spanish court of the 1920s. The Duchess of Westminster describes a polo match she attended in 1928: "It was a very select affair. The Queen and the Infantas and the cream of Spanish Society were watching, and King Alfonso was captaining one of the teams. I had always heard that the etiquette at the Spanish Court was very stiff and uncomfortable, and sure enough, we had not a moment's peace, for every time the King galloped past (and in polo the riders never stop thundering up and down the field) we all had to rise and make a deep curtsey. Hardly had we sat down than we had to spring up again, and really, by the time the game was over, we were almost as exhausted as the players. To me it seemed an utterly ridiculous scene, but the Spaniards accepted it as being absolutely right and natural" (1961:133).

Since royalty are quite adept at concealing their feelings, we do not know how they feel about the fact that their companions have "occasion to observe the behavior of their masters being privy to many of their secrets" (Coser 1974:76). We do know, however, that Queen Victoria was acutely aware of such opportunities. Thus, she tried to prevent her Private Secretary, Sir Frederick Ponsonby, from marrying. Ponsonby's daughter provides the following description of what royal service entailed:

> Far from being grateful for all the trouble he took the Queen accepted it as a matter of course. She had been a domestic autocrat for so long that she had become very selfish indeed and when my father wanted to get married she forbade it on the grounds that men always tell their wives everything and she did not choose that her affairs should be talked about all over London. (Westminster 1961:27)

Eventually, Victoria relented and allowed Ponsonby to marry. That did not end her interference in his private life, though. Even though the Ponsonbys had a house near Windsor, Victoria insisted that Sir Frederick abandon his family and stay with her in the Castle when he was "in waiting." Living with Queen Victoria does not seem to have been fun. As Ponsonby himself wrote: "We subdue our voices considerably while eating the royal beef" (St. Aubyn 1979:126).

Although royal service can have its drawbacks, as the Ponsonby anecdote indicates, it also has its advantages. These advantages are both objective and subjective. Just as kings of yore tied their courts to them with gifts and favors, so does the modern Royal Family. If ordinary servants are incorporated into the households of their masters, royal ones are incorporated into the very family making them quasimembers of the Royal Family. This incorporation is effected through a series of exchanges. Anthropologists have long recognized that exchange (as described earlier in the discussion of gifts) is a kind of social glue, holding social relationships together. This is no less true of royal relationships.

Coser also noted that greedy institutions were those which sought "exclusive and undivided loyalty" from their personnel (1974:4). Royalty is a greedy institution. Most individuals have a number of separate social identities that can be assumed or divested as circumstances dictate. On the job they are one kind of person; they change when they go home. Royalty and courtiers cannot do this so easily: they are always royalty and courtiers. Even in the rough and tumble of the polo field, Charles is ever the Prince of Wales. To compensate for the insatiable demands that royalty as an institution places upon its personnel, there are substantial compensations. These compensations involve exchanges that take place between royal masters and their noble companions, cementing their relationship. Although some exchanges are symmetrical, the overriding one is the asymmetrical one of loyalty for social honor. Let us look, then, at some of these.

## Grace and Favour Houses

One material advantage that makes royal service highly desirable is the granting of grace and favour houses. Servants live in the houses of their masters. So do many of the Household. But, unlike the servants, say, in "Upstairs-Downstairs," the Household are not relegated to the drafty cramped spaces under the eaves of Buckingham Palace or Balmoral Castle. Instead, they are often given what are called "grace and favour" houses.

These are rent-free premises that are made available at the discretion of the Queen to members of her family, Household, and other retainers (e.g., Edward VIII's butler, Amos, was given one after the Abdication). Packard tells us that there are 121 such houses. Hampton Court Palace has 27, Kensington Palace 13, and St. James's Palace 20 (1981:83). This tally leaves just over half unaccounted for. Hibbert noted that there used to be about 140 grace and favour residences, but managed to denigrate the advantage by observing that since most are so uncomfortable and expensive to modernize "they are not being reallocated when the occupants die" (1979:209). Grace and favour residences are a prime example of a coveted British honor about which everyone knows, but about which it is especially difficult to learn anything of substance.

The Ponsonbys enjoyed the use of two grace and favour houses: one at Windsor, called The Saxon Tower, and one in St. James's Palace. St. James's is not, "as its name might suggest, one big solid mansion. It is more like an assortment of college buildings clustered around a group of small courtyards" (Westminster 1961:49). Even though having one's servants live under the same roof has been a way of dominating them, the possession of a grace and favour house is not so much a sign of domination as it is a mark of distinction. So potent is this honor that it impressed even the fabulously wealthy Duke of Westminster when he was courting Loelia Ponsonby: "With a wave of his hand he summoned the Rolls-Royce which was waiting by the door and when I said I lived in St. James's Palace he thought it was a joke" (1961:146).

Courtiers are of course still billeted in St. James's Palace, as they were in Sir Frederick Ponsonby's day. The following anecdote was provided by a biographer of Prince Philip: "One morning I accosted the Queen's

[then] private secretary, Sir Michael Adeane, walking toward the front of the building. While he sympathetically heard out some problem that was teasing me, I got the impression, faint as an echo, that he would like to be moving on. It was another minute or two before he said, 'I do hope you'll forgive me, but I've just heard that my house is on fire. I wouldn't mind, but as it's a part of St. James's Palace'" (Boothroyd 1970:xi).

Not all courtiers have a grace and favour house. Others are merely allowed to lease (naturally for undisclosed amounts) houses on one or another royal estate. "Scattered near Sandringham are a number of ordinary looking houses. There is nothing on the outside to suggest that their occupants are special in any way, but in fact they are courtiers of varying degrees" (Lacey 1982:10).

One such house is Park House, on the Sandringham estate, a few hundred yards from the main house with its 365 rooms. It was leased by the then Viscount Althorp when he was a royal Equerry. It was there that his daughter, Diana Spencer, was born. Not only is royal service hereditary but so is the tenancy of houses on royal estates. Diana's mother was born in the same room as she was. Diana's grandfather, the fourth Baron Fermoy, had leased the house from George V.

Diana's father and maternal grandfather were royal tenants, as is her brother-in-law.

> Her middle sister Jane married Robert Fellowes, assistant private secretary to the Queen, and this intensified her contact with the royal family. She quite frequently drove up from Coleherne Court (where she shared a flat with three roommates) to see her sister in Kensington Palace, where the Fellowes had a home, and when she was spotted with Prince Charles on the banks of the Dee in September 1980, one reason for her being there was to help her sister look after her new born baby girl. (Lacey 1982:15)

The title "assistant private secretary" may sound inconsequential to Americans, but this passage is revealing. Not just anybody has a flat at Kensington Palace. It is one of the world's most exclusive addresses. Kensington, like St. James's, is also a collection of buildings, mostly Georgian in style. It has aptly been called a "royal village." To wit, the *pied à terre* of the Prince and Princess of Wales is in Kensington Palace, as are those of the Duke and Duchess of Gloucester, the Dowager Duchess of Gloucester, Princess Margaret, Prince and Princess Michael of Kent, the Ogilvys (Princess Alexandra), and the late Duke of Beaufort, to name a few. Robert and Lady Jane Fellowes keep very good company.

It may be arguable that tenancy of Kensington Palace does not make one a quasi-member of the Royal Family. It does, however, make one a royal neighbor. If royal neighbors do not exactly exchange cups of sugar across the back fence, they certainly are in a position to trade other, more impressive commodities. These exchanges are social in nature and bind royalty and nobility to one another. They are hospitality, marriage partners, and godparentage.

These interactions obliquely affirm the superior social status of those who participate in them. Unlike those of royalty and ordinary people, say, on the occasion of a factory visit, these transactions do not seem to be characterized by graciousness on the part of the donor and gratitude (often abject) on the part of the donee. Was Lord Spencer "grateful" when Prince Charles spent a shooting weekend at Althorp? Probably not, though he no doubt enjoyed the honor of having a member of the Royal Family under his roof. This sense of honor was also evident in the comment made by Mark Phillips's grandmother at the time of his engagement to Princess Anne: "It's quite a feather in the family's cap to have a member become engaged to a Royal."

## Royal Marriages: The Aristocratic Connection

Royal marriages are publicly celebrated yet remain private transactions that forge alliances between families. The families who are able to form such alliances with the Royal Family are those of consequence. Royal marriages have not united the Royal Family with a wide cross-section of society. To date, royal in-laws have been aristocratic. When Prince Charles was looking for a wife, he did not date secretaries, nurses, or shopgirls. They were not part of his world of country weekends. Any courtship by Prince Charles was mostly conducted at friends' homes. "When he was invited away for a shooting or fishing weekend, the current girlfriend was generally invited too. They were then in the company of a great many other people. The Prince's love life was fraught with difficulty" (Barry 1983:178).

Prince Charles has said that he chooses his friends from among those who share his interests, such as shooting. Other royals also find their marriage partners among those who share their interests. The romance of Prince Andrew and Sarah Ferguson seems to have begun with a food fight during the Ascot Races. "There are always humble beginnings. It's got to start somewhere," Prince Andrew said at a news conference after his engagement was made public.

Lady Elizabeth Bowes-Lyon also met her husband through her social contacts with George VI's sister, Princess Mary. The two women had become friends through their work with Girl Guides. Princess Anne met Mark Phillips through their involvement with horses and competitive riding. Lady Diana caught the Prince of Wales's eye while he was her father's house guest. The Duke of Kent met his wife, Katharine Worsley, when her father, the Lord Lieutenant of the North Riding of Yorkshire, brought him home for a visit.

Let us examine this last example. Probably there were many fathers in England, let alone Yorkshire, who would have liked to have been able to have introduced their daughters to a Royal Duke. Warwick describes Katharine Worsley as "an ordinary girl brought up against a typically English background of windswept Yorkshire moors" (1980:91). Although he neglects to mention that her father was Lord Lieutenant, Warwick goes on to say that her father had his own cricket team, and that one of her brothers was an MP. Warwick's disingenuous description of Katharine Worsley as "ordinary" can be seen as either the denial of the existence of the aristocracy, or as the identification of all that is quintessentially English with the aristocracy.

Marriage is inextricably linked with country socializing. This has been so since Edwardian times, when Edward VII, occasionally accompanied by Alexandra, visited one or another of the great country houses (actually palaces in their own right). Until comparatively recently, the Court Circular would publish the names of those who entertained members of the Royal Family, either singularly or en masse. Indeed, the practice persisted well into the reign of Elizabeth II. In the 1950s it was routinely published that on such and such a weekend the Princess Margaret had been a house guest of, say, the Duke and Duchess of Buccleuch (gossip had it that she was linked romantically with the Duke's heir, the Earl of Dalkeith). That practice has now fallen into abeyance, perhaps for considerations of security.

House parties are still an important fixture of royal and aristocratic socializing. Since the practice of chronicling that social life in the Court Circular has lapsed, it is easy to assume that the Royal Family have no private life apart from one another. This is not true, although a great deal of their socializing does take place with members of the family. Lacey does identify a few of the friends at whose homes the Queen and Prince Philip often stay for weekends. For example, they often visited the late Lord Rupert Nevill, brother of the Marquess of Abergavenny, at his home near Uckfield. There they went to the theatre in nearby Brighton.

> Visiting their country houses for weekends, she would normally attend the parish church on Sunday mornings, but her fellow worshippers saw her presence as a secret to be kept. They did not tip off the local press. (Lacey 1977:235)

In addition to the estates of her extensive and "invisible" family, the Queen visits those of nonrelatives. For instance, in 1956, the Suez Crisis caught the Queen at Arundel Castle, the home of the Duke of Norfolk. She was his guest for the Goodwood races. She watched the races from a private room in the Duke of Richmond's box (Lacey 1977:210–11). Presumably, both Dukes have enjoyed the Queen's hospitality at Royal Ascot, which is down the road from Windsor Castle.

## Godparentage

Royals and aristocrats are also godparents to one another's children. Royal godchildren and godparents are fascinating topics, but difficult to research. Again, one has to depend upon serendipity to learn of these particular bonds that tie royal and aristocratic families. One instance of such serendipity was the marriage of the Prince of Wales and Diana Spencer. The attendant publicity revealed, among other things, another connection between the Windsors and the Spencers. The Queen is Diana's brother's godmother; Queen Mary and the Prince of Wales (later the Duke of Windsor) were godparents to Diana's father. Edward VII was the godfather of her grandfather, the seventh Earl Spencer. (Diana is the only member of her family without a royal godparent.) True to form the Fergusons have been tied to the Royal Family this way. Major Ferguson's son, Andrew, by his second wife is a godson of Prince Charles.

Godparentage is the modern derivative of the medieval institution of wardship, in which the children of upper-class families were sent away to the homes of prominent individuals to learn social graces, often by serving at table. Wardship was a form of clientship in which children were the nexus between families. Nonetheless, many contemporary writers were troubled by this peculiar desire of the English to banish their own children from their homes. This British antipathy to the young does not seem to have passed with the transition to modern times despite what Ariès felt is the age's characteristic concern for the integrity of the family. In the nineteenth century upper-class children were segregated in the nursery, replete with nanny and separate nursing staff. The "green baize door" relegated the children of the household to the same drafty and creepy outer reaches of the house that were occupied by the servants. Today fewer households can afford to maintain such an elaborate and separate nursery world. Nonetheless, upper-class children are still sent away rather heartlessly, it would seem, to prep schools when they are but eight years old. Writing in *Tatler,* one Hugo Williams recalls the experience: "Our mothers were only 28 or 29 but they put on serious clothes and took us to Daniel Neal's, the ante-room to prepdom. We held their hands and got our first whiff of homesickness and the world" (10/ 85:146).

This photograph of Prince William's christening is a tantalizing glimpse of court life. Standing, left to right, are Prince Philip, Princess Alexandra, King Constantine, Lady Susan Hussey, Prince Charles, Lord Romsey, the Duchess of Westminster, Lord Spencer, Lady Fermoy, Sir Laurens van der Post, and Prince Edward. Seated, left to right, are Princess Anne, the Queen, the Princess of Wales holding Prince William, the Queen Mother, and Mrs. Shand Kidd. *Fox Photos Ltd.*

There was, of course, a positive side to wardship. It was a way of securing powerful mentors who could promote the interests of the children. Furthermore, wardship insured that children had guardians should their own parents die. The Earl of Essex had been made a ward of Elizabeth I by his father, who feared (and rightly so) that he would not live to see his own son grown (Pearson 1957:75). (Elizabeth eventually had this particular ward beheaded.) Assuming the wardship of a child, however, was not an entirely altruistic proposition. Guardians could avail themselves of the substantial sums that were provided wards as their living expenses.

Although modern christenings have assumed a religious dimension, elements of wardship are not entirely absent. The hope of securing a powerful patron for one's children still seems to be a motivating force in the modern practice of British godparentage. And ordinary—though well-connected—individuals have no illusions about the "kind invitation"; they accordingly limit the number of children they sponsor (Barr and York 1982:57). Of course, there could be no more powerful patron for a child than a member of the Royal Family. One wonders what limits royals place on the number of godchildren they will accept.

Although Prince Charles's valet never commented on Prince Charles as godfather, he made an interesting observation that may also apply to royal godparentage: "Most of his ex-girlfriends have married and he usually gets invited to the wedding. He rarely goes. As he says, 'If I accepted every wedding invitation I'd be buying presents morning, noon, and night and never be out of a morning coat'" (1983:171). And if he accepted every invitation to sponsor a child that no doubt comes his way, he would never be out of a baptistry.

Christenings do more than incorporate the child into the fold of the Church, a preliminary step in the long process of taming that presumably ends in adulthood. The selection of godparents also incorporates the child into a wider social network extending beyond the family. Godparents contribute to the godchild's portion in life. Expensive gifts are *de riguer;* and if parents are able to enlist a socially powerful patron for their child, so much the better. For example, Debrett's writes:

> It is a great compliment to be invited to stand as a godparent to a child, and a thoughtful godparent is a precious gift for a child to acquire at birth. . . .
>
> The duties of a godparent do not end with the ceremony and traditional christening gift. As the child grows, the link forged at baptism should become a bond; only the godparent can ensure that this occurs. . . .
>
> [And, most significantly,] the golden rule of choosing presents is probably to think in terms of the future and not the present. A gift of money is appropriate and antiques of all kinds, including silver, porcelain and glass, maps, prints and books are suitable. Wine is a traditional gift and port, claret and burgundy can be purchased for laying down for the future. (1981:17–20)

Royal wedding gifts are put on display; unfortunately, royal christening presents are not. So much the pity, because it would be wonderful to know what royal children receive from their godparents, or, for that matter, what the Queen gives her godchildren.

One can learn a little about godparentage in royal circles from the christenings of royal children, though. Christenings remain the one royal rite of passage that has not been added to the roster of royal public events. In the nineteenth century, as we have seen, royal weddings and funerals were private. Royal births, in contrast, were comparatively public occasions with the birthing chamber crammed with all manner of folk. For example, when Queen Victoria was born the process was watched by the Duke of Wellington, the Archbishop of Canterbury, the Bishop of London, the Marquess of Landsdowne, the Rt. Hon. George Canning, the Rt. Hon. Nicholas Vansittart, the Chancellor of the Exchequer, Earl Bathurst, the Duke of Sussex (Victoria's father's brother), the Duke of Kent (Victoria's father), and Lt. Gen. Wetherall (Dewhurst 1980:145). Today marriages and funerals are public, while royal births are private. Christenings have also remained out of the public eye. This is puzzling. Certainly the baptism of a royal child—the little child lost in the immense Honiton lace dress first used for the christenings of Victoria's children and doused by the Archbishop with water from the River Jordan—would be as edifying and ceremonial a spectacle as a royal wedding or investiture. Royal christenings have probably remained private because of the importance of godparents on these occasions. They are either close personal friends (often courtiers) or relatives, both close and distant. To broadcast a royal christening might penetrate too far into the private sphere of royal life. A royal wedding can be broadcast because the principal players, the bride and groom, are familiar to all. A christening, however, might give too much away.

Royal christenings may not be public, but they are not entirely hidden. Both Prince William's and Prince Harry's christenings received a great deal of press attention, the latter's no less because of the reputed rift between his parents and his aunt, Princess Anne, who spent the day killing rabbits.

Debrett's says that under Church of England canon law a boy has two godfathers and one godmother, and girls vice versa. Royal children always have more than this. Prince William had six godparents. They were King Constantine (late of Greece), Lord Romsey, Sir Laurens van der Post, Princess Alexandra, the Duchess of Westminster, and Lady Susan Hussey. Let us look briefly at these individuals. Constantine is a cousin of both the Queen and Prince Philip. His mother, Queen Frederika, was a great-granddaughter of Victoria, and the granddaughter of Kaiser Wilhelm II. Constantine's mother's brother, Prince George of Hanover, is married to Prince Philip's sister Sophie. The ex-King is one of two royal godparents of William. Princess Alexandra is the other. Besides being the granddaughter of George V, Alexandra's maternal grandmother was the Grand Duchess Helen of Russia, who married Prince Nicholas of Greece, Philip's father's brother. (The Grand Duchess Helen was a sister of Czar Nicholas II. Her mother, the Czarina Marie Feodorovna, was the sister of Queen Alexandra. This genealogical snippet shows not only that Princess Alexandra is variously related to the Queen, but also the generally convoluted relationships of the Royal Family.)

Lord Romsey, grandson of Earl Mountbatten, will someday be the third Earl Mountbatten of Burma, succeeding his mother, Countess Mountbatten (one of Charles's godmothers). Lord Romsey, Norton Knatchball, is a relative who has also been a close friend of Prince Charles since their Gordonstoun schooldays. Charles was best man at his wedding and is godfather to the Romseys' son.

Sir Laurens van der Post was a rather surprising choice of godfather. *People* magazine described him as being a friend of the Queen Mother's family, an assertion difficult to ascertain. Looking him up in *Who's Who*, however, revealed that not only is he a most prolific writer, he had also once been a member of Lord Mountbatten's staff. Given the affection and respect for Lord Mountbatten reportedly felt by Prince Charles, Sir Laurens may not have been such an odd choice after all.

As for the godmothers, the Duchess of Westminster, like Lord Romsey, seems to have been chosen on the basis of personal friendship. The Princess of Wales is godmother to the Duchess's second daughter, Lady Edwina Louise Grosvenor. But with the then twenty-one-year-old Duchess, we once again find a strong Mountbatten connection. She is the granddaughter of the late Lady Zia Wernher, a friend of the Queen. Lady Zia was a daughter of the Grand Duke Michael of Russia, brother of the Czar. Her sister, Nada, married Lord Mountbatten's brother, the second Marquess of Milford Haven. (After his marriage, the Marquess was "no longer short of money" [Hough 1981:55].)

The inclusion of Lady Susan, was also something of a surprise choice. Lady Susan, daughter of the Earl Waldegrave, is the Queen's youngest Lady-in-Waiting. *People* wrote that she was chosen because she had helped Lady Diana learn royal etiquette during her engagement. Barry writes that prior to his marriage Lady Susan was one of the most influential women in Prince Charles's life (1983:183).

The godparents of Prince William are very different from those who sponsored Prince Charles, Princess Anne, and Prince Edward. Previously, royal godparents were just that—royal—and rather closely related to the child (which seems to waste a relative). The shift to noble godparents parallels the one from royal to aristocratic spouses.

Oddly enough, Prince Andrew's christening does not seem to have been in *The Times* (London). He was born February 19, 1960; royal christenings normally take place six weeks to two months after the birth. On March 23, *The Times* reported that Andrew's birth had been formally registered. The announcement was accompanied by a picture of the

Royal Family with the baby in the Honiton lace christening robe. The caption read: "This picture was recently taken in the Music Room at Buckingham Palace [the site of royal christenings]." From this I deduce that Andrew's christening took place but was not publicized.

Prince Charles's godparents were Princess Margaret; the Queen Mother (who at the time was Queen); the Queen Mother's brother, David Bowes-Lyon; the King of Norway (a grandson of Edward VII); the Dowager Marchioness of Milford Haven (the maternal grandmother of Prince Philip and Lord Mountbatten's mother); Prince George of Greece (Philip's uncle); and Lady Brabourne, now Countess Mountbatten (Philip's matrilateral cross-cousin). The strategy seems to have been one of aligning further the two families of the baby's parents. The seven godparents were drawn evenly from the mother's and father's sides, with the King of Norway straddling the two. What immediately strikes one, however, is that the sponsors from the mother's side, her mother and sister, were close relations, while the patrilateral relations were more distantly related. Why, for example, were not Prince Philip's sisters chosen? Perhaps because Prince Charles was baptized December 15, 1948, not long after the war with Germany. It would not have been very politic to have Philip's sisters as godmothers since they were married to German princes who had been officers in Hitler's army.

The situation seems to have changed somewhat when Princess Anne was baptized October 21, 1950, by the Archbishop of York in the Music Room of Buckingham Palace. Her five sponsors were her maternal grandmother the Queen (now the Queen Mother); Princess Andrew (Philip's mother, for whom Princess Alice, Countess of Athlone, stood proxy); Princess Gottfried of Hohenlohe-Langenburg (Philip's sister Margarita); Lord Mountbatten; and the Hon. Andrew Elphinstone (the Queen Mother's nephew).

The sponsors of Charles and Anne had been predominantly royal. It was with the christening of Prince Edward on May 2, 1964, at Windsor Castle, with the Dean of Windsor officiating, that we begin to see a preference for indigenous aristocrats over foreign royals emerge. Prince Edward's five sponsors were the Duchess of Kent (née Katharine Worsley, for whom her mother-in-law, Princess Marina, stood proxy); Princess George of Hanover (Philip's father's sister); Prince Richard of Gloucester (now the Duke of Gloucester); the Earl of Snowdon; and Prince Louis of Hesse (the brother-in-law of Philip's dead sister, Cecile).

Aside from the enormous cachet that accrues to an individual able to say, "I was visiting my godmother, the Queen," it is difficult to learn what exactly royal godparentage involves. One hint lies with the choice of bridesmaids for Princess Margaret's wedding in May 1960. There were eight, including the chief bridesmaid, Princess Anne. Their names and the briefest of biographical sketches were published in *The Times* (3/25/60). The bridesmaids were Catherine Vesey, daughter of Viscountess de Vesci (the groom's sister); Lady Rose Nevill, daughter of the Marquess of Abergavenny, who was described as "a cousin of the bride"; Miss Angela Nevill, daughter of Lord Rupert Nevill, the Marquess's brother, and thus also a cousin; Marilyn Wills, both a goddaughter of the bride and a cousin through her mother; Annabel Rhodes, a goddaughter of the Duke of Edinburgh, and the daughter of a niece of the Queen Mother; Lady Virginia Fitz Roy, a daughter of Lord and Lady Euston before they succeeded to the Dukedom of Grafton; and Miss Sarah Lowther, a goddaughter of Princess Margaret, and, probably not uncoincidentally, the daughter of one of Margaret's Ladies-in-Waiting.

What is interesting about Margaret's bridesmaids is that all were connected to families of the bride or groom, except perhaps Sarah Lowther, who was a fictive or quasirelative by virtue of being the godchild of the Princess. Three royal goddaughters served as bridesmaids; two, Annabel Rhodes and Marilyn Wills, were also blood relatives. Moreover, four—the two cousins Nevill, Virginia FitzRoy, and Sarah Lowther—were children of courtiers. There is a certain confluence among the categories of courtier, blood relative, and fictive relative. Obviously, relatives and courtiers have a very good chance of having their children accepted as godchildren by members of the Royal Family. Moreover, the choice of bridesmaids at Margaret's wedding reveals to some extent the ways that royal godparents strengthen the bonds between themselves and their godchildren, the latter getting to go to some pretty snazzy parties.

Social visits, courtship, and gifts to godchildren are examples of exchanges that bind royalty and courtiers. These are, for the most part, hidden transactions. There is, however, one that publicly affirms the bonds of loyalty and companionship that bind royal and aristocrat. That is the Order of the Garter.

Today there are six orders of knighthood: The Garter, The Thistle, The Bath, St. Michael and St. George, The Royal Victorian Order, and The British Empire. Although most knighthoods, like other honors, are politically distributed, three orders have remained the personal gift of the Sovereign: The Garter, The Thistle, and The Royal Victorian Order.

The premier order is that of the Garter, founded in 1348 "as a Noble Fraternity by King Edward III consisting of himself and twenty-five knights, to be designated the 'Knights of Saint George' or the 'Knights of the Blue Garter' who were to consist of his children and the bravest in the land" (De la Bere 1964:55).

The Thistle is the Scottish equivalent of the Garter in terms of prestige. It supposedly antedates the Garter; legend has it that it originated in the eighth century. (Thus, Knights of the Thistle think their own order outranks the Garter.) The Thistle Knights are predominantly Scottish noblemen, such as the erstwhile fourteenth Earl of Home, now Lord Home of the Hirsel; the Duke of Buccleuch and Queensberry; and Lord Maclean, the ex-Lord Chamberlain.

The Royal Victorian Order was founded by Queen Victoria and thus is far more recent than either The Garter or The Thistle. Nonetheless, it is a highly coveted honor, being awarded to those in the Sovereign's personal service such as all her Ladies-in-Waiting and other high ranking courtiers like the Lord Chamberlain, and the Master of the Horse. It can also include lower-ranking individuals such as palace gardeners. The Garter and Thistle have no internal rankings. The Royal Victorian, however, has five: "Knights or Dames Grand Cross (GCVO); Knights or Dames Commander (KCVO/DCVO); Commanders (CVO); Members, Fourth/Fifth Class (MVO)" (Paget 1979:95).

The Garter is still a male preserve, even though the Sovereign of the Order is technically female. Occasionally, women are admitted, as were Queen Elizabeth (the Queen Mother) in 1936, and Princess Elizabeth in 1948. Foreign royal ladies are also incorporated as Extra Ladies of The Garter, as was Queen Juliana of The Netherlands in 1958. These "Ladies of the Garter" do not place the letters of signification (KG) after their names, but are described as such in formal documents (De la Bere 1964: 83).

The Garter is about the greatest honor a man can receive (though Knights of the Thistle may dispute this). So potent is the honor that *Who's Who*, for example, notes not only whether a man is a Garter Knight but also if his father, father-in-law, brother, or uncle is. A KG after one's name is a primary form of adornment that distinguishes one above most others. The Garter is such a great distinction because it is the Sovereign's personal gift. But it is not given freehold. It literally comes from the Sovereign's hands and into those hands it must return. Ironically, that is a source of the Garter's great distinction.

The Cenotaph wreath and the Maundy coins are given for keeps; the Garter insignia are not. They cannot be hoarded and made into family heirlooms. They must be kept in circulation. De la Bere ruefully noted that it was only in 1948 "that any accurate record was kept to show by whom particular collars had been worn in the past, but now collars of all British Orders are marked by the Central Chancery in such a way that in the future the names of former holders will be known. The object of this is to endeavor, if such an occasion should arise, to make it possible, when a new knight is appointed, for him to be invested with the collar which was worn by one or more of his ancestors" (1964:76), making it a *de facto* heirloom.

When a Knight dies, his son, grandson, or nearest male relative personally returns the Lesser George and the Star to the Sovereign. (The other pieces of Garter insignia are returned more informally to the Central Chancery of Knighthoods.) The Sovereign, then, has very personal contact with both the Knight and his family. The significance of the Queen's expressing her condolences can be grasped when one considers that the Sovereign is normally isolated from the death of those outside her own family. The grief of Garter Knights and their families is the Queen's grief.

The Order of the Garter is one of the most public acknowledgments of the exchange of honor and trust between the Queen and those of her ilk. The intimacy of the Queen and her companions is symbolized by the actual investment of the Knight-elect. This the Sovereign does herself. She buckles the Garter about his leg, places the Riband with the Lesser George (the badge with St. George Stabbing the Dragon) over his left shoulder (other orders wear the riband over the right), pins the Star under his left breast, drapes the Mantle over his shoulders, and finally puts on the ornate gold chain called the Collar.

To put a garter around a man's knee means that the Queen must come into close body contact with him. Bodies in general are symbolically dangerous because they are messy. There is no messier region than that of the groin near which the Queen must bring her head in order to strap the garter around the man's leg. But the very danger of the act signals the Queen's trust in her companion. Previously, much has been made of how royal companions are converted into servants. Here we have a certain role reversal. The physical intimacy required to invest the Knight transforms the Queen into the Knight's valet, his body servant. There is no greater honor than that.

The Garter, then, is a form of aristocratic exchange whose purpose is prestige rather than economic gain. The ceremonial objects (i.e., the insignia) move among representatives of the uppermost echelons of British society (at last count there were three Dukes, one Marquess, and four Earls). This movement is accompanied by feasts and social displays—the luncheon hosted by the Queen in the Waterloo Chamber of Windsor Castle before the service, the tea served there afterwards, and the colorful procession from the Castle of St. George's Chapel. Even the lugubrious return of the insignia to the Sovereign is marked by a private, though nonetheless ceremonial, audience with the Queen.

Circulation of the insignia is accelerated by the practice of generally appointing older men to the Order. This can be seen in the following list of Knights of the Garter. The numbers in parentheses are the Knights' ages when admitted to the Order. The asterisk denotes royal service, including Lord Lieutenancies and Her Majesty's Representatives in the Boroughs of London. The Garter is most prestigious; one clearly has a far greater chance of attaining it if one is in royal service.

The Duke of Northumberland,* 1959 (45)
The Viscount De L'Isle, 1968 (59)
The Lord Ashburton,* 1969 (71)
The Lord Cobbold,* 1970 (64)
Sir Cennydd Traherne,* 1970 (60)
The Earl Waldegrave,* 1971 (66)
The Earl of Longford, 1971 (66)
The Lord Rhodes,* 1972 (77)
The Earl of Drogheda, 1972 (62)
The Lord Shackleton, 1974 (63)
The Marquess of Abergavenny,* 1974 (60)
The Lord Wilson of Rievaulx, 1976 (60)
The Duke of Grafton, 1976 (57)
The Earl of Cromer,* 1977 (59)
The Lord Elworthy,* 1977 (61)
The Lord Hunt, 1979 (69)
Sir Paul Hasluck, 1979 (74)
Sir Keith Holyoake, 1980 (76)
Sir Richard Hull,* 1980 (73)
The Duke of Norfolk,* 1983 (68)
The Lord Lewin, 1983 (63)
The Lord Richardson of Duntisbourne,* 1983 (68)
*Whitaker's Almanac*

As we have seen, aristocrats are bound to the Royal Family through marriage or through the exchange of godparents, godchildren, and christening gifts. These exchanges do more than merely tie a number of individuals to one another. They also create an organic solidarity between the Royal Family and the indigenous aristocracy. The value of that solidarity works both ways. On the one hand noble marriages have made the Royal Family more English and thus more secure. On the other, intimate association with royalty, affirmed through reciprocal exchanges, is a mark of social honor. Paradoxically, these marks are all the more distinctive because they are hidden. More importantly for our purposes, however, is that these interactions are a tantalizing indication of just how privileged these friends and associates of royalty really are. They lead charmed lives.

# XI

⟨☙⟩

# The Coronation

Court life revolves around informal country weekends spent shooting, hunting, or fishing, as well as more formal weddings and baptisms. These are largely hidden activities involved as they are with the ambiguous private life of the Queen. The court, however, does appear in public though the identities of courtiers are obscured by bearskins or garter ribands. Nevertheless, these occasions are those times when the Queen calls her courtiers to her side to share her importance with them (Walzer 1974:28). They establish the Queen's position at the peak of the social hierarchy and make clear that she is not alone on this pinnacle.

A hierarchy is a particularly solid social structure. Its strength derives from the sharing of power by those on top with those beneath them. This sharing can take the form of the delegation of real authority or the bestowing of honor, social advantage, or rank. The latter are easily given, binding favored individuals all the more closely to their patron (Simmel 1950:208). At no other time is this symbiosis more apparent than at the Coronation.

The Queen is crowned in Westminster Abbey, the ritual center of Great Britain where Sovereigns have been consecrated for nearly a thousand years. Kings or queens cannot be crowned without the participation of their nobles. Nor may they even accede to the throne without that participation. The Accession of the Sovereign, supposedly automatic, must first be proclaimed by the Accession Council, an elite group composed of the Privy Council, the Princes of the Blood, the Lords Spiritual and Temporal, and "other principal gentlemen of quality."

Some eighteen months after the Accession, the Coronation takes place with a similarly elite group in attendance. The roles that aristocrats play on this most solemn occasion literally entitle them to their social privilege. The moment the Sovereign is crowned, the peers and peeresses in the Abbey lower their coronets upon their own heads. The Sovereign is the Fountain of Honour after all. The Coronation consecrates both the Queen's sovereignty and the Court's privilege. It underscores the interdependence of Sovereign and nobility.

## The Order of Service

Within the Abbey, the Sovereign is crowned in what is called the Coronation Theatre. This carefully delineated ritual space is bounded on the east by the Altar and on the west by the Throne placed on a raised dais. The Royal Gallery and peers are on the south with the peeresses and bishops on the north. St. Edward's Chair, where the Queen is actually crowned, is between Altar and Throne, emblems of heavenly and earthly power. The Coronation Theatre is more than merely an area of the Abbey set apart for the service. It is a highly condensed microcosm of the world oriented along an east–west axis with its connotations of life and death. The placement of Altar and Throne implies that this world is bounded by spiritual and temporal powers that act in harmony to consecrate the Queen. Significantly this microcosm is itself enclosed within a gathering of the most socially distinct of the land.

Let us look briefly at the broader outlines of the ceremony, which begin with the presentation of Elizabeth by the Archbishop of Canterbury to those assembled. The people signal their recognition of their "undoubted Queen" by shouting, "God Save Queen Elizabeth!" After the Queen has made her Coronation Oath, the Archbishop intones, "Render therefore unto Caesar the things which are Caesar's," and the Queen is stripped of her earthly finery. Elizabeth enters the Abbey in "Her Royal Robes of Crimson Velvet, hemmed with ermine and bordered with gold lace, wearing the Collar of the Garter; on her head a Diadem of Precious Stones" (Barker 1976:164). One by one these are removed by the Mistress of the Robes and the highborn Maids of Honour. A simple white tunic* is placed over the gown richly embroidered with symbols of Great Britain and the Commonwealth (the Thistle of Scotland, the Maple Leaf of Canada, etc.). Thus stripped, the Queen is anointed with holy oil which prepares her for the investment. She stands and is dressed by the Mistress of the Robes and the Dean of Westminster. First comes the *Colobium Sindonis,* a muslin undergarment worn by the Byzantine emperors for their Coronations. Over this is placed the cloth of gold *Supertunica,* made fast by a golden girdle. From the Altar are brought the Spurs, the Sword for the Offering (a Queen Regnant merely touches the sword that would be attached to the girdle of a King), the Armills or Bracelets, the Stole Royal, the Pallium, or Robe Royal, and then the Regalia proper: the Orb, the Ring, the Glove, the Sceptres, and finally the Crown of St. Edward. Thus arrayed, she "takes seisin of her dominion" (Barker 1976:180).

The Queen mounts the five steps to the dais, the western boundary of the Theatre, where she sits on the Throne to receive the Homage of her Lords Spiritual and Temporal. The first to swear fealty is the Archbishop of Canterbury, who kneels before her, placing his hands between hers, saying,

> I Geoffrey, Archbishop of Canterbury, will be faithful and true, and faith and truth will bear unto you, our Sovereign Lady, Queen of this realm and Defender of the Faith, and unto your heirs and successors according to law. So help me God.

As he makes this pledge, all the bishops kneel and do likewise. The first Temporal Lord to pay homage is the Duke of Edinburgh, his oath a slight variation of the Archbishop's.

> I Philip, Duke of Edinburgh, do become your liege man of life and limb, and of earthly worship; and faith and truth I will bear unto you, to live and die, against all manner of folk. So help me God.

And so through all the ranks of peerage, the senior in each rank actually swearing fealty, "while the peers of the same degree knelt in their places to repeat the words" (Barker 1976:186).

---

*Queen Victoria described this tunic as "a funny little shift bordered with lace." Edwards wrote: "Hartnell did better for his Queen [Elizabeth II] [than a funny little shift.] Made in fine white linen, sunray pleated to fall from the neckline, and modestly covered, as it was symbolically designed to do, the vainglorious dress. But even here the practical demands of the situation had to be carefully considered, for the Mistress of the Robes who had to put on the white shift would be wearing long white gloves. Fiddly fastenings were therefore out of the question, modern zips notoriously tricky, and tiny buttons impossible to manipulate, so in the end large buttons with large buttonholes were chosen. On such small details can dignity and decorum depend" (Edwards 1977:56).

The ceremony concludes with the Queen and the Duke of Edinburgh taking Communion. After the Communion, the Queen, carrying the two sceptres, returns briefly to the raised Throne, before retiring to St. Edward's Chapel to exchange the very heavy (five pounds) St. Edward's Crown for the lighter Imperial Crown. Emerging from the Chapel she wears the Robe of Purple Velvet and carries the Sceptre with the Cross, and the Orb. The golden vestments, however, have also been put aside so that the embroidered Coronation dress can once again be seen. And so the Queen progresses out of the Abbey and through the streets of London to Buckingham Palace.

## Betwixt and Between

A coronation is a rite of passage. It is a ceremony that marks the transformation of the social person from one status to another. One emphasis of the Coronation was the progression from Princess to Queen of the realm.

Legally, Princess Elizabeth automatically became Queen the instant her father died. In the interim between his death and her Coronation there was, however, a certain amount of ambiguity. For example, in November 1952 Elizabeth opened Parliament as Sovereign but did not actually wear the Crown. The Crown was instead displayed on a cushion near the Throne where the Queen sat. This ceremonial interregnum, then, approximates the situation of an Egyptian Pharaoh who "was born a god but between his birth and the moment of his enthronement lost some of his sacredness" (Van Gennep 1966:111).

Rites of passage draw heavily upon images of liminality which enhance the sense of being on the threshold. Evidence of liminality abounded at the Coronation of Elizabeth II. Like initiates everywhere the Queen was set apart from her family who watched from the Royal Gallery. The white tunic she wore resembled both a winding sheet that binds the dead and a swaddling cloth that wraps the newborn. The Queen was crowned on St. Edward's Chair suspended between heaven and earth.

As Victor Turner wrote, neophytes are both passive and malleable (1967:101). They must first be "ground down" so that their new identity can be built up. The malleability of the Queen was expressed in her passivity throughout the ceremony. She allowed herself to be stripped of her rank, rendering her symbolically naked. The opulent Robe of Velvet Crimson, Garter Collar, and Diadem of Precious Stones were taken from her; her secular clothing—the costly Coronation Dress—covered with the simple white tunic. The surest sign of her nakedness was the unadorned hair. Even as a child, and seemingly far from the Throne, Elizabeth did not appear in public with her head uncovered. The High and Mighty Princess Elizabeth had been brought low so that her new regal persona could be raised.

## The Regalia as Sacra

As Victor Turner also noted, though neophytes remain passive through much of their initiations, the process itself is hardly a passive one. Neophytes are aggressively transformed by instructors who impart sacred and esoteric knowledge through the use of *sacra*. It is the communication of such lore that "grows" men and women (Turner 1967:102). The clergy were the Queen's instructors, the Regalia the *sacra*. The Moderator of the Church of Scotland advised her, "Here is Wisdom; this is the royal law; these are the lively Oracles of God"; the Archbishop of Canterbury cautioned her to "render unto Caesar those things which are Caesar's."

The Regalia are *sacra*, a means of communicating *gnosis*, the wisdom essential to transform the Queen's body natural into the body politic. Like most *sacra* the Regalia are essentially simple items—a glove, a spur, a crown, a sword; the meanings associated with them are complex. They are "the outward and visible signs of an inward and spiritual grace" that comes from God. They are signs of God's election. They are encrusted with history—the Black Prince's Ruby, Elizabeth I's earrings, St. Edward's Sapphire. Thus, in the Regalia are fused the past and the present, the temporal and the eternal. Furthermore, each piece is an abstraction of an aspect of kingliness. The Armills are symbols of sincerity and wisdom; the Spurs symbolize the ideals of Christian chivalry. As the Queen is invested with each of these Regalia, she absorbs the powers with which they are imbued.

On Coronation Day, the Regalia were brought to the Abbey and kept in a room called the Jerusalem Chamber. Before the Queen arrived, the Dean and Prebendaries carried them to the entrance where the Regalia were handed over to the Peers to be carried before the Queen to the Theatre. The Peers were entrusted with (if not invested with) the Regalia before the Queen.

The Order of the Queen's Procession into the Abbey was as follows:

The Beadle and Canons of the Abbey carrying Crosses
Six Pursuivants [officers of the College of Arms]
The Barons of the Cinque Ports
The Ring, the Armills, and the Sword for the Offering
carried for the Keeper of the Jewel House by

Lord Hardinge of Penshurst
Two Pursuivants
Four Knights of The Garter [who later held
the Canopy for the Anointing]
Commonwealth Ministers
The Prime Minister (W. Churchill)
The Cross of York and its Archbishop
The High Cross of Canterbury and its Archbishop
Heralds and Lyon King of Arms
Philip

| *Lord Bearers* | *Regalia* |
|---|---|
| Earl of Ancaster | St. Edward's Staff |
| Viscount Portal of Hungerford (KG) | The Sceptre with the Cross |
| Lord Hastings and Lord Churston | The Golden Spurs |
| Duke of Buccleuch | The Third Sword of Temporal Justice |
| Earl of Home | The Second Sword of Temporal Justice |
| | |
| Duke of Northumberland | Curtana, the Sword of Mercy |
| Marquess of Salisbury | The Sword of State |
| Duke of Richmond and Gordon | The Rod with the Dove |
| Earl Alexander of Tunis | The Orb |
| The Lord High Steward | St. Edward's Crown |
| (Viscount Cunningham of Hyndhope) | |

The Queen
and the Six Maids of Honour

(Barker 1976:160–64; 77)

The peers carried the Regalia into the Abbey. They also assisted the clergy in the investment of the Sovereign, affirming the interdependence of the spiritual and temporal in the order of things. After the Anointing, the Lord Great Chamberlain, the Marquess of Cholmondely (pronounced "Chumly") was given the Spurs by the Dean of Westminster. He held these while the Queen touched them. The Lord Chamberlain, the Earl of Scarbrough, gave the Sword for the Offering to the Archbishop, who placed it in the Queen's right hand. The Queen brought the Sword to the Altar, dedicating it to the service of God. The Marquess of Salisbury redeemed it and carried it before the Queen for the rest of the ceremony. When the Armills were placed on the Queen's wrists by the Archbishop, the Lord Great Chamberlain, in accordance with his traditional duties of the Wardrobe, assisted the Mistress of the Robes in dressing the Queen in the Robes Royal. The Lord Great Chamberlain even fastened the clasps, an intimate act for a man to perform.

Once the Queen had been adorned with the symbols of majesty, she was ready to be transfigured by the Regalia. The Orb, Sceptres, and

Crown were handed to the Archbishop by another clergyman, the Dean of Westminster. But two pieces were handled by peers. The Keeper of the Jewel House brought the Coronation Ring to the Archbishop, who placed the "wedding ring of England" on the Queen's finger. The Chancellor of the Duchy of Lancaster, Lord Woolton, brought the Glove to the Queen, who put it on her right hand. The investiture was complete when St. Edward's Crown was placed on the Queen's head as she held the Sceptres of Mercy and Justice.

## The Regalia Absorb Their Lord Bearers

The Regalia, like all *sacra,* were potent, infused as they were with a force powerful enough to transform the person of Princess Elizabeth into the Queen of England. They also had an effect on the Lord Bearers. Even though they were insulated on scarlet cushions, the inanimate pieces of the Regalia "absorbed" the identities of their Bearers. The peers who carried the Regalia *became* the Regalia, so to speak. For example, Barker wrote of the procession into the Abbey: "Here were coming some of the glittering splendours of the Regalia, St. Edward's Staff, the Sceptre with the Cross, the Golden Spurs" (1976:164). He could just as easily have written, "Here were coming the Earl of Ancaster, Viscount Portal of Hungerford, the Lords Hastings and Churston, [etc.] *carrying* the Regalia." His description implies that the Regalia were moving on their own. This was not merely an idiosyncracy of Barker. John Snagge and Howard Marshall, BBC commentators at the Coronation, did the same. At one point in the ceremony, one intoned, "With the Great Sword of State preceding her, the Queen . . ." instead of "With the Marquess of Salisbury carrying the Sword of State preceding her, the Queen. . . ." The Lord Bearers were as instrumental in transforming the Queen as were the Clergy.

The Lord Bearers were also courtiers *par excellence.* They participated in the Coronation because they had the hereditary right to do so. That right was earned by personal service to, or attendance upon, the Sovereign by one of their forebears. But the Lord Bearers were not just attendants; they were also symbols in the ritual. Their participation revealed certain truths even while it camouflaged others. This is not a peculiarity of English royal ritual. It is a constant of belief systems of all people.

> Groups have symbolic codes, or systems of signs, which give order to the beliefs held by their members. . . . [These symbolic codes]

represent a condensation of a complex set of motives, experiences, knowledge, and desire, which they help to shape and express *at the same time that they keep so much of it unsaid and below the surface.* (Dolgin et al. 1977:6) (emphasis added)

This perspective also informs much of Victor Turner's *Forest of Symbols*. Influenced by Freud's work on dream symbolism, Turner was fascinated by the ability of ritual symbols to reveal as well as to conceal simultaneously. Symbols, then, are like secrets. They compel because they tantalize. They offer a vision, but as we reach out to that vision, it recedes. Like secrets (and cosmetics), symbols hide realities by positive and negative means.

The anonymity of the Lord Bearers is one such symbolic device which keeps the privileged relationship of the aristocracy below the surface, even while the Coronation ceremony flaunts the exclusivity of that relationship. The Lord Bearers were not anonymous to all; they were friends and acquaintances of many present in the Abbey (*see* Appendix D).

## The Coronation and the Secret Society

Rites of passage actually include two rather different kinds of rituals. One kind, the so-called puberty rite, "converts irresponsible immature minors into morally responsible adults" (Beidelman 1971:101). The Coronation did mark the attainment of a certain kind of majority by the Queen. The second type of passage is an opposite of the first which incorporates individuals into mundane worlds. The latter separates individuals from those spheres, bringing "about admission to age groups and secret societies [as well as] the ordination of a priest or a magician, the enthroning of a King, the consecration of monks and nuns or of sacred prostitutes and so forth" (Van Gennep 1960:65). The Coronation marked the Queen's formal admission to a secret society whose charter is to shape and express certain fundamental beliefs even while keeping these ideas well beneath the surface, leaving much unsaid.

The aristocrats who participated in the Coronation did not appear solely as the Queen's attendants, or instructors; they were also the inhabitants of the world into which she was inducted. Many parts were played by the "descendants" of "great Lords who had strutted in Norman courts, or rode in the lists of Chivalry," such as the Lord High Steward of England, the Lord High Constable, the Lord Great Chamberlain, the Lord Chamberlain, the Earl Marshal, and the Master of the Horse. "The history of their offices is part of the complicated pattern of English history" (Barker 1976:72). The descendants thus inhabited a mythic realm tied to the heroic past. Evidence that the Queen was being inducted into a secret society can be found in the relationship of the Lord Bearers to the Regalia. They were entrusted with them even before she was invested. Their task was to carry them into the Abbey and hand them from the Altar to the Archbishop. They had a proprietary relationship with the *sacra*. But more significant was the Canopy held by the four Knights of the Garter during the most sacred part of the Ceremony.

## The Anointing

The Coronation was preeminently a religious ceremony. It was conducted in a church by an Archbishop, and it incorporated the sacrament of communion. The form of the modern Coronation can be traced to the tenth-century Archbishop of Canterbury, Dunstan, who set it down for the crowning of Edgar in 973 (Tanner 1952:15). Although the service has become identified with the "coronating" of the Sovereign, the most sacred moment is not the crowning but the Anointing. "Throughout the centuries the Anointing has been regarded by the Church as the central act and purpose of the ceremony" (Barker 1976:126). "Nothing which goes before and nothing which follows can approach the anointing in significance. Without it the King cannot receive the royal ornaments, without it, in a word, he is not King" (Barker 1976:126). So solemn was this moment that the Queen was hidden even from the elite assemblage in the Abbey. To this end, four Knights of the Garter held a canopy made of cloth of gold over her.

The Queen was sprinkled with holy oil by the Archbishop on her hands, breast, and head. (Queen Victoria had been anointed only on her head and hands. Elizabeth I had complained to Bishop Oglethorpe that the holy oil "was greasy and smelt ill" [Tanner 1952:74].) Once anointed, the Queen could receive the vestments of majesty and the symbols of sovereignty.

The raising of the canopy (and the turning away of the cameras) signaled the importance of the moment. But more importantly, the canopy held by the knights was a potent tableau of the social relations that exist between royal and aristocrat, a world within that world bounded by the Coronation Theatre. A sign of their trustworthiness was their being made privy to the Queen's nakedness. So sacred and secret was this Anointing that none could see it except the Knights and Clergy.

The Canopy Knights—Viscount Allendale, Earl Fortescue, the Duke

In preparation for the
Anointing, the Knights
of the Garter hold the
golden canopy over the
symbolically naked Queen.
*Keystone Press Agency Ltd.*

of Wellington, and the Duke of Portland—were not the only Garter
Knights participating in the Coronation. The others were the Duke of
Norfolk, the Earl Marshal; the Duke of Beaufort, the Master of the
Horse, who rode behind the Queen's carriage; the Marquess of Salisbury,
who carried the Sword of State; Viscount Portal of Hungerford, who
carried the Orb of England; the Lord Chamberlain, the Earl of Scarbrough; Viscount Montgomery of el-Alamein, who carried the Royal
Standard; Lord Harlech, who carried the Standard of the Principality of
Wales; and the Duke of Edinburgh, the first Temporal Lord to swear
allegiance to the Queen—nine in all. Given that in 1953 there were more
than nine hundred peers, and only twenty-five Knights Companion of
the Garter, the part played by the Order was out of all proportion to its
numbers.

Rituals present highly condensed visions of the social relations that inform the societies in which they are found; no less so the Coronation. The image presented on that occasion resembled a series of Chinese boxes within boxes. The smallest and thus most exclusive was the golden canopy whose treasure was the Queen. This canopy was a chrysalis of sorts out of which the unformed Queen emerged to assume all the glorious ornaments of Kingship.

The Canopy over St. Edward's Chair was contained within the Coronation Theatre, bounded by Altar and Throne. The Theatre, in turn, was secure within the Abbey, which, too, had its own box, the Royal City of Westminster; and beyond that the Empire that Britain still ruled in 1953. Entry to each of these special spheres was determined by secret knowledge and social connections. The Coronation seemed to be an essentially religious service; it was, however, an affirmation of social hierarchy whose strength derived from the reciprocal sharing of intimacy, services, secrets and social honor. At the Apex sat the Sovereign, supported and protected by the Lords Spiritual and Temporal (individuals who owed their own privileged position to a Sovereign). Around the Queen were gathered the Court—the Royal Family, the peers, and bishops. Beyond the walls of the Abbey could be found those who form the immense, truly anonymous base of the social pyramid, equally essential for the support of the apex.

But those outside were not really part of the ceremony. The Coronation was a convocation of the aristocracy. The Queen, of course, had been born into that group, but like the Egyptian Pharaohs, seems to have lost some of her sacredness (Van Gennep 1960:111). Not only was she inducted; she was also installed, or enthroned, at the apex establishing "with absolute clarity her position at the peak of the hierarchical system and greatly enhancing the public's sense of the power and mystery of kingship" (Walzer 1974:28).

The Coronation had been seen by some as an act of national communion affirming the moral values by which Britain lived, namely, "generosity, clarity, loyalty, justice in the distribution of opportunities and rewards, reasonable respect for authority, the dignity of the individual, and his right to freedom" (Shils and Young 1975:141–43). These are important values in British society, but it is difficult to see how the Coronation affirmed them. Indeed the Coronation Committee had been adamantly opposed to the televising of the ceremony, lest "chaps in pubs watch the Coronation over their third pint" (Barker 1976:130), hardly an affirmation of the dignity of the working-class individual.

The Coronation did indeed confirm the moral values of British society, but those values were the solidarity of the upper class, the exclusion of the lower ones, the importance of social distance, the unequal distribution of social honor, and the domination of society by an hereditary elite. But this was not apparent at the time. As Ziegler noted:

> Britain in 1953 was in a mood to celebrate. The painful years of austerity that had followed the war seemed at last to be ending. . . . All that was needed was some strong stimulus to catalyze the growing sense of hope and confidence. . . . The Coronation was therefore to be a rebirth; the new Elizabethans would march united into a brave new world. (1978:97)

Or, as a Yorkshire worker put it, "What people like is the sheer excess of it. We lead niggling enough lives these days. Something a bit lavish for a change is good for the soul" (Shils and Young 1975:146–47).

# XII

# Royal Power

## Appearance and Reality

Oddly enough, the aristocracy, a group of people who in the cosmic lottery have fared so much better than their fellows, are not so much envied for their material and nonmaterial advantages as they are admired, deferred to, and regarded as part of the national heritage. As Joseph Chamberlain pithily observed, every Englishman dearly loves a lord. This anomaly was neatly phrased by Hollowood, who described the British as "an odd lot," who "look with awe upon the faces of nitwits labeled with cherished surnames and titles [yet] are a people who subscribe passionately to the tenets of democracy."

This apparent anomaly exists because domination is an extremely seductive process. This work took as its starting point an examination of one ritual system in a complex society. The symbolism and imagery of that system contribute to the domination of the aristocracy—whose influence, as Stacey (1960) wrote, is out of all proportion to its size.

Domination is a form of social interaction that results in the superordination of one group over others. But this superordination rarely, if ever, results from force and coercion. Rather, it proceeds by the erosion of the "internal resistance of the subjugated" (Simmel 1950:181). The subjugated are, in effect, courted. Domination makes the obligatory pleasurable. Rape and seduction are both expressions of power asserted in a sexual idiom. The rapist achieves his ends solely by external coercion and in the process humiliates his victims. Seducers, on the other hand, convince their quarry of the desirability of their intended interaction, that is, they break down internal resistance. They co-opt the objects of their desire. Seduction proceeds by "sweet talk," language which paints a glowing picture of what ought to be. Aristocratic domination secures willing compliance by using language that draws very heavily upon the corpus of symbols employed by royal imagery. These symbols can have many referents. This is particularly true of the symbols employed in royal aristocratic imagery. They relate the social relations of privilege to cosmology in diverse ways. For instance, photographs of royals engaged in robust country pursuits suggest all the hearty, manly, and unpretentious values associated with the countryside. Since royal persons also signify the nation, the implication is that these virtues constitute the "Englishness" imbuing all the Queen's subjects. Yet what is unsaid is that these pastimes, requiring vast acreage, can be enjoyed by only a tiny proportion of individuals on this overpopulated island. Thus pictures of the Queen in her unattractive country clothes entice us to believe the fiction of her "common touch." The Queen's head scarf and boxy jacket conceal the enormous privilege of country events. Symbols, in short, can be as much involved with concealment as they can with revelation. That is the secret of symbols.

The Queen's frumpy clothing notwithstanding, average persons are not always taken in. They know that the Queen enjoys very privileged pastimes, no matter how rain-soaked or mud-splattered she becomes. "Just like a mum," effused Paul McCartney after receiving his MBE. But he fooled no one: the Queen is the Queen. The point of this concealment is not to fool or dupe but rather to allow people to participate in the royal spectacle as spectators who are, after all, as essential as the prime players.

Perhaps a clearer example of royal imagery's ability to conceal and reveal simultaneously is the convention of never identifying most individuals who appear with the Royal Family. The existence of these courtiers/companions is revealed even while their identities are concealed. Thus they exist and do not exist at the same time. They are kept secret.

But the moral authority of such persons is not secret. It is the linchpin in the relationship of super- and subordination. Moreover, authority "presupposes, in a much higher degree than is usually recognized, a freedom on the part of the person subjected to [that] authority" (Simmel 1950:183). The deference with which aristocrats are treated is evidence of the acquiescence of free persons to the moral authority of the upper class. This subjugation is also made manifest by the deference, esteem, and voluntary homage paid the Queen and her courtiers that is so much in evidence on minor occasions.

This voluntary homage is not something paid only to the very top by the majority of British. Rather, it is evident at all levels of society. Priestly (1973) feels that it is so integral an aspect of British national character that even lifeboat survivors would begin to observe their necessary class distinctions almost immediately after having escaped a watery death. The class system is not imposed by those on top even though they benefit most by it. The truth seems to be that all strata are comfortable with inequality. It is part of their social baggage.

In a television interview John Le Carré observed that espionage is a natural endeavor for the British since they are always "reading" one another, searching for clues which will help them sort and categorize one another; in *The Honourable School Boy* he wrote of the "secret plumage of privilege."

Private clubs, ranked railway cars, and royal occasions present highly condensed versions of the class system. Privilege is modeled in space. Anyone who has traveled by rail in Britain knows that first-class people ride in one set of cars, while the rest do so in another. Similarly, on a royal occasion, the distribution of social honor is directly related to proximity to the Queen.

Let us return to the special ability of symbols to keep secrets. In fact, much of what Simmel wrote apropos the secret can also be applied to symbols. Both offer the possibility of a second world alongside the manifest one. As Durkheim told us, "One must know how to go underneath the symbol to the reality which it represents and which gives it meaning" (1965:14). Symbols, like secrets, hide the reality of that second world, even while they are clues to its existence. Moreover, the realities of the "second world" are hidden by both positive and negative means—thus their ability to tantalize. This tantalization derives from the dynamic quality of both secrets and symbols. Presumably everyone who throngs to a royal event would like to be admitted to the secrets of that second world by, say, being invited to enter the Queen's coach. But that, of course, is not possible. Symbols are cultural secrets that are shared differently by different categories of persons.

For example, the royal establishment (the Royal Family and their Households) may regard royal persons as signs, or direct forms of representation and communication, that must be presented in such a way so as to exude the essential mysteriousness of symbols to the people "out there." Part of that presentation involves the observation of royal etiquette. Prince Charles rarely calls Elizabeth II "my mother"; rather, he publicly refers to her as "the Queen." The assumption of anonymity in the royal presence and the absolute discretion serve to preserve the body and personal secrets of royals.

In Britain participation in royal secrets is a matter of hierarchy. Even though the Queen and the Royal Family, in a sense, belong to everyone, those at the top know more than the rest. There are two, especially well-kept, secrets: how much money the Queen has and the Queen's role in government.

The first is not so interesting. Whether the Queen has two million, ten million, or a hundred million, she has more than most. The second one corresponds to an anomaly in the British character: the love of liberty and democracy coupled with that of deference and aristocratic principles. The democratic principle is after all associated with the principle of publicity (Simmel 1950:365), the aristocratic one with that of secrecy. Because Britain is a democratic country, the workings of its government must presumably be publicized. Yet the British constitution is largely unwritten but for a few exceptions such as the Act of Settlement and the Parliament Acts. Because it is unwritten, government proceeds according to precedent, its agents knowing "what is done" and "what just is not done."

Government in Britain is aristocratic in style. Its ethic, with its insistence upon silence, knowledge of precedence, good form, and the exclusion of outsiders (e.g., the media), is aristocratic. Its personnel are still largely drawn from the upper class. For example, two of the Queen's Ladies-in-Waiting, Lady Susan Hussey and Miss Mary Morrison, have brothers who are, or were, Members of Parliament. At the time of her engagement, the Duchess of Kent's brother was a Member of Parliament. There is a great deal of overlap between royal circles and those of government. This is not to say that there are no Members of Parliament who have not come up through the ranks; Bernadette Devlin did. But if one is not "aristocratic" when one enters those circles, one often seems to be when one leaves. Obviously, government service cannot make individuals aristocrats of the blood, but it seems to introduce them to the aristocracy as a style.

Margaret Thatcher is a case in point. The greengrocer's daughter from Lincolnshire used her Oxford education as a springboard to higher social status and was able to ingratiate herself with the members of the Tory Party. Not surprisingly, Mrs. Thatcher affects an upper-class style—a "plummy" accent, strands of pearls, and a coiffure similar to the Queen's. She is, after all, the leader of the Tory Party. But Mrs. Thatcher is not an isolated, nor special, example. In fact, service in the upper circles of government transforms Labourites into aristocrats. Ramsay MacDonald put on the dog, affecting the tweeds and manner of a country squire. Subsequent Labour leaders have not been any more successful in resisting such temptations. The "aristocratization" of those morally, or at least politically, opposed to the upper class is a testament to the seductive power of that class. Heads still shake in wonder or condemnation at the "co-optation" of Ramsay MacDonald some sixty years ago, but the process continues.

James Callaghan, "the first Prime Minister since Ramsay Mac-Donald to have been neither to Oxbridge nor to a public school" (Marwick 1981:342), had a cabinet of which one-quarter were "traditional upper class figures." They had been to an Oxbridge college or public school. Moreover, Callaghan, like his predecessor Harold Wilson, sent his children to public school.

A less blatant example of co-optation was Richard Crossman (1975), another Labourite, who, in his memoirs, railed against the Privy Council meetings, over which the Queen presides, as the "purest form of mumbo-jumbo." Yet passages from these same memoirs make it clear that Crossman was charmed by the Queen. This Communist (Crossman had been the editor of the anthology, *The God That Failed*) obviously relished tête-à-têtes with Her Majesty. As Duncan so dryly observed, having a drink with the Queen is a universally recognized status symbol (1970:12), one which is not only admired from Clacton to Calcutta, but one which has considerable clout with Labour and Tory alike.

Even Labour Party members who would resist the temptation to emulate the upper class find themselves in a losing battle. Tony Crosland perversely wore what in England is so uneuphonically called a "lounge suit" to occasions on which those around him sported either morning coats or white tie and tails. This sartorial perversity was in part ideological. After all, "in the Labour Party the symbol of the sell out by their first Prime Minister, Ramsay MacDonald, was his donning the Tories' white tie and tails" (Crosland 1982:340). (And in part it was self-indulgence: "Why on earth should one be expected to hire ludicrous garments from Moss Bros?")

Despite his resistance and insistence upon a plain dark suit, Crosland came off neither as working class (which he was not), nor classless (which, as a socialist, he presumably would have preferred). Reviewing the tapes of a 1960s television appearance, Crosland, then Secretary of State, objected to the "upper middle class figure" he cut.

> "I wish to God, I didn't sound like that, Fred."
> "Like what, Secretary of State?"
> "So bloody lah dee dah."
> [Fred] Goshawk thought the Secretary of State's full bodied voice was marvelous. "People much prefer to hear someone talking with an educated voice." (Crosland 1982:154)

For "lah dee dah," "full bodied" and "educated," read "upper class." The response of Fred Goshawk (a lifelong socialist) is particularly interesting and tells much about the pervasiveness of class attitudes. His response shows that homage paid the upper class is not only voluntary, it is involuntary.

The governance of Britain, then, is an aristocratic undertaking; the aristocratic ethic of silence and exclusion is made manifest by not publicizing the workings of government as they are in the United States. Yet Britain is also a democratic nation—and the principle of democracy is that the workings of government should be publicized so that citizens can be familiar with both the structure and function of that government. This collision of values presents a dilemma: the desire to conceal, the need to reveal. The Queen's role in government is an example of the problem; it is also part of the solution, reconciling as it does the contradictory demands of government in Britain. Briefly, the Queen is a highly visible person, yet *all* conversations with her are privileged, whether they take place at a horse show or at a meeting with cabinet ministers. At the former, silence is enjoined by discretion (i.e., taste and breeding); at the latter it is enforced by legal statute (i.e., to divulge what transpires at such a meeting would be a breach of the Official Secrets Act, a prime example of the gradation of manners into law). Thus the publicized picture of the Queen's role in government is limned by these two contradictory aspects—great visibility and the strictest of secrecy.

The Queen's constitutional duties are integral to the domination by the ruling class. Domination is the assertion of power. But that power must appear attractive and desirable. "Cosmetics" must be applied, and symbols are those cosmetics. The denser a symbol is, the more effective it can be in "cosmeticizing" the relations of superordination and subordination. Royal symbols are especially compact, their referents simultaneously cosmological, historical, and social. Nowhere is the paradoxical use of the misleading to lead clearer than in the popular and necessarily cloudy public presentation of the Queen's role in government. On the one hand, the Queen is a kind of metaphor that helps in the understanding of government; government agents are the Queen's ministers, their work described as "Her Majesty's Service." In contrast, we are constantly reminded that the Queen has no political power. The Queen reigns but does not rule despite her portrait or profile on stamps and money, her coat of arms adorning public buildings.

Hibbert, another popularizer, writes that "the monarch in Britain has virtually no effective power, except in extraordinary circumstances" (1979:152). Yet this virtually powerless monarch routinely reads and signs all state papers and is privy to the policies of the Foreign Office as well as the secret proceedings of Cabinet meetings. Moreover, the Queen can confer with any Cabinet Minister whenever she wishes, and when in London she meets once a week with her Prime Minister, who *must* con-

consult the Queen on government business and whom the Queen has the right to warn or encourage as she sees fit. These are not inconsequential activities. Stewart describes the Queen as "an expert adviser to her Ministers, comparable to a highly placed Civil Servant" (1967:40). The Queen may lack formal authority but her informal authority is clearly immense. But the way British government is constituted makes it difficult to determine, with any precision, many governmental roles, let alone the Queen's.

The constitutional duties of the Queen are certainly glossed in popular books on the monarchy (e.g., Howard 1977a; Hibbert 1979; Longford 1983). These books are part of the corpus of royal iconography that determines *popular* ideas about kingship. The constitutional role is given short shrift in popular literature, partially because it is boring (and difficult to understand) and partially because it can only be assessed by those in a "special coign of vantage" such as the Prime Minister. And Prime Ministers do not tend to write popular books on the monarchy. Rather, the ceremonial role of the monarch is stressed, using ritual to camouflage (and to "cosmeticize") the relations of power and authority in British society.

This is not a particularly novel concept. Walter Bagehot, writing in the nineteenth century, prescribed that the monarchy be the dignified facade behind which the real government cranks away. A. M. Hocart, writing in the aftermath of the Abdication, inverted Bagehot's prescription. He felt that the popular belief that the King was an administrator (i.e., part of efficient government) was a facade behind which was hidden the Sovereign's dignified and ceremonial role. Regardless of what hides what, it is interesting that both Hocart and Bagehot endorsed the role of dissimulation in the popular perception of the monarch's constitutional role. Moreover, each propounds the belief that the monarch has no real role in government. But the truth of the matter is that the Queen's very real role, even if it is only being privy to all government information, is obscured by the belief that the Queen is merely a "figurehead." Here we are faced with a paradox.

The Queen as figurehead, as a symbol of the body politic, *is* a facade behind which the government works away busily and efficiently. But the Queen, as an individual, is also behind that very facade herself, busily warning, encouraging, being consulted, "doing the Boxes," signing documents, conferring with Cabinet Ministers, and talking over drinks with Privy Councillors at Buckhingham Palace or Balmoral. The symbolic properties of the Queen, aspects of her body politic, deny the participation of the Queen in these activities, by insinuating that the Queen's participation in government is merely that of a cipher.

The Queen's constitutional role, then, exhibits the same "now you see it, now you don't" properties of her ceremonial role. But this constitutional role demonstrates much more clearly than the ceremonial that the Queen and the aristocracy *are* the ruling class. Domination may proceed by seduction, by dissimulation and camouflage. And association with the Queen and the Royal Family does make certain members of the aristocracy, and by extension the whole class, appear to be entitled to their privilege even while their extraordinary anonymity denies that privilege. But the glossing of privilege is only part of the picture of domination. Domination also involves the assertion of power, the subjugation of others measurable in the lack of privilege. Yet the monarchy is shielded from the messy aspects of power and subjugation by being dismissed: (a) it has no power, and (b) royal rituals are merely colorful spectacles somehow tacked onto real life. Knights of the Garter, the Peers of the Realm, and even the Royal Family appear to be emblems of a

> superficial continuity with the pre-industrial past, [a past] symbolized by all those things which, by their very rarity in the modern world, attract the foreign sightseer and a fortunately increasing amount of foreign tourist currency: Queen and Lords, the ceremonials of long-obsolete or archaic institutions [sic] and the rest. (Hobsbawm 1969:15).

But the whole point of this work has been that these "emblems" of a bygone age are not merely colorful atavisms. Rather, they epitomize a small group of people who exercise extraordinary social, economic, and political power. The Queen, royal public events, and royal iconography are not only the cosmetics of that power, they are also instruments of rule.

# Reference Matter

# APPENDIX A

# Visit by Her Majesty The Queen to Worthmore House

## PROGRAMME

2.30 All residents and staff should be in their place, which will be notified to them by the Wardens.

3.00 The Queen arrives outside the main entrance to [the residence] and is received by the Mayor, who presents the Town Clerk and [the MP].

At the entrance doorway Lord Seagram (Chairman of the Trust) will present the Chairman of the Management Committee (Dame Prudence Peake), the Director and the Warden of Worthmore House.

In the entrance hall of Worthmore House Lady Crossby, Lady Worthmore, some of the Governors and members of the Management Committee and the Senior Staff are presented.

(Members of the staff of Worthmore House will be grouped behind on the right hand side of the hall.)

3.05 The Royal party proceeds across the car park to the entrance of Crossby Court where the Architect and four representatives of the builders and of the Trust's maintenance staff are presented.

(Residents of Wessex House [the residence of male students] will be lining the way across the car park. If wet they will stand on the stairs in the main building.)

3.10 Miss Cranach is presented and the Queen visits two flats on the ground floor of Crossby Court and then goes down to the Playroom and the Nursery in the basement, where children and some of their parents will be present. A bouquet will be presented by one of the children.

3.35 The Queen returns to the entrance of Crossby Court and goes back across the car park to the Worthmore House dining room.

In the dining room will be gathered five groups each of twenty residents divided into countries as follows:

<blockquote>

1. Australia & New Zealand
2. Canada
3. Africa
4. United States of America
5. Europe, Asia, West Indies

</blockquote>

Two members of each group will be presented, and the Queen will speak to each group in turn. Approximately fifty other residents of Worthmore House will also be present.

4.00  The Queen goes through into the Small Common Room where the Warden of Wessex House will present six Wessex House residents, and the Director will present four long-service members of the staff.

(Other members of the Wessex House staff will also be present.)

4.05  The Queen goes up the stairs to the Large Common Room on the first floor where the Governors and others who were presented to her on arrival will be gathered, together with twenty residents of Worthmore House who will be presented to her. Tea will be served.

4.25  After signing the Visitors Book and a portrait which is to be hung in Crossby Court, Her Majesty leaves.

4.30  Lord Seagram takes his leave at the entrance of Worthmore House, and the Mayor takes her leave at Her Majesty's car.

NOTE

1. Admission to Worthmore House after 2.00 P.M. will not be permitted except on production of an admission card, which will be issued to residents and staff by Wardens.

2. The entire cul-de-sac opposite the entrance to Worthmore House will be closed to all cars. Residents are accordingly warned that they should park their cars elsewhere on that day.

3. Smoking will not be allowed in Worthmore House until the Royal party has left.

4. No-one, other than the official photographer, will be permitted to take photographs during the Royal visit, and no person will be permitted to bring autograph books.

|  |  | Total number in room | Total Presented To H.M. | See List |
|---|---|---|---|---|
| Arrival | Received by Mayor |  |  |  |
| Entrance Hall | Senior staff | 6 | 6 |  |
| Door/Anteroom | Clerk of the Works. | 6 | 6 |  |
| or |  |  |  |  |
| Small Common Room | Management Committee, Senior staff (then go to L.C.R.) | 19 | 7<br>12 | A<br>B |
| Dining Hall | (Tables pushed against walls and into centre, so that H.M. walks in large inverted "U" from door to S.C.R. towards Anteroom through corridor of staff & residents, those to be presented being spaced round room.) | 190 |  |  |
|  | Worthmore House residents | | 20 | C |
|  | Flat tenants<br>$(2 \times 30 = 60)$ | | $2 \times 6$ | D |
|  | Sec'ys & recepts. (5)<br>Linen room. Porters. | | 4 | E |
|  | O.C.S. Supervisors<br>(8)<br>Catering staff $(6 + 3)$ | | 1 | F<br>G |
|  | Accounts Dept. (3) | | | H |
| Bar Anteroom | Club Committee and Committee Chairman, presented by Eric, plus Messrs Whadcoat, Blanchet, Kane, Bielby, Martin Andrew | 25? | 15 | I |
| Entrance Hall |  |  |  |  |
| Car Park | Could be lined by staff and residents not otherwise included |  |  |  |

## Synopsis of Royal Visit (continued)

|  |  | Total number in room | Total Presented To H.M. | See List |
|---|---|---|---|---|
| Crossby Court | Visit two flats on ground or first floor |  | 4 | J |
|  | *Nursery.* 2 × 19 adults, 2 staff, children | 40+ | 2 × 5 | K |
|  | *Rumpus room,* 2 × 16 adults, children | 32+ (children) | 2 × 4 | L |
| Return to House | (Possibly visit single room on way to Large Common Room? Only one suitable: Karim Weule (German) |  |  |  |
| Large Common Room | (Management Committee (7) already presented, + J.D., J.M. P.F.) (FS!FL.FP) | 25 + 28 |  |  |
|  | F. and G.F. Committee (10) (4 already presented) |  | 6 | M |
|  | Club Committee (10 girls, 2 × 9) |  | 28 | N |
|  | Lady Crossby, Lady Worthmore, Brig. Pepper. Dame Jocelyn. Miss Cummins. |  | 5 |  |
|  | After presentations, H.M. sits on sofa at car park end of room and is offered tea. Individuals could be brought up to her if time permits. (Signs visitor's book.) |  |  |  |

## Synopsis of Royal Visit (continued)

| | | Total number in room | Total Presented To H.M. | See List |
|---|---|---|---|---|
| Departure | Entrance hall roped so that children can line walls. Bouquet presented by child. | | | |
| | Cheering mob of residents from both Houses on pavement from entrance towards departure route. | | | |
| | (Tea, or something stronger, then served to Governors, Management Committee and senior staff in large common room.) | | | |

# The Most Noble Order of the Garter: The Installation Service

*13th June 1983*

## INSTALLATION SERVICE

TO BE HELD IN THE QUEEN'S FREE CHAPEL
OF ST GEORGE ON MONDAY THE THIRTEENTH DAY
OF JUNE 1983 AT 3.0 P.M.

BY COMMAND OF

## THE SOVEREIGN

———————

*The National Anthem will be sung by all present.*

> God save our gracious Queen,
> Long live our noble Queen,
> God save the Queen.
> Send her victorious,
> Happy and glorious,
> Long to reign over us;
> God save the Queen.
>
> Thy choicest gifts in store
> On her be pleased to pour,
> Long may she reign.
> May she defend our laws,
> And ever give us cause
> To sing with heart and voice
> God save the Queen.

*The congregation will remain standing.*

THE SOVEREIGN *will say*

It is Our Pleasure that the Knights Companion newly Invested
be Installed.

*The Chancellor will call the name of*
THE MOST NOBLE MILES FRANCIS STAPLETON,
DUKE OF NORFOLK
*and Garter will conduct him to his Stall.*

*The Chancellor will then call the name of*
ADMIRAL OF THE FLEET THE RIGHT HONOURABLE TERENCE THORNTON,
BARON LEWIN
*and Black Rod will conduct him to his Stall.*

*The Chancellor will then call the name of*
THE RIGHT HONOURABLE GORDON WILLIAM HUMPHREYS,
BARON RICHARDSON OF DUNTISBOURNE
*and Garter will conduct him to his Stall.*

THE SOVEREIGN
*will then be conducted by Garter to the Sovereign's Stall.*

*After which Black Rod will conduct the Chancellor to his Stall.*

*The congregation still standing, the Register will say to the Knights installed*

THE Lord be with you in your going out and your coming in henceforth and
for evermore. Amen.

*Then the congregation will kneel, and join with the Knights installed in saying*

THE LORD'S PRAYER

*After which the Register will say*

|  | O Lord, save these thy servants; |
| *Answer.* | Who put their trust in thee. |
| *Register.* | Be thou to them a tower of defence; |
| *Answer.* | From the face of their enemies. |
| *Register.* | Let the enemy have no advantage over them; |
| *Answer.* | Nor the wicked approach to hurt them. |
| *Register.* | O Lord, hear our prayer; |
| *Answer.* | And let our cry come unto thee. |

O LORD, who didst give to thy servant Saint George grace to lay aside the fear of man, and to be faithful even unto death: Grant that we, unmindful of worldly honour, may fight the wrong, uphold thy rule, and serve thee to our lives' end; through Jesus Christ our Lord. *Amen.*

GOD save our gracious Sovereign, and all the Companions, living and departed, of the Most Honourable and Noble Order of the Garter. *Amen.*

*All then stand for the solemn Thanksgiving.*

### Te Deum Laudamus

WE praise thee, O God; we acknowledge thee to be the Lord. All the earth doth worship thee, the Father everlasting. To thee all angels cry aloud, the heavens, and all the powers therein; to thee Cherubin and Seraphin continually do cry,

> Holy, Holy, Holy, Lord God of Sabaoth;
> Heaven and earth are full of the majesty of thy glory.

The glorious company of the apostles praise thee; the goodly fellowship of the prophets praise thee; the noble army of martyrs praise thee. The holy Church throughout all the world doth acknowledge thee,

> The Father, of an infinite majesty;
> Thine honourable, true, and only Son;
> Also the Holy Ghost, the Comforter.

THOU art the King of glory, O Christ; thou art the everlasting Son of the Father. When thou tookest upon thee to deliver man, thou didst not abhor the virgin's womb. When thou hadst overcome the sharpness of death, thou didst open the kingdom of heaven to all believers. Thou sittest at the right hand of God, in the glory of the Father. We believe that thou shalt come to be our judge. We therefore pray thee, help thy servants, whom thou hast redeemed with thy precious blood. Make them to be numbered with thy saints in glory everlasting.

> O Lord, save thy people, and bless thine heritage;
> Govern them, and lift them up for ever.

> Day by day we magnify thee;
> And we worship thy name ever world without end.

> Vouchsafe, O Lord, to keep up this day without sin;
> O Lord, have mercy upon us, have mercy upon us.

> O Lord, let thy mercy lighten upon us;
> As our trust is in thee.

> O Lord, in thee have I trusted;
> Let me never be confounded.

*( from the Service "Collegium Regale"*
*by Herbert Howells 1892–1983)*

*The congregation will remain standing and, facing East, say aloud together*

### The Apostles' Creed

I BELIEVE in God the Father Almighty, Maker of heaven and earth: And in Jesus Christ his only Son our Lord, Who was conceived by the Holy Ghost, Born of the Virgin Mary, Suffered under Pontius Pilate, Was crucified, dead, and buried, He descended into hell; The third day he rose again from the dead, He ascended into heaven, And sitteth on the right hand of God the Father Almighty; From thence he shall come to judge the quick and the dead.

I believe in the Holy Ghost; The holy Catholic Church; The Communion of Saints; The Forgiveness of sins; The Resurrection of the body; And the Life everlasting.   Amen.

*Then, all being seated, the Prelate will read*

### The Lesson

Ephesians 6. 10–18.

*After which will be sung*

### The Anthem

### The Twelve

Without arms or charm of culture,
Persons of no importance
From an unimportant Province,
They did as the Spirit bid,
Went forth into a joyless world
Of swords and rhetoric
To bring it joy.

When they heard the Word, some demurred,
Some mocked, some were shocked:
But many were stirred and the Word spread.
Lives long dead were quickened to life;
The sick were healed by the Truth revealed;
Released into peace from the gin of old sin,
Men forgot themselves in the glory of the story
Told by the Twelve.

Then the Dark Lord, adored by this world,
Perceived the threat of the Light to his might.
From his throne he spoke to his own.
The loud crowd, the sedate engines of State,
Were moved by his will to kill.

It was done. One by one,
They were caught, tortured, and slain.

O Lord, my God,
Though I forsake thee
Forsake me not,
But guide me as I walk
Through the valley of mistrust,
And let the cry of my disbelieving absence
Come unto thee,
Thou who declared unto Moses:
"I shall be there."

Children play about the ancestral graves,
For the dead no longer walk.
Excellent still in their splendour
Are the antique statues:
But can do neither good nor evil.
Beautiful still are the starry heavens:
But our fate is not written there.
Holy still is speech,
But there is no sacred tongue:
The Truth may be told in all.

Twelve as the winds and the months
Are those who taught us these things:
Envisaging each in an oval glory,
Let us praise them all with a merry noise.

*(W. H. Auden 1907–1973)*                    *(William Walton 1902–1983)*

*Then, all kneeling, the Register will say*

Let us give thanks for the foundation of this Most Noble Order:

ALMIGHTY God, in whose sight a thousand years are but as yesterday: We give thee most humble and hearty thanks for that thou didst put it into the heart of thy servant, King Edward, to found this order of Christian chivalry, and hath preserved and prospered it through the centuries unto this day. And we pray that, rejoicing in thy goodness, we may bear our part with those illustrious Companions who have witnessed to thy truth and upheld thine honour, through the grace of our Lord Jesus Christ, himself the source and pattern of true chivalry; who with thee and the Holy Spirit liveth and reigneth, ever one God, world without end. *Amen.*

GOD of our fathers, we offer thee our praise for all thy mercies to our land, and to kindred nations in allegiance to our Sovereign; for the devotion of rulers and lawgivers; for deliverance from strife and foreign foes. Grant us, we beseech thee, to treasure our inheritance, and let thy blessing rest still upon this kingdom, that turning to thee with all our heart, and ever seeking thy kingdom and righteousness, we may in thy strength conquer every adverse power and be made fit instruments of thy purpose; through Jesus Christ our Lord. *Amen.*

O HEAVENLY Father of our Saviour Jesus Christ, assist continually with thy Holy Spirit our Sovereign Queen Elizabeth, and grant her to abound in every good work for the advancement of thy glory; and to all the Companions of this Most Noble Order give such virtue and grace, that thy name may be thereby magnified, the commonwealth be well served, and their good fame remain to their posterity. Grant this, O Father, for the merits of the same Jesus Christ, who with thee and the same Holy Spirit liveth and reigneth, one God, world without end. *Amen.*

*All then stand*

HYMN

O WORSHIP the King
All glorious above;
O gratefully sing
His power and his love:
Our Shield and Defender,
The Ancient of days,
Pavilioned in splendour,
And girded with praise.

O tell of his might,
O sing of his grace,
Whose robe is the light,
Whose canopy space.
His chariots of wrath
The deep thunder-clouds form,
And dark is his path,
On the wings of the storm.

This earth, with its store
Of wonders untold,
Almighty, thy power
Hath founded of old;
Hath stablished it fast
By a changeless decree,
And round it hath cast,
Like a mantle, the sea.

Thy bountiful care
What tongue can recite?
It breathes in the air,

It shines in the light;
It streams from the hills,
   It descends to the plain.
And sweetly distils
   In the dew and the rain.

Frail children as dust,
   And feeble as frail,
In thee do we trust,
   Nor find thee to fail;
Thy mercies how tender!
   How firm to the end!
Our Maker, Defender,
   Redeemer, and Friend.

O measureless Might,
   Ineffable Love,
While Angels delight
   To hymn thee above,
Thy humbler creation,
   Though feeble their lays,
With true adoration
   Shall sing to thy praise.

*All then kneeling, the Prelate will say*

WE commend unto thy mercy, O Lord, the Founder and Benefactors of this house of God and College. Prosper with thy blessing their good intentions; and grant that all who serve thee here may work together for the good of each other, to thy honour and glory. *Amen.*

*After which he will give*

THE BLESSING

———————

*The Service being ended a Procession will be formed and will move from the Quire to the West Door in the order prescribed overleaf:*

The Constable and Governor of Windsor Castle

The Military Knights of Windsor

The Officers of Arms

The Knights Companions

His Royal Highness The Prince of Wales

and

Her Majesty Queen Elizabeth The Queen Mother

The Officers of the Order

THE SOVEREIGN

accompanied by

His Royal Highness The Prince Philip, Duke of Edinburgh

*followed by*

*The Silver Stick in Waiting and the Field Officer in Brigade Waiting
and their Adjutants*

Members of the Royal Family not members of the Order

*The Lady in Waiting and the Equerry in Waiting to the Sovereign,
and the Lady in Waiting to Her Majesty Queen Elizabeth The Queen Mother*

The Gentlemen at Arms

The Choristers and Lay Clerks

The Minor Canons and Canons

*Ladies of the Knights Companions and of the Officers of the Order*

As THE SOVEREIGN enters the Nave a fanfare of trumpets will be sounded.

Her Majesty's Body Guard of the Honourable Corps of Gentlemen at Arms
and the Queen's Bodyguard of the Yeoman of the Guard will be on duty in
the Chapel.

―――――

*All visitors in the Quire and Nave are requested to remain in their places until the Procession has passed out of the Nave.*

# Reports on the Post Mortem Examinations on the Bodies of His Royal Highness William Henry, Duke of Gloucester, and His Mother, Her Majesty Queen Anne

## (Drewhurst 1980:189–191)

William Henry, Duke of Gloucester
(Blenheim M/S FI 16a)

Upon the death of His Highness William, Duke of Gloucester, which happened on Monday, 29th July about midnight, the right honourable the Earl of Marlborough, one of their Excellencies the Lords Justices of England and Governor to his late Highness, was pleased to give order, that the Body should be opened.

Accordingly the surgeons appointed by his Lordship (whose names are subscribed) in the presence of Dr. Hannes, who was commanded to assist at the operation, and of several other spectators, made the Dissection; and afterwards jointly with the Dr. gave in the following report on it, on Wed. July 31, 1700.

1. On the inspection of the outward surface of the body, the Head, Chest, Abdomen and Arms appeared livid and tainted more than usual, the legs and thighs not much altered from their proper colour.

2. The Abdomen was first opened, and these observations were made upon the parts contained:

The Omentum was found as is natural.

The Gutts from the Rectum inclusively upwards to the Duodenum, had the common appearances; excepting only that a few inflammatory spotts were seen disperse upon the small gutts, and that the plerus glandulares of the same gutts were become florid, and therefore more conspicuous than is usual.

The Duodenum and stomack and gullet were highly inflamed, especially the stomack which had in its cavity wind and a small quantity of liquor.

In the Pancreas, spleen, liver and bladder of gall was nothing remarkable only the spleen and liver were more livid than usual: the substance of the kidneys carried a colour deeper than ordinary: besides which they were not noted to have anything preternatural: as neither had the glandulae renales or the ureters of the urinary bladder or the Urine expressed from the bladder.

3. Next after the abdomen, the Thorax or chest was examined. Here the Pleura was inflamed to the most intense degree.

The Diaphragm and mediastinum and pericardium were thought not to differ from the constitution given them by nature: excepting that the Diaphragm was some thing inflamed.

The Humor of the Pericardium was red: and perhaps not without a mixture of blood: And even the Thorax and abdomen were judged to have more blood in their Cavitys than could well proceed from the mouth of the vessels cut by the knife at the time the respective venters were laid open:

In the Larynx, the membranes that joint the cartilages, cricoides and Thyreoides were very dark with inflammation.

The membrane that links the Epiglottis at the root of the tongue was also inflamed insomuch that the glandulae miliares of it which are scarce visible at other times, were much distended and very conspicuous.

4. In the mouth, we found the palate inflamed, as also the uvula: the membrane of which was swelled.

The almonds of the ears were swelled and had in them purulent matter, there being prest out of one of them, as much of it as filled a tea spoon.

5. Last of all, the head was opened, and out of the first and second ventricles of the cerebrum was taken about four ounces and halfe of a lympid humour.

The Heart was extremely flaccid and weak in its texture, the right ventricle had very little blood, and the left ventricle was altogether empty.

The Lungs in both sides were filled with blood to the height of an inflammation.

The neck was swollen and upon dissection the condition of the contained parts appeared such as is observed in bodys strangled. At the place where the jugulares arise above the claviculae, the inflammation approaches very near to a mortification.

The glandula thyreoidea were almost black with the inclosed blood: and being putt into scales were found above five drachms in weight.

The gullet was much inflamed, as was said above.

The windpipe also was affected in the same kind, especially the upper parts of it called the larynx.

In this region nothing besides was found particular or differing from the natural state and disposition of it.

Signed: Edward Hannes M.D., Charles Bernard, Edward Greene, William Cowper

Queen Anne
*The British Medical Journal,* 12 November 1910, p. 1530
At the Council Chamber, St. James's, 3 August 1714

Present:
The Excellencys the Lords Justices in Council.

The Physicians called in and Dr. Laurence delivered the following paper, containing an Acct. of what was observed at the opening of her late Maj$^{ys}$ Body.

Kensington Palace,
2 August 1714

Upon opening the Body of her late Majesty of Blessed Memory, We found a small Umbilical hernia Omentalis without any excoriation, a large Omentum well Coloured. No water in the Cavity of the Abdomen. The Stomach thin, and its inward coat too smooth. The Liver not Schirous, but very tender and Flaccid, as were all the rest of the Viscera of the lower belly. The Gall Bladder, Kidneys, and Urinary bladder without any stone. There was a very small Scorbutic Ulcer on the left leg. We can give no further account, being forbid making any other inspection than what was absolutely necessary for Embalming the Body.

The Physicians' Report to their Excellencys deliver'd by Dr. Lawrence as Principal Physician.

(Signed)

| | |
|---|---|
| Thos. Laurence, | Hans Sloane, |
| Davd. Hamilton, | Amb. Dickins, |
| Jno. Arburthnott, | Rd. Blundell. |
| Jo. Shadwell, | |

A true Copy.
(Signed)
Edward Southwell.

## APPENDIX D

# Excerpt from the Diary of Sir Henry Channon

The Coronation sanctifies the new sovereign's possession of the sovereignty. It is also a celebration of the in group, as this passage (describing the 1937 Coronation of George VI) from the diary of Sir Henry Channon indicates. Sir Henry, or Chips, as he was known, kept a wonderful, eminently readable diary that chronicled the London social scene of the 1930s. Chips had had an English mother but had been born an American. In his youth he inherited a fortune that enabled him to do pretty much what he wanted. He went to England and, becoming a British subject, ran for Parliament. He married a Lady Honor Guinness, the daughter of the 1st Earl Iveagh. (This Lord Iveagh, whose family had made their fortunes in the brewery business, was a member of that segment of the peerage that Nancy Astor contemptuously dismissed as the "beerage." For an interesting look at the Guinness family today, see Mary Killen's article, "Guinnessty" in the September 1985 issue of *Tatler*.)

Chips was something of a social climber; in fact, Mary Killen, writing in *Tatler*, noted that Chips "was felt to be overkeen on his own social advancement." He hoped to follow in his father-in-law's footsteps and be raised to the peerage. Although he never made it, he had picked out a title for himself, Lord Westover of Kelvedon.

12 May
   At 5:30 the Lord and Lady of Kelvedon [an ironic reference to Chips and his wife—their country house was Kelvedon] woke, thrilled and eager to get to the Abbey, and as I dressed I thought, not only of the approaching ceremony but of Kelvedon: shall I one day take its name? Lord Westover of Kelvedon? Ten years in the Whips' Office might do it, I think. But shall I ever get there? . . .
   My baby boy, sleepy but laughing, was brought down to my room to watch his father get into his finery, my velvet Court suit. Honor looked splendid in grey, all her sapphires and diamond tiara. Will Paul remember us, togged in our finery, as we stooped to kiss him?
   At exactly 7 o'clock we stepped into the car, and already a crowd had gathered, and they cheered us. Soon we were in a stream of cars all proceeding towards the Abbey; they were wonderful to watch. Some contained friends, the Warrenders, the Marlboroughs, some funny Peers and vast frumpy Peeresses, unknowns, in fact the world and his wife driving off . . . Everyone was laughing and gay and the thin crowds cheered the few State coaches—I counted only three.

At 7:30 we arrived at the Poet's Corner Door, one hour too soon, so we crossed over to the Commons, and meeting the Willoughby d'Eresbys joined them for breakfast. Much chaff as to the possible bladder complications, if we ate or drank too much. Then we returned to the Abbey at 8:30 and found it already filling up. We were conducted by a Gold Staff Officer to seats in the South Transept, where we sat immediately behind the Viscounts and Barons.

The panorama was splendid, and we felt we were sitting in a frame, for the built-up stands suggested Ascot, or perhaps—more romantically—the tournaments of medieval England—the chairs were covered with blue velvet; the church atmosphere, I fear, had completely gone; we had an excellent view and we settled down to wait. I looked about me; on all sides were MPs I knew and their be-plumed, be-veiled, be-jewelled wives. Some were resplendent but my Honor stood out. The Peeresses began to take their places, the Duchesses in front, and in front of them the four of their Order who had been chosen to hold the canopy, Mollie Buccleuch, Kakoo Rutland, Mary Roxburghe and Lavinia Norfolk. My mother-in-law, on the Countesses' bench, looked magnificent as her glorious diamond riviere made a circle of blazing light. It sparkled as she moved . . . the North Transept was a vitrine of bosoms and jewels and bobbing tiaras. I recognised many, Eileen Sutherland, Loelia Westminster wearing a heavy necklace of rubies. In the "theatre," half-way between the two transepts, stood the two thrones, whilst facing the altar was St. Edward's chair. There was an excited pause, then a hush as the regalia was carried in and then out again. Then again half an hour to wait, and I went out to prowl, and gossip with friends. The lavatory arrangements were excellent: "Peeresses"—"Peers" "Gentlemen," and several of these three orders were smoking cigarettes on the outer built-up balcony. I talked to Vansittart, very dashing in his robes; Winston Churchill, Duff and Diana Cooper and others. Soon the processions began: the foreign Royalties and their suites; our own tuppenny Royalties, i.e., the Carisbrookes, Mountbattens, Carnegies, etc. Then, a pause. And I looked about again, dazzled by the red, the gilt, the gold, the grandeur. After a little the real Royalties arrived, the Princess Royal looking cross, the tiny Princesses [i.e., Elizabeth and Margaret] excited by their coronets and trains, and the two Royal Duchesses looking staggering. The Duchess of Gloucester looked so lovely that for a moment I thought she was Princess Marina. Another pause, till the gaunt Queen of Norway [Princess Maud, daughter of Edward VII, and George VI's aunt] appeared, followed by Queen Mary, ablaze, regal and over-powering. Then the Queen's procession, and she appeared, dignified but smiling and much more bosomy. Then, so surrounded by dignitaries carrying wands, sceptres, orbs and staffs, as to be overshadowed, George VI himself. He carried himself well. The Peers clustered around him, Lord Zetland, Honor's uncle Halifax, others. And soon the long ceremony began: it seemed endless, and the old

Archbishop intoned in his impressive clear voice that was heard so well over the amplifiers. The ceremonies were complicated, but thanks to the books which we found on our seats we could follow the Service with ease. After communion [the Order of Service was somewhat different from that in 1952 when the ceremony concluded with the Communion] the King resumed St. Edward's Chair and we watched him as he undressed and the Canopy carried by 4 Knights of the Garter was held over him. Then he was anointed. Then the homage of the Peers, led by the Archbishop, with all the other Bishops kneeling in a row, looking like a Gentile Bellini. Opposite me, near the throne, sat the 8 representatives of the Free Churches, like crows at a Feast, in their drab "Elders of the Kirk" black cloth. They looked so glum and disapproving that they reminded me of the present Government as it sat decreeing the Abdication, relentless, perhaps right, but forbidding . . . The sun shone through the windows and the King looked boyish suddenly. Then it was the Queen's turn, and followed by her train-bearers, "Liz" Paget, Ursula Manners and two others, she advanced towards the altar. Once again the Golden Canopy was brought forward, and for a brief moment the four Duchesses held it over her. The second Service was shorter and soon she mounted her throne. And my thoughts travelled back to the old days when I called her "Elizabeth" and was a little in love with her.

. . . The end of the Service was long, too much of the Archbishop, too little of the Sovereigns; and Honor complained of feeling ill. The heat and airlessness were indeed overpowering. Then at last the procession formed up, and we watched, spellbound, as it uncurled and slowly progressed down the nave. With Hailsham looking, as he invariably does, like a Gilbert and Sullivan Lord Chancellor in his robes and his wig, and Ramsay MacDonald, old hypocrite, who, as Lord President of the Council, had stood almost behind the throne throughout the Service, the Archbishop and others. I wondered what were Queen Mary's thoughts as she swept out? Personally I believe she is a worldly old girl; certainly she and the Court group hate Wallis Simpson to the point of hysteria, and are taking up the wrong attitude: why persecute her now that all is over? Why not let the Duke of Windsor, who has given up so much, be happy? They would be better advised to be civil if it is beyond their courage to be cordial . . . There was a long wait after the Royalties and processions left, and impatience broke out. Chocolates were munched, and flasks slyly produced; I tried to remember the great moments of the ceremony: I think the shaft of sunlight, catching the King's golden tunic as he sat for the crowning; the kneeling Bishops drawn up like a flight of geese in deploy position; and then the loveliest moment of all, the swirl when the Peeresses put on their coronets: a thousand white gloved arms, sparkling with jewels, lifting their tiny coronets. By now there was much general chaff and when one of the Gold Staff Officers lost his sense of humour, and called "I say, a Baron has got out before the Viscounts," there was a roar of laughter.

The few Socialists and their wives seemed subdued and impressed by the ancient Service and the grandeur of the feudal capitalistic show. One of them remarked to me, "Why should we sit behind these Peer Johnnies?" "It's their show, after all. You are lucky to be here at all," I answered, and he stopped smiling.

At home, at 7.45, friends began to arrive, Winston with his wife and youngest daughter Mary; Coopers, Eric Dudley, Jim Wedderburn, others. We listened to Mr. Baldwin on the wireless and then to the King, who was adequate, and everyone said "well done," and the party became riotous. Duff held Brigid Guinness' hand, Winston held forth, champagne flowed, people came in. The party was too hilarious to go out into the wet streets but now and then one heard the hurrahs of the soaked crowds cheering outside Buckingham Palace. At 1.30 our guests left, and Honor with some of them went to a night-club. Then Emerald (Cunard) arrived with Thomas Beecham and the Birkenheads and Basil Dufferin and we sat up until the dawn, a bit tight, drinking and talking.

I must really try and be a Peer before the next Coronation. (1967:123–26)

The Coronation was a convocation of the Aristocracy (and would-be aristocracy, viz., Chips Channon). It expressed the premier value of the secret aristocratic society: the few separate themselves from the many "because they do not want to make common cause with them, because they wish to let them feel their superiority" (Simmel 1950:364). Secret societies "offer a very impressive schooling in the moral solidarity among men" (Simmel 1950:348). To most people the identities of the Lord Bearers and others in the Abbey were hidden. But to Chips, and other spectators, they were everyday acquaintances. This sense of possession of secret knowledge is most palpable. As Simmel wrote, apropos of secrecy, the knowledge that others must do without makes possession all the sweeter (1950:332). Channon was obviously very aware that others—such as the crowds outside his home, the token socialists, or even the "crows at the feast, the Elders of the Kirk"—must do without, and so he savored the sweetness of the occasion all the more.

# Bibliography

Adam, Thomas R.
   1964   "The Queen as political symbol in the British Commonwealth." *In* Symbols and Society: Conference on Science, Philosophy and Religion, 14th Symposium. T. Bryson, L. Lyman, Louis Finkelstein, Hudson Hoagland, and R. M. Maciver, eds. New York: Cooper Square Publishers Inc.

Alice, Princess
   1983   *The Memoirs of Princess Alice, Duchess of Gloucester.* London: Collins.

Alsop, Susan Mary
   1978   *Lady Sackville: A Biography.* Garden City: Doubleday.

Angelo, Bonnie
   1981   "An inside look at royal riches." *Money* (July), pp. 28–34.

Argy, Josy, and Wendy Riches
   1977   *Britain's Royal Brides.* London: Sphere Books.

Arnstein, Walter L.
   1973   "The survival of the Victorian aristocracy." In *The Rich, the Well-born and the Powerful: Elites and Upper Classes in History.* Frederic Cople Jaher, ed. Urbana, Chicago, and New York: University of Illinois Press.

Ashdown, Dulcie M.
   1976   *Ladies-in-Waiting.* New York: St. Martin's Press.

Asquith, Margot
   1922   *The Autobiography of Margot Asquith: Political Events and Celebrities.* London: Thornton Butterworth Ltd.

Auchincloss, Louis
   1979·  *Persons of Consequence: Queen Victoria and Her Circle.* New York: Random House.

Aylmer, G. E.
  1961 *The King's Servants: The Civil Servants of Charles I.* New York: Columbia University Press.
Bagehot, Walter
  1964 *The English Constitution.* London: C. A. Watts & Co. Ltd. First published 1867.
Bailey, Anthony
  1977a "Profiles: Queen Elizabeth II—Part I." *The New Yorker* (11 April).
  1977b "Profiles: Queen Elizabeth II—Part II." *The New Yorker* (18 April).
Baker, Richard
  1977 "Royal occasion." In *The Queen: A Penguin Special.* London: Penguin Books.
Barker, Brian
  1976 *When the Queen Was Crowned.* London and Henley: Routledge and Kegan Paul.
Barr, Anne, and Peter York
  1982 *The Official Sloane Ranger Handbook: The First Guide to What Really Matters in Life.* London: Ebury Press.
Barry, Stephen
  1983 *Royal Service: My Twelve Years as Valet to Prince Charles.* New York: Macmillan.
Bartimus, Tad
  1985 Queen Elizabeth visits Wyoming: British monarch savors the land and the people. *American West* (March/April), pp. 29–39.
Barwick, Sandra
  1982 *The Royal Baby: HRH Prince William of Wales.* London: Pitkin Pictorials.
Beaton, Cecil
  1973 *The Strenuous Years: Diaries 1948–55.* London: Weidenfeld and Nicolson.
Bedford, John, Duke of
  1959 *A Silver Plated Spoon.* Garden City, NY: Doubleday and Company.
Bedford, Nicole, Duchess of
  1974 *Nicole Nobody: The Autobiography of the Duchess of Bedford.* Garden City, NY: Doubleday and Company.
Beidelman, Thomas
  1966 "Swazi royal ritual." *Africa* 36:373–405.
  1968 "Some Nuer notions of nakedness, nudity, and sexuality." *Africa* 38:113–32.
  1971 *The Kaguru: A Matrilineal People of East Africa.* New York: Holt, Rinehart and Winston.
Bennett, Daphne
  1977 *King Without a Crown: Albert Prince Consort of England 1819–1861.* Philadelphia: J. B. Lippincott & Company.

Berger, Peter, and Thomas Luckmann
  1967   *The Social Construction of Reality: A Treatise in the Sociology of Knowledge.* Garden City, NY: Doubleday and Company.
Birnbaum, Nathan
  1955–56  "Monarchs and sociologists: A reply to Professor Shils and Mr. Young." In *Sociological Review,* vols. 3 and 4.
Bloch, Marc
  1973   *The Royal Touch: Sacred Monarchy and Scrofula in England and France.* J. E. Anderson, trans. London: Routledge and Kegan Paul, Ltd., and McGill-Queen's University Press.
Blow, Simon
  1983   *Fields Elysian: A Portrait of Hunting Society.* London and Melbourne: J. M. Dent & Sons, Ltd.
Bocock, Robert
  1974   *Ritual in Industrial Society: A Sociological Analysis of Ritualism in Modern England.* London: George Allen and Unwin Ltd.
Boothroyd, Basil
  1971   *Prince Philip: An Informal Biography.* New York: The McCall Publishing Company.
Bott, Elizabeth
  1957   *Family and Social Network: Roles, Norms, and External Relationships in Ordinary Urban Families.* London: Tavistock Publications.
Bottomore, T. B.
  1964   *Elites and Society.* Harmondsworth: Penguin Books.
British Information Services
  1975a  *The Monarchy in Britain.* London: Central Office of Information.
  1975b  *Honours and Titles in Britain.* London: Central Office of Information.
Brooks-Baker, H. B.
  1978   Foreword to *U and Non-U Revisited,* edited by Richard Buckle. London: Debrett's Peerage Ltd.
Brown, Craig, and Lesley Cunliffe
  1982   *The Book of Royal Lists.* New York: Summit Books.
Brown, Tina
  1985   "The mouse that roared: How has marriage changed Princess Diana?" *Vanity Fair* (October), pp. 58–119.
Bryan, J. III, and Charles J. V. Murphy
  1979   *The Windsor Story.* New York: William Morrow and Company.
Buckle, Richard, ed.
  1978   *U and Non-U Revisited.* London: Debrett's Peerage Ltd.
Bullough, D. A.
  1974   "Games people played: Drama as propaganda in medieval Europe." *Royal Historical Society Transactions* 24:97–122.
Burke, Edmund
  1941   "Letter on a regicide peace." In *Victorian Prelude: A History of English Manners, 1700–1830.* New York: Columbia University Press.

Butler, Col. Sir Thomas
    1976   *The Crown Jewels and Coronation Ritual.* London: Pitkin Pictorials Ltd.
Caffrey, Kate
    1976   *The 1900s Lady.* London: Cremonsi.
Cannadine, David
    1977   "The not so ancient traditions of monarchy." *New Society* (June 2), pp. 438–40.
    1983   "The context, performance and meaning of ritual: The British monarchy and the 'invention of tradition,' c. 1820–1977." In *The Invention of Tradition.* Eric Hobsbawn and Terence Ranger, eds. Cambridge: Cambridge University Press.
Channon, Henry
    1967   *Chips: The Diaries of Sir Henry Channon.* Robert Rhodes James, ed. London: Weidenfeld and Nicolson.
Cole, George D. H.
    1955   *Studies in Class Structure.* London: Routledge and Kegan Paul. Reprint edition, 1976.
Coser, Lewis A.
    1974   *Greedy Institutions: Patterns of Undivided Commitment.* New York: The Free Press.
Crocker, J. Christopher
    1977   "The social function of rhetorical forms." In *The Social Use of Metaphor: Essays on the Anthropology of Rhetoric.* Philadelphia: University of Pennsylvania Press.
Crosland, Susan
    1982   *Tony Crosland.* London: Jonathan Cape.
Crossman, Richard
    1975   *Diaries of a Cabinet Minister,* 3 vols. New York: Holt, Rinehart and Winston.
Dangerfield, George
    1935   *The Strange Death of Liberal England: 1910–1914.* New York: Capricorn Books.
David, Edward, ed.
    1978   *Inside Asquith's Cabinet: From the Diaries of Charles Hobhouse.* New York: St. Martin's Press.
Debrett's
    1981   *Debrett's Etiquette and Modern Manners.* Elsie Burch Donald, ed. New York: The Viking Press.
De la Bere, Ivan
    1964   *The Queen's Orders of Chivalry.* London: Spring Books.
Derber, Charles
    1979   *The Pursuit of Attention: Power and Individualism in Everyday Life.* Cambridge, MA: Schenkman Publishing Company.
Dewhurst, Sir Jack
    1982   *Royal Confinements.* London: Weidenfeld and Nicolson.

Dolgin, Janet, David Kemnitzer, and David Schneider
  1977  "As people express their lives, so they are." Introduction to *Symbolic Anthropology: A Reader in the Study of Symbols and Meanings*. New York: Columbia University Press.

Donaldson, Frances
  1974  *Edward VIII: The Road to Abdication*. Philadelphia: J. B. Lippincott and Company.
  1975  *Edward VIII: A Biography of the Duke of Windsor*. Philadelphia: J. B. Lippincott and Company.
  1977  *King George and Queen Elizabeth*. Philadelphia: J. B. Lippincott and Company.

Duff, David
  1973  *Elizabeth of Glamis*. London: Frederick Muller Ltd.

Duncan, Andrew
  1970  *The Reality of Monarchy*. London: Heineman.

Dunkin, Mary
  1977  *One Hundred and Forty-Four Picture Postcards of Her Majesty Queen Elizabeth II and Her Family*. London: Omnibus Press.

Durkheim, Emile
  1965  *The Elementary Forms of the Religious Life*. Joseph Ward Swain, trans. New York: The Free Press. First published, 1915.

Durkheim, E., and Marcel Mauss
  1965  *Primitive Classification*. Rodney Needham, trans. Chicago: University of Chicago Press. First published, 1903.

Edgard, Donald
  1979  *Britain's Royal Family in the Twentieth Century: King Edward VII to Queen Elizabeth II*. New York: Crown Publishers Inc.

Edwards, Anne
  1977  *The Queen's Clothes*. London: Express Books.

Elias, Norbert
  1978  *The Civilizing Process: The Development of Manners*. Edmund Jephcott, trans. New York: Urizen Books. First published, 1939.
  1983  *The Court Society*. Edmund Jephcott, trans. New York: Pantheon Books. First published, 1969.

Erickson, Carolly
  1980  *Great Harry*. New York: Summit Books.

Evans-Pritchard, E. E.
  1962  "Anthopology and history." In *Social Anthropology and Other Essays*. New York: The Free Press.

Fallers, Lloyd A.
  1974  *The Sociological Anthropology of the Nation-State*. Chicago: Aldine Publishing Company.

Fashion Institute of Technology
  1982  *The Undercover Story* (The catalogue from the show, "The Undercover Story," 11/8/82–5/7/83). New York: The Galleries at the Fashion Institute of Technology.

Fisher, Graham, and Heather Fisher
1972 *The Crown and the Ring: The Story of the Queen's Years of Marriage and Monarchy*. London: Robert Hale.

Fleming, Patricia
1973 "The politics of marriage among non-Catholic European royalty." *Current Anthropology* (June), pp. 207–42.

Ford, Colin, ed.
1977 *Happy and Glorious: Six Reigns of Royal Photography*. New York: Macmillan Publishing Company.

Fortes, Meyer
1969 Introduction to *The Developmental Cycle in Domestic Groups*. Jack Goody, ed. Cambridge: Cambridge University Press.

Fraser, Antonia
1979 *Royal Charles: Charles II and the Restoration*. New York: Delta Publishers.

Fraser, J. T.
1978 *Time as Conflict: A Scientific and Humanistic Study*. Basel & Stuttgart: Birkhauser.

Fraser, Kennedy
1970–81 *The Fashionable Mind: Reflections on Fashions*. New York: Alfred A. Knopf.

Fritz, Paul S.
1981 "From 'public' to 'private': The Royal Funerals in England, 1500–1830." In *Mirrors of Mortality: Studies in the Social History of Death*. Joachim Whaley, ed. London: Martins Publishing Group.
1982 "The trade in death: The Royal Funerals in England, 1685–1830." *Eighteenth-Century Studies* (Spring).

Geertz, Clifford
1977 "Centers, kings and charisma: reflections on the symbolics of power." In *Culture and Its Creators: Essays in Honor of Edward Shils*. J. Ben-David and T. Clark, eds. Chicago: University of Chicago Press.

Gerth, Hans, and C. Wright Mills
1953 *Character and Social Structures: The Psychology of Social Institutions*. New York and Chicago: Harcourt, Brace and World Inc.

Giddens, Anthony, and Philip Stanworth, eds.
1974 *Elites and Power in British Society*. Cambridge: Cambridge University Press.

Giesey, Ralph
1960 *The Royal Funeral Ceremony in Renaissance France*. Geneva: Librarie E. Droz.

Girouard, Mark
1978 *Life in the English Country Home: A Social and Architectural History*. New Haven and London: Yale University Press.

Glynn, Prudence
1978 *In Fashion: Dress in the Twentieth Century*. New York: Oxford University Press.

1982    *Skin on Skin: Eroticism in Dress*. New York: Oxford University Press.
Goffman, Erving
1959    *The Presentation of Self in Everyday Life*. Garden City, NY: Doubleday and Company.
1961    *Asylums: Essays on the Social Situation of Mental Patients and Other Inmates*. Garden City, NY: Doubleday and Company.
1963    *Stigma: Notes on the Management of Spoiled Identity*. Englewood Cliffs, New Jersey: Prentice-Hall.
1976    "Gender advertisements." *Studies in the Anthropology of Visual Communication* 3(2).
Goldthorpe, John H.
1980    *Social Mobility and Class Structure in Modern Britain*. Oxford: Clarendon Press.
Grosvenor, Peter, ed.
1978    *"We Are Amused": The Cartoonists' View of Royalty*. London, Sydney and Toronto: The Bodley Head.
Grunfeld, Nina
1984    *The Royal Shopping Guide*. New York: William Morrow and Company, Inc.
Gurvitch, Georges
1964    *The Spectrum of Social Time*. Myrtle Korenbaum, trans. and ed. Dordrecht: B. Reidel Publishing Company.
Guttsman, W. L.
1963    *The British Political Elite*. New York: Basic Books Inc.
Guttsman, W. L., ed.
1969    *The English Ruling Class*. London: Weidenfeld and Nicolson.
Hall, Edward
1955    "The anthropology of manners." *Scientific American* 192:85–89.
Hall, Ron
1969    "The family background of Etonians." In *Studies in British Politics: A Reader in Political Sociology*. Second edition. New York: Macmillan, St. Martin's Press.
Hardie, Frank
1935    *The Political Influence of Queen Victoria, 1861–1901*. London: Oxford University Press.
1970    *The Political Influence of the British Monarchy*. London: B. T. Batsford Ltd.
Hardy, Alan
1980    *The Kings' Mistresses*. London: Evans Brothers Ltd.
Harrison, Rosina
1975    *Rose: My Life in Service*. New York: The Viking Press.
Havighurst, Alfred F.
1962    *Twentieth Century Britain*. Second edition. New York: Harper and Row.

Hayden, Ilse
1975 *The King Never Dies: The Funeral of George VI.* Unpublished M.A. thesis.
Heald, Tim
1984 *Old Boy Networks: Who We Know and How We Use Them.* New York: Ticknor and Fields.
Heald, Tim, and Mayo Mohs
1979 *H.R.H.: The Man Who Will Be King.* New York: Arbor House.
Hecht, J. Jean
1980 *The Domestic Servant in Eighteenth-Century England.* London: Routledge and Kegan Paul.
Hibbert, Christopher
1964 *The Court At Windsor: A Domestic History.* New York: Harper and Row.
1979 *The Court of St. James's: The Monarch at Work from Victoria to Elizabeth II.* London: Weidenfeld and Nicolson.
Hinde, Thomas
1983 *Stately Gardens of Britain.* New York and London: W. W. Horton and Company.
Hobsbawm, E. J.
1969 *Industry and Empire. The Pelican History of Britain, Vol. 3: From 1750 to the Present Day.* Harmondsworth: Penguin.
Hobsbawm, E. J., and Terence Ranger
1983 *The Invention of Tradition.* Cambridge: Cambridge University Press.
Hocart, A. M.
1927 *Kingship.* London: Oxford University Press.
1970a "In the grip of tradition." In *The Life Giving Myth and Other Essays.* London: Methuen and Company. Originally published, 1952.
1970b *Kings and Councillors: An Essay in the Comparative Anatomy of Human Society.* Chicago and London: University of Chicago Press.
Holden, Anthony
1979 *Prince Charles: A Biography.* New York: Atheneum.
Honeycombe, Gordon
1981 *Royal Wedding.* London: Michael Joseph Ltd.
Hough, Richard
1981 *Mountbatten: A Biography.* New York: Random House.
Howard, Philip
1970 "Fifty years at the Cenotaph." *The Times* (November 9).
1977a *The British Monarchy.* London: Hamish Hamilton.
1977b "The changing monarchy." *The Illustrated London News* (February).
Howe, James
1981 "Fox hunting as ritual." *American Ethnologist* (August), pp. 278–300.
Hultkrantz, Åke
1973 "Response to Fleming's 'The politics of marriage among non-Catholic European Royalty.' *Current Anthropology* (June), p. 243.

Itzkowitz, David C.
  1977   *Peculiar Privilege: A Social History of English Foxhunting 1735–1885.*
         Hassocks (Sussex, U.K.): The Harvester Press.
Junor, Penny
  1982   *Diana: Princess of Wales.* London: Sedgwick and Jackson.
Kantorowicz, Ernst
  1957   *The King's Two Bodies: A Study in Medieval Political Theology.* Prince-
         ton: Princeton University Press.
Kapuscinski, Ryszard
  1983   *The Emperor: Downfall of an Autocrat.* William R. Brand and Kata-
         ryzna Mroczkowska-Brand, trans. San Diego, New York and Lon-
         don: Harcourt, Brace and Jovanovich.
Killen, Mary
  1985   "Guinnessty." *Tatler,* September.
Kuper, Hilda
  1972   "The language of sites in the politics of space." *American Anthropolo-
         gist* 74:411–25.
Lacey, Robert
  1977   *Majesty: Elizabeth II and the House of Windsor.* New York: Harcourt,
         Brace and Jovanovich.
  1982   *Princess.* New York: Times Books.
Laird, Dorothy
  1976   *Royal Ascot.* London: Hodder and Stoughton.
Lant, Jeffrey L.
  1980   *Insubstantial Pageantry: Ceremony and Confusion at Queen Victoria's
         Court.* New York: Taplinger Publishing Company.
Laski, Harold J.
  1932   *The Crisis and the Constitution.* London: Hogarth Press.
Leach, Edmund
  1966   "Time and false noses." In *Rethinking Anthropology.* London: The
         Athlone Press.
Lee, Sir Sidney
  1927   *King Edward VII: A Biography. Vol. II: The Reign, 22nd January 1901
         to 6th May 1910.* New York: The Macmillan Company.
Leete-Hodge, Lornie
  1981   *The Country Life Book of the Royal Wedding.* London: Country Life
         Books.
  1982   *The Country Life Book of Diana, Princess of Wales.* New York: Crescent
         Books.
Levron, Jacques
  1968   *Daily Life at Versailles in the 17th and 18th Centuries.* Claire Elaine En-
         gel, trans. London: George Allen and Unwin Ltd.
Longford, Elizabeth
  1964   *Queen Victoria: Born to Succeed.* New York: Harper and Row.
  1977   "Personal styles in twentieth century monarchy." In *The Queen: A
         Penguin Special.* London: Penguin Books.

1983    *The Queen: The Life of Elizabeth II.* New York: Alfred A. Knopf.

McKerron, Jane

1982    "Bystander: Gold Cup Day at Ascot." *Tatler* (September), p. 53.

Martin, Kingsley

1962    *The Crown and the Establishment.* London: Hutchinson of London.

Martin, Ralph G.

1973    *The Woman He Loved.* London: W. H. Allen.

Marwick, Arthur

1965    *The Deluge: British Society and the First World War.* New York: W. W. Norton and Company.

1980    *Class: Image and Reality in Britain, France and the USA Since 1930.* London: William Collins.

Mauss, Marcel

1967    *The Gift: Forms and Function of Exchange in Archaic Societies.* Ian Cunnison, trans. New York: W. W. Norton and Company. Originally published, 1925.

1979    *Sociology and Psychology: Essays.* Ben Brewster, trans. London, Boston, and Henley: Routledge and Kegan Paul.

Maxwell, Susan

1982    *The Princess of Wales: An Illustrated Biography.* London and Sydney: Queen Anne Press.

Millar, Fergus

1977    *The Emperor in the Roman World.* London: Duckworth.

Mingay, G. E.

1976    *The Gentry: The Rise and Fall of a Ruling Class.* London and New York: Longman.

Mitford, Nancy

1945    *The Pursuit of Love.* New York: Random House.

1955    "The English aristocracy." *Encounter* (September), pp. 5–12.

Montagu of Beaulieu

1970    *More Equal Than Others: The Changing Fortunes of the British and European Aristocracies.* London: Michael Joseph.

Montague-Smith, Patrick

1976    *The Country Life Book of the Royal Silver Jubilee.* London: Country Life Books.

1977    *Debrett's Correct Form: An Inclusive Guide to Everything from Drafting a Wedding Invitation to Addressing an Archbishop.* New York: Arco Publishing Company.

Morley, John

1971    *Death, Heaven and the Victorians.* Pittsburgh: University of Pittsburgh Press.

Morris, James [Jan]

1968    *Pax Britannica: The Climax of an Empire.* New York: A Harvest/Harcourt Brace Jovanovich Book.

1973    *Heaven's Command: An Imperial Progress.* New York: A Harvest/Harcourt Brace Jovanovich Book.

Morrow, Ann
  1983   *The Queen*. London, Toronto, Sydney, New York: Granada.
Murray, Jane
  1974   *The Kings and Queens of England*. New York: Charles Scribner and Sons.
Murray-Brown, Jeremy
  1969   *The Monarchy and Its Future*. London: George Allen and Unwin Ltd.
Mursell, Norman
  1982   *Come Dawn, Come Dusk: Fifty Years a Gamekeeper*. New York: St. Martin's Press.
Needham, Rodney
  1970   Introduction to *Hocart's Kings and Councillors: An Essay in the Comparative Anatomy of Human Society*. Chicago and London: University of Chicago Press.
  1979   *Symbolic Classification*. Santa Monica, CA: Goodyear Publishing Company Inc.
Nelson, Michael
  1976   *Nobs and Snobs*. London: Gordon and Cremonesi.
Nicolson, Nigel
  1973   *Portrait of a Marriage*. London: Weidenfeld and Nicolson.
Nicolson, Philippa
  1983   Foreword to *Vita Sackville-West's Garden Book*. P. Nicolson, ed. New York: Atheneum.
Ormond, Richard
  1977   *Royal Faces: 900 Years of British Monarchy*. London: Her Majesty's Stationery Office.
  1978   *The Face of Monarchy: British Royalty Portrayed*. Oxford: Phaidon Press Ltd.
Packard, Jerold M.
  1981   *The Queen and Her Court: A Guide to the British Monarchy Today*. New York: Charles Scribner's Sons.
Paget, Julian
  1979   *The Pageantry of Britain*. London: Michael Joseph.
Pearson, Lu Emily
  1957   *Elizabethans At Home*. Stanford, CA: Stanford University Press.
Perrott, Roy
  1968   *The Aristocrats: A Portrait of Britain's Nobility and Their Way of Life Today*. New York: The Macmillan Company.
Picknett, Lynn, ed.
  1980   *Royal Romance: An Illustrated History of the Royal Love Affairs*. New York: Crescent Books.
Ponsonby, Frederick
  1951   *Recollections of Three Reigns*. London: Eyre and Spottiswoode.
Priestley, J. B.
  1973   *The English*. New York: Viking Press.

Ranum, Orest
  1980  "Courtesy, absolutism, and the rise of the French State, 1630–1660."
        *The Journal of Modern History* (September), pp. 426–51.
Raven, Simon
  1962  *The Decline of the Gentleman*. New York: Simon and Schuster.
Reed, Jane, ed.
  1977  *Jubilee*. London: IPC Magazines Ltd.
Reynolds, Roger
  1982  *Who's Who in the Royal Family: The First One Hundred and Fifty in Line
        of Succession to the British Throne*. London: Proteus Books.
Richards, Audrey
  1960–61  "African kings and their royal relatives." *Journal of the Royal Anthro-
        pological Institute*, pp. 135–50.
  1968  "Keeping the king divine." *Proceedings of the Royal Anthropological In-
        stitute*, pp. 23–35.
Rose, Richard
  1968  *Studies in British Politics: A Reader in Political Sociology*. New York: St.
        Martin's Press.
  1980  *Politics in England: An Interpretation in the 1980s*. Boston and Toronto:
        Little, Brown and Company.
The Royal Jubilee Trusts
  1981  *The Royal Wedding: The Marriage of H.R.H. The Prince of Wales and
        The Lady Diana Spencer, St. Paul's Cathedral, 29 July 1981*. London:
        The Royal Jubilee Trusts.
Rubinstein, W. D.
  1977  "Wealth, elites, and the class structure of modern Britain." *Past and
        Present*, no. 76.
Sackville-West, Vita
  1975  *The Edwardians*. New York: Avon Books. Originally published,
        1930.
  1983  *Vita Sackville-West's Garden Book*. Philippa Nicolson, ed. New York:
        Atheneum.
St. Aubyn, Giles
  1979  *Edward VII: Prince and King*. New York: Atheneum.
Sapir, J. David
  1977  "The anatomy of metaphor." In *The Social Use of Metaphor: Essays on
        the Anthropology of Rhetoric*. Philadelphia: University of Pennsylvania
        Press.
Schramm, Percy
  1937  *The History of the English Coronation*. Oxford: Clarendon Press.
Service, Alastair
  1979  *London 1900*. New York: Rizzoli International Publications.
Sharpley, Anne
  1977  "Face to face with the Queen." In *Elizabeth II: The First Twenty-Five
        Years, a 32-page souvenir guide*. London: The Evening Standard.

Shils, Edward A.
    1956   *The Torment of Secrecy: The Background and Consequences of American Security Policies.* Glencoe, IL: The Free Press.

Shils, Edward A., and Michael Young
    1975   "The meaning of the Coronation." In *Centers and Peripheries: Essays in Macrosociology.* Edward A. Shils, ed. Chicago: University of Chicago Press.

Simmel, Georg
    1950   *The Sociology of Georg Simmel.* Kurt H. Woolf, trans. Glencoe, IL: The Free Press.

Sinclair, Andrew
    1969   *The Last of the Best: The Aristocracy of Europe in the Twentieth Century.* London: Weidenfeld and Nicolson.

Smith, Clifford
    1931   *Buckingham Palace: Its Furniture, Decoration, and History.* London: Country Life Ltd.

Stacey, Margaret
    1960   *Tradition and Change: A Study of Banbury.* London: Routledge and Kegan Paul.

Starkey, David
    1977   "Representation through intimacy: A study in the symbolism of monarchy and court office in early-modern England." In *Symbols and Sentiments: Cross-Cultural Studies in Symbolism.* Ioan Lewis, ed. London: Academic Press.

Stewart, Michael
    1967   *The British Approach to Politics.* London: George Allen and Unwin Ltd.

Stone, Lawrence, and Jean C. Fawtier Stone
    1984   *An Open Elite?: England 1540–1880.* Oxford: Clarendon Press.

Strong, Roy
    1973   *Splendour at Court: Renaissance Spectacle and the Theatre of Power.* Boston: Houghton Mifflin Company.

Sutherland, Douglas
    1965   *The Yellow Earl: The Life of Hugh Lowther, 5th Earl of Lonsdale, K. G., GCVO, 1857–1944.* New York: Coward-McCann Inc.
    1978   *The English Gentleman.* London: Debrett's Peerage Ltd.
    1979a  *The English Gentleman's Wife.* New York: Viking Press.
    1979b  *The English Gentleman's Child.* Harmondsworth: Penguin Books.

Talbot, Godfrey
    1978   *The Country Life Book of Queen Elizabeth, The Queen Mother.* New York: Crescent Books.
    1980   *The Country Life Book of the Royal Family.* London: Country Life Books.

Tanner, Lawrence E.
    1932   *The Story of Westminster.* London: Raphael-Tuck and Sons Ltd.
    1952   *The History of the Coronation.* London: Pitkin.

Tindall, Gillian
   1977   "If you own a golden coach, why use a bicycle?" In *Elizabeth II: The First Twenty-Five Years*. London: The Evening Standard.
Trent, Christopher
   1966   *The Buckingham Palace of Festivals and Events in Britain*. London: J. M. Dent & Sons Ltd.
Trevelyan, G. M.
   1953   *History of England*. Garden City, NY: Doubleday Anchor Books.
Turner, E. S.
   1959   *The Court of St. James*. New York: St. Martin's Press.
Turner, Victor
   1967   *The Forest of Symbols: Aspects of Ndembu Ritual*. Ithaca, NY: Cornell University Press.
Van Gennep, Arnold
   1960   *The Rites of Passage*. Chicago: University of Chicago Press.
Viktoria, Luise
   1977   *The Kaiser's Daughter: Memoirs of H.R.H. Viktoria Luise, Duchess of Brunswick and Lüneburg, Princess of Prussia*. Robert Vacha, trans. and ed. Englewood Cliffs, NJ: Prentice-Hall Inc.
Vogue
   1969   *Vogue's Book of Etiquette and Good Manners*. New York: By Conde Nast Publications Inc., in association with Simon and Schuster.
Wagner, Sir Anthony
   1967   *Heralds of England: A History of the Office and College of Arms*. London: Her Majesty's Stationery Office.
Walvin, James
   1982   "Dust to dust: Celebrations of death in Victorian England." *Historical Reflections* (Fall), pp. 353–71.
Walzer, Michael, ed.
   1974   *Regicide and Revolution: Speeches at the Trial of Louis XVI*. London and New York: Cambridge University Press.
Warren, Gregory
   1977   *Royal Souvenirs*. London: Orbis Publishing.
Warwick, Christopher
   1980   *Two Centuries of Royal Weddings*. New York: Dodd, Mead and Company.
Waugh, Auberon
   1986   "Blue Wales." *Tatler*.
Weinberg, Ian
   1967   *The English Public Schools: The Sociology of Elite Education*. New York: Atherton Press.
Westminster, Duchess of, Loelia
   1961   *Grace and Favour*. New York: Reynal and Company.
Whitaker, James
   1981   *Settling Down*. London: Quartet Books.

Wilkinson, Rupert
    1964   *Gentlemanly Power: British Leadership and the Public School Tradition: A Comparative Study in the Making of Rulers.* New York and London: Oxford University Press.

Williams, Hugo
    1985   "After eight." *Tatler* (October).

Winchester, Simon
    1982   *Their Noble Lordships: Class and Power in Modern Britain.* New York: Random House.

Windsor, Duke of
    1951   *A King's Story: The Memoirs of the Duke of Windsor.* New York: Putnam.

Woodham-Smith, Cecil
    1972   *Queen Victoria: From Her Birth to the Death of the Prince Consort.* New York: Alfred A. Knopf.

Woodward, Kathleen
    1923   *Queen Mary: A Life and Intimate Study.* London: Hutchinson & Company.

Wright, Peter A., C.V.O.
    1973   *The Pictorial History of the Royal Maundy.* London: Pitkin Pictorials.

York, Rosemary
    1971   *Charles in His Own Words.* New York and London: Omnibus Press.

Zerubavel, Eviatar
    1981   *Hidden Rhythms: Schedules and Calendars in Social Life.* Chicago: University of Chicago Press.

Ziegler, Philip
    1978   *Crown and People.* London: Collins.

# Index

*About the Author*

ILSE HAYDEN became interested in anthropology through fieldwork she did as an archaeology student in Wyoming, Majorca, England, and New Jersey. She later taught anthropology for six years at Adelphi University, Hofstra University, Brooklyn College, and John Jay College. As part of her research for writing this book, she traveled to London where she talked her way into both Buckingham Palace and Clarence House (the Queen Mother's residence). She is currently writing a book on the anthropology of food, sex, and sin.